C++ Weekend
Crash Course

Stephen R. Davis

Hungry Minds™

Best-Selling Books • Digital Downloads • e-Books • Answer Networks • e-Newsletters • Branded Web Sites • e-Learning

New York, NY ◆ Cleveland, OH ◆ Indianapolis, IN

C++ Weekend Crash Course
Published by
Hungry Minds, Inc.
909 Third Avenue
New York, NY 10022
www.hungryminds.com

Library of Congress Card Number: 00-101537
ISBN: 0-7645-4689-9
Printed in the United States of America
10 9 8 7 6 5
1B/QZ/QY/QR/FC
Distributed in the United States by Hungry Minds, Inc.
Distributed by CDG Books Canada Inc. for Canada; by Transworld Publishers Limited in the United Kingdom; by IDG Norge Books for Norway; by IDG Sweden Books for Sweden; by IDG Books Australia Publishing Corporation Pty. Ltd. for Australia and New Zealand; by TransQuest Publishers Pte Ltd. for Singapore, Malaysia, Thailand, Indonesia, and Hong Kong; by Gotop Information Inc. for Taiwan; by ICG Muse, Inc. for Japan; by Intersoft for South Africa; by Eyrolles for France; by International Thomson Publishing for Germany, Austria and Switzerland; by Distribuidora Cuspide for Argentina; by LR International for Brazil; by Galileo Libros for Chile; by Ediciones ZETA S.C.R. Ltda. for Peru; by WS Computer Publishing Corporation, Inc., for the Philippines; by Contemporanea de Ediciones for Venezuela; by Express Computer Distributors for the Caribbean and West Indies; by Micronesia Media Distributor, Inc. for Micronesia; by Chips Computadoras S.A. de C.V. for Mexico; by Editorial Norma de Panama S.A. for Panama; by American Bookshops for Finland.

For general information on Hungry Minds' products and services please contact our Customer Care Department within the U.S. at 800-762-2974, outside the U.S. at 317-572-3993 or fax 317-572-4002.

For sales inquiries and reseller information, including discounts, premium and bulk quantity sales, and foreign-language translations, please contact our Customer Care Department at 800-434-3422, fax 317-572-4002, or write to Hungry Minds, Inc., Attn: Customer Care Department, 10475 Crosspoint Boulevard, Indianapolis, IN 46256.

For information on licensing foreign or domestic rights, please contact our Sub-Rights Customer Care Department at 212-884-5000.

For information on using Hungry Minds' products and services in the classroom or for ordering examination copies, please contact our Educational Sales Department at 800-434-2086 or fax 317-572-4005.

Please contact our Public Relations Department at 212-884-5163 for press review copies or 212-884-5000 for author interviews and other publicity information or fax 212-884-5400.

For information on using Hungry Minds' products and services in the classroom or for ordering examination copies, please contact our Educational Sales Department at 800-434-2086 or fax 317-572-4005.

For press review copies, author interviews, or other publicity information, please contact our Public Relations department at 317-572-3168 or fax 317-572-4168.

For authorization to photocopy items for corporate, personal, or educational use, please contact Copyright Clearance Center, 222 Rosewood Drive, Danvers, MA 01923, or fax 978-750-4470.

Hungry Minds™ is a trademark of Hungry Minds, Inc.

About the Author

Stephen R. Davis

A 43-year-old father and husband, works as a programmer for Valtech (Valtech.com), a software training, mentoring and consulting company.

Credits

Acquisitions Editor
Greg Croy

Project Editor
Matthew E. Lusher

Technical Editor
Greg L. Guntle

Copy Editors
S.B. Kleinman
Rich Adin

Media Development Specialist
Jason Lusher

Permissions Editor
Lenora Chin Sell

Media Development Manager
Stephen Noetzel

Project Coordinators
Linda Marousek
Louigene A. Santos
Marcos Vergara

Graphics and Production Specialists
Robert Bihlmayer
Jude Levinson
Michael Lewis
Ramses Ramirez
Victor Pérez-Varela
Dina F Quan

Quality Control Specialist
Laura Taflinger

Proofreading and Indexing
York Production Services

Illustrators
Mary Jo Richards
Brent Savage

Cover Design
Clark Creative Group

to my wonderful new nieces, Christa and Sarah

Preface

C++ *Weekend Crash Course* teaches the reader C++ in one admittedly busy weekend: 30 sessions of a half-hour each, for 15 hours stretching from Friday evening to Sunday afternoon. At the end of each part of the book, you'll get a chance to pause, reflect, and review what you've just learned before pushing on through the rest. Good luck!

What is C++?

C++ is the most popular programming language in use today. C++ is used in applications from the micro-programs that drive your microwave oven, your clothes washer and your TV up through the huge, hardcore programs that control nuclear missiles and Mars rockets — heh, you can't blame the Mars rockets on C++.

In the late 1980s C began to show signs of age. For one, C does not support the object-oriented programming style. At the time, the object-oriented wave was taking the world by storm. Employers were throwing money at object-oriented programmers. All you had to do was work the phrase "new paradigm" into the conversation in order to gather a crowd of admirers.

The problem was that every program worth its salt was written in C (there were a few programs written in Pascal like early versions of Windows, but they don't count — if you are familiar with the earliest versions of Windows, you know why). There was no way that companies were going to rewrite all that code just to ride the object-oriented wave.

Object-oriented concepts had to be grafted onto the existing C language. The result was called C++.

C++ is a superset of C. Any well written C program can be rebuilt with a C++ tool to generate a working program. That meant the companies could upgrade their software in pieces. Existing code could remain in C while new code adopted the extra features of C++.

Fortunately for us, C++ is a standardized language. The American National Standards Institute (ANSI) and International Standards Organization (ISO) agree on what C++ is. They issued a detailed description of the C++ language. This standardized language is often known as ANSI or ISO standard C++ or simply Standard C++.

Standard C++ is not controlled by a single company such as Microsoft (or Sun, for that matter). The Standard C++ community is not held hostage to the whims of any one corporate giant. In addition, companies do not stray. Even Microsoft's Visual C++ holds tightly to the C++ standard.

The programs in *C++ Weekend Crash Course* in can be built using any Standard C++ implementation.

The Object-Oriented Paradigm

Object-oriented programming is not all hype. Object-oriented programming really is a different approach to programming than its predecessor. Object-oriented programs are easier to write and maintain. Object-oriented modules can be reused with greater ease than those written in older styles.

C++ Weekend Crash Course presents more than just the C++ language. You need to learn the object-oriented paradigm in order to make complete use of the power of C++. *C++ Weekend Crash Course* uses C++ examples to teach you the object-oriented view of the world. Anyone who claims to program in C++ without understanding OO concepts is just using C++ as a "better C".

Who

C++ Weekend Crash Course is intended for the beginner through the intermediate reader.

This book serves the beginner by not assuming any knowledge of programming or programming concepts. The first few lessons go over real-world, non-techie explanations of what programming is.

This book is also great for the home programmer. The multiple examples demonstrate programming techniques used in modern, high speed programs.

The serious programmer or student needs C++ in his quiver of programming skills. The ability to speak knowledgeably of C++ can make the difference between getting that job and not.

What

C++ Weekend Crash Course is more than just a book: it's a complete development package. A CD-ROM containing the famous GNU C++ environment is included with the book.

You need a word processor, such as Microsoft Word, in order to do word processing. Similarly, you need a C++ development environment in order to build and execute programs in C++.

Many readers will already own a programming environment such as Microsoft's ubiquitous Visual C++. For those who do not own a C++ environment already, *C++ Weekend Crash Course* includes the standard GNU C++.

GNU C++ is not some stripped down, limited time program. The GNU C++ package included with the book is a complete, no-holds-barred development environment. *C++ Weekend Crash Course* provides complete instructions on how to install and use both GNU C++ and Visual C++.

How

C++ Weekend Crash Course follows a one-weekend format. Start with Friday evening; conclude Sunday afternoon.

This "One weekend" format is:

- ideal for the student who wants to catch up with the rest of the class,
- ideal for the one-time programmer who wants to brush up on his skills, and
- ideal for anyone who wants to learn C++ while the kids are off at Grandma's house.

Of course, you can proceed through the book at a more leisurely pace, if you prefer. Each section of 4 to 6 lessons can be read independently.

The reader should be able to complete each of 30 sessions in 30 minutes. Time markers in the lesson margin help keep the reader on pace.

Each session is followed by a set of review questions to allow the reader to judge her comprehension of the material. A set of more involved problems is provided at the end of each part to help drive home knowledge gained during the weekend session.

Overview

C++ Weekend Crash Course presents its sessions in groups of 4 to 6 chapters, organized into 6 parts:

Friday evening — Introduction to programming.

This part introduces programming concepts and progresses you through your first program.

Saturday morning — Basic C++

This part covers beginning topics such as statement syntax, operators and basic function.

Saturday afternoon — Structures and pointers.

Here the reader delves the slightly more complicated topic of pointer variables including their application in linked lists, arrays and objects.

Saturday evening — Introduction to object based programming.

This is the jumping-off point — topics such as C++ structures, which form the basis for object-oriented programming are discussed.

Sunday morning — Object-oriented programming.

Here it is — the mother lode. This part delves into both the syntax and the meaning of object-oriented programming.

Sunday afternoon — Wrap up

This part wraps up some of the more involved topics such as error handling using exceptions and overloading operators.

Each part ends with a discussion of debugging techniques for finding and removing the inevitable errors from your programs. The level of complexity of these techniques is chosen to match the reader's ability glean from that session.

The appendix includes more involved programming problems for each lesson.

Layout and Features

No one should try to simply power through this material without a break. After each session, and at the end of each part, you'll find some questions to check your knowledge and give you a little practice at exercising your new-found skills. Take a break, grab a snack, refill that coffee mug, and plunge into the next one!

Along the way, you'll find some features of the book to help you keep track of how far along you are, and point out interesting bits of info you shouldn't miss. First, as you're going through each session, check for something like this in the margin:

20 Min. To Go

This icon and others like it let you know how much progress you've made through each session as you go. There are also several icons to point out special tidbits of info for you:

 This is a flag to clue you in to an important piece of info you should file away in your head for later.

 This gives you helpful advice on the best ways to do things, or a neat little technique that can make your programming go easier.

 Don't do this! 'Nuff said.

 This highlights information you'll find on the CD-ROM that accompanies this book.

We also occasionally highlight text passages that explain key concepts of C++ syntax, like so:

SYNTAX ▶ A **function** is a logically separate block of C++ code. The function construct has the form:

```
<return type> name(<arguments to the function>)
{
    // ...
    return <expression>;
}
```

Conventions Used in this Book

Aside from the icons you've just seen, such as *Tip*, there are only three conventions in this book:

- To indicate a menu choice, we use the ⇨ symbol, as in:

  Choose File ⇨ Save Project to save your work.

- To indicate programming code within the body text, we use a special font, like this:

  Likewise, when writing main(), I could concentrate on handling the summation returned by sumSequence(), while thinking only of what the function did, and not about how it worked.

- To indicate a programming example that's not in the body text, we use this typeface:

```
float fVariable1 = 10.0;
float fVariable2 = (10 / 3) * 3;
fVariable1 == fVariable2;   // are these two equal?
```

What's left?

Nothing. Open your work book to the first page and start the clock. It's Friday evening: you have two days.

Acknowledgments

Writing a book like C++ Weekend Crash Course is a challenge, especially since it's one of the first titles in a new series. I'm pleased to have had the opportunity to help launch a new way to teach readers the basics of programming.

I'd first like to thank Greg Croy, acquisitions editor, for spearheading this new series and selecting me as an author. I'd also like to thank my agent, Claudette Moore, for her work with Greg and me to get this project moving.

The editorial staff at IDG Books has been very helpful, and their contributions have made this a better book: Matt Lusher, project editor; S.B. Kleinman and Rich Adin, copy editors; and the production staff directly responsible for the look of what you now hold in your hands. Greg Guntle, technical editor, provided a sharp eye for accuracy and detail.

Finally, and most of all, I'd like to thank my family, whose support of my writing makes it all worthwhile.

Contents at a Glance

Contents

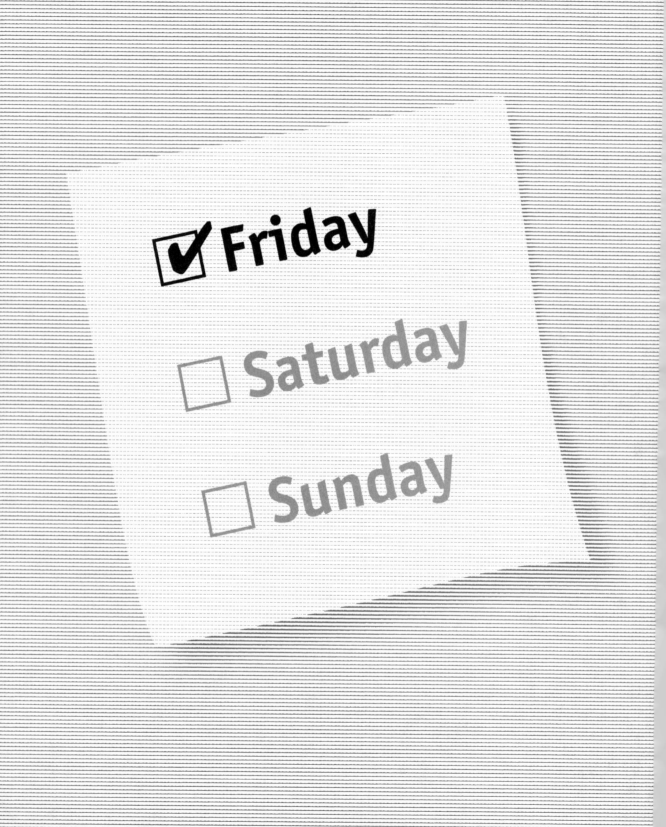

Part I — Friday Evening

PART

I

Friday Evening

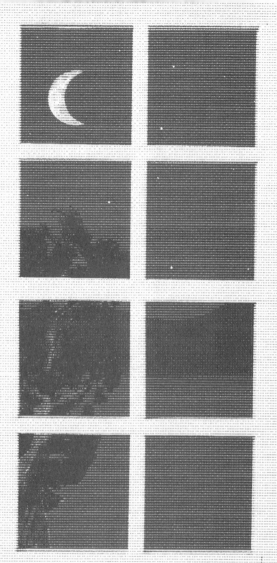

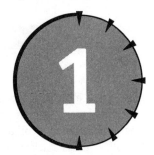

What Is Programming Anyway?

Session Checklist

✔ Learn the principles of programming

✔ Learn to be a human computer processor

✔ Learn to change a tire

**30 Min.
To Go**

Webster's New World College Dictionary lists several definitions for the noun "program." The first definition is "a proclamation, a prospectus, or a syllabus." Not much help there. It wasn't until the sixth definition that I found something reasonable: "a logical sequence of coded instructions specifying the operations to be performed by a computer in solving a problem or in processing data."

After thinking for a minute, I realized that this definition is a bit restrictive. First, in the phrase "a logical sequence of coded instructions . . . ," I don't know whether the instructions are encrypted, that is coded, or not, but I know the term "logical" is overly restrictive. I have written programs that don't do much of anything before crashing — actually, most of my programs crash before doing anything. That doesn't seem logical. Second, ". . . solving a problem or in processing data." What about the computer that drives the climate control system in my car?

It doesn't solve any problem that I'm aware of. I like my air conditioner the way it is — push a button to turn it on, push the button again to turn it off.

The biggest problem with Webster's definition is the phrase ". . . operations to be performed by a computer . . ." A program does not need to involve a computer at all. (Unless you count that muddy stuff between your stereo headsets. In that case, you can claim that anything you do involves "a computer.") A program can be a guide to anything possessing some modicum of intelligence — even me. (Assuming, of course, that I don't fail the modicum of intelligence limitation.) Let's consider how we might write a program to guide human behavior.

A Human Program

Writing a program to guide a human is much easier than writing a program to guide a machine. We have a lot familiarity with and, therefore, understanding of a human. The most important familiarity is that we share a common language. In this section, let's write a "human program" and study its parts. Let's consider the problem of changing a flat tire.

The algorithm

Changing a tire is relatively simple. The steps go something like this:

```
1.   Raise the car.
2.   Remove the lug nuts that affix the tire to the car.
3.   Remove the faulty tire.
4.   Mount the new tire.
5.   Install the lug nuts.
6.   Lower the car.
```

(I know that the words tire and wheel are not synonymous — you don't remove a tire from a car, you remove a wheel. Jumping back and forth between the words wheel and tire gets confusing, however. Just assume that the word tire includes the wheel on which the tire is mounted.)

At its core, this is the basis for a program. I could use these instructions to repair any of the many flats that I have experienced. More precisely, this is an algorithm. An algorithm is a description of the steps to be performed, usually at a high level of abstraction. An algorithm is to a program as a description of the principles of TV is to a TV circuit board.

**20 Min.
To Go**

The processor

To make anything happen, an algorithm must be combined with some type of "do"er or processor. Our tire repair program assumes, for example, that there is someone to man (uh, I mean *person*) the jack, remove the lug nuts, and lift the tire into place. The objects mentioned — car, tire, and nuts — are powerless to move on their own.

Let's assume that our processor understands only a few words of English and understands them very literally. Let's assume that our processor understands these nouns, which are common in the tire-changing industry:

```
car
tire
nut
jack
wrench
```

(The latter two objects were not mentioned in the tire-changing algorithm, but were implied in phrases such as "replace tire." That's the problem with algorithms — so much goes unsaid.)

Let's further assume that our processor understands these verbs:

```
grab
move
release
turn
```

Finally, our processor person needs to be capable of counting and making simple decisions.

This is all that our tire-changing processor person understands. Any other command generates a blank stare.

The program

Given the vocabulary of our processor, it is clear that the processor cannot perform an operation such as "Remove the lug nuts from the car." The word "remove" is not in the processor's vocabulary. Further, no mention is made of the wrench with which to remove the lug nuts. (These are the types of things that go unsaid in normal speech.)

The following steps define the phrase "remove lug nuts" using terms that the processor understands:

```
1.  Grab wrench
2.  Move wrench to lug nut
3.  Turn wrench counterclockwise five times
4.  Remove wrench from lug nut
5.  Release wrench
```

Let's go over each step of this program in detail.

The processor begins with Step 1 and continues through each step in turn until reaching Step 5. In programming parlance, we say that the program flows from Step 1 through Step 5 even though the program doesn't go anywhere — it's the processor person.

In Step 1, the processor person retrieves the wrench. It is possible that the processor already has the wrench in hand; however, we cannot assume that. Step 2 places the wrench on the lug nut. Step 3 loosens the lug nut. Finally, Steps 4 and 5 return the wrench.

One problem with this algorithm jumps out immediately. How do we know that turning the wrench five times is sufficient to remove the lug nut? We could just make the number of turns large enough that it would remove the lug nut from any wheel. Not only is this solution wasteful, it may not even work. What will our processor do if the lug nut falls off and she is asked to turn the wrench again? Will the processor become confused and stop?

The following updated program utilizes our processor's limited decision-making capabilities to remove a lug nut properly:

```
1.  Grab wrench
2.  Move wrench to lug nut
3.  While lug nut attached
4.  {
5.      Turn wrench counterclockwise
6.  }
7.  Remove wrench from lug nut
8.  Release wrench
```

**10 Min.
To Go**

Here the program flows from Step 1 through Step 2 just as before. Step 3 is something completely different. The processor person is asked to repeat all of the steps contained in the parentheses immediately following Step 3 until some condition is satisfied. In this case, to continue turning until the lug nut comes off. After the lug nut is no longer attached, the processor person continues executing at Step 7. Steps 3 through 6 are known as a processing loop because the processor loops in a circle.

This solution is far superior because it makes no assumptions about the number of turns required to remove any particular lug nut. Furthermore, this program is not wasteful by requiring more turns than necessary, and it does not ask the processor to turn a nut that is no longer there.

As nice as it is, this program still has a problem: it only removes a single lug nut. Most medium-size cars have five lug nuts on each wheel. We could repeat Step 2 through Step 7 five times, once for each lug nut. Removing five lug nuts doesn't work very well either. Compact cars typically have four lug nuts and large-size cars and most small trucks have six lug nuts.

The following program expands the previous solution to all of the lug nuts on a wheel, irrespective of the number of nuts holding the wheel in place.

```
 1.  Grab wrench
 2.  For each lug nut on the wheel
 3.  {
 4.      Move wrench to lug nut
 5.      While lug nut attached
 6.      {
 7.          Turn wrench counterclockwise
 8.      }
 9.      Remove wrench from lug nut
10.  }
11.  Release wrench
```

This program begins just as before with grabbing the wrench. Beginning with Step 2, the program loops through Step 10 once for each lug nut on wheel. Step 9 moves the wrench from one lug nut to the next before starting over at Step 2.

Notice how Steps 5 through Step 8 are still repeated until the given lug nut comes off the wheel. Steps 5 through 8 are known as an inner loop, while Steps 2 through 10 are the outer loop.

The complete program consists of the combination of similar solutions for each of the six steps in the original algorithm.

Computer processors

A computer processor works much like our human processor. A computer processor follows literally a string of commands built from a limited vocabulary.

Removing a wheel from a car seems like a simple task, and yet our processor person requires 11 commands to remove just a single wheel. How many instructions are required to move each of the thousands of pixels that make up a window on the computer screen when the user moves the mouse?

Done!

Unlike a human processor, a silicon processor is extremely fast. A Pentium II computer processor can execute roughly 100 million steps in a second. It still requires millions of commands to move the window around, but because the computer processor can execute them so quickly, the window appears to move smoothly across the screen.

REVIEW

This chapter introduced the principles of programming by describing how you might write a program to instruct a very stupid but extremely obedient mechanic in the intricacies of tire replacement.

- Computers do exactly what you tell them — no less, and certainly no more.
- Computer processors have a limited but well-defined vocabulary.
- Computer processors are smart enough to make simple decisions.

QUIZ YOURSELF

1. What are some nouns that a "human processor" that washes dishes might need?
2. What are some verbs?
3. What kind of decisions would a processor need to make?

Creating Your First C++ Program in Visual C++

Session Checklist

✔ Creating your first C++ program using Visual C++

✔ Building your C++ source statements into an executable program

✔ Executing your program

✔ Getting help when programming

**30 Min.
To Go**

hapter 1 looked at how you might program a human. This chapter and the
next describe how to program a computer in C++. This chapter centers on
writing programs in Visual C++, while the next concentrates on the public
domain GNU C++, which is contained on the enclosed *C++ Weekend Crash Course*
CD-ROM.

> **Don't get too worried about the designation Visual C++ or GNU
> C++. Both compilers represent true implementations of the C++
> standard language. Either compiler can compile any of the pro-
> grams in this book.**

The program we are about to create converts a temperature entered by the user
from degrees Celsius to degrees Fahrenheit.

Installing Visual C++

You need to install the Visual C++ package on your computer before you can write a Visual C++ program. The Visual C++ package is used to write your C++ programs and to convert them to .EXE programs that the computer can understand.

Visual C++ does not come with this book. You need to purchase Visual C++ separately, either as a part of the entire Visual Studio package or on its own. The very capable GNU C++ compiler is included.

Consult Appendix A if you need help installing Visual C++.

Creating Your First Program

A C++ program begins life as a text file containing the C++ instructions. I will lead you step-by-step through this first program.

Start the Visual C++ package. For Visual Studio 6.0, click Start followed by Programs and the Microsoft Visual Studio 6.0 menu options. From there, select Microsoft Visual C++ 6.0.

Visual C++ should start with two empty windows labeled Output and WorkSpace. If other windows appear or Output or WorkSpace is not empty, then someone has been using your Visual C++ on your machine. To close out whatever they were doing select File followed by Close Workspace.

Create an empty text file by clicking on the small New Text File icon at the left of the menu bar as shown in Figure 2-1.

Don't worry too much about indentation — it isn't critical whether a given line is indented two spaces or three spaces; case, however, is critical. C++ does not consider "Cheat" and "cheat" to be the same word.

(You can cheat and copy the Conversion.cpp file contained on the accompanying CD-ROM.)

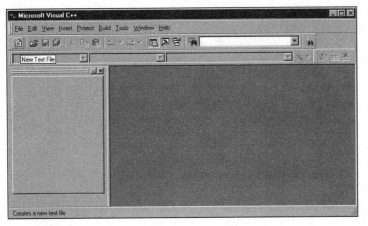

Figure 2-1
You begin writing your C++ program by using the New Text File button to create an empty text file.

Enter the following program exactly as written below.

```
//
//  Program to convert temperature from Celsius degree
//      units into Fahrenheit degree units:
//      Fahrenheit = Celsius  * (212 - 32)/100 + 32
//
#include <stdio.h>
#include <iostream.h>
int main(int nNumberofArgs, char* pszArgs[])
{
    // enter the temperature in Celsius
    int nCelsius;
    cout << "Enter the temperature in Celsius:";
    cin >> nCelsius;

    // calculate conversion factor for Celsius
    // to Fahrenheit
    int nFactor;
    nFactor = 212 - 32;

    // use conversion factor to convert Celsius
    // into Fahrenheit values
```

```
    int nFahrenheit;
    nFahrenheit = nFactor * nCelsius/100 + 32;

    // output the results
    cout << "Fahrenheit value is:";
    cout << nFahrenheit;

    return 0;
}
```

Save the file under the name Conversion.cpp. The default directory is in one of the Visual Studio folders. I prefer to navigate to a folder that I created in a more convenient spot before saving the file.

Building Your Program

We used a limited set of commands in Session 1 to instruct the human computer in changing the tire of a car. Although restricted, even these instructions were understandable to the average human (at least the average English-speaking human).

The Conversion.cpp program you just entered contains C++ statements, a language that doesn't look much like anything you would read in the morning paper. As cryptic and crude as these C++ commands might appear to be, the computer understands a language much more basic than even C++. The language your computer processor understands is known as *machine language*.

The C++ compiler converts your C++ program into the machine language of the microprocessor CPU in your PC. Programs you can execute from the Programs option of the Start menu, including Visual C++ itself, are nothing more than files consisting of these machine instructions.

It is possible to write a program directly in machine language, but it is much more difficult to do than it is to write the same program in C++.

The primary job of your Visual C++ package is to convert your C++ program into an executable file. The act of creating an executable .EXE is known as *building*. The build process is also known as *compiling* (there is a difference, but it is not relevant at this point). That part of the C++ package that performs the actual build process is known as the *compiler*.

To build your Conversion.cpp program, click the Build menu item under the Build menu option. (No, I was not stuttering.) Visual C++ responds by warning you that you have yet to create a Workspace, whatever that is. This is shown in Figure 2-2.

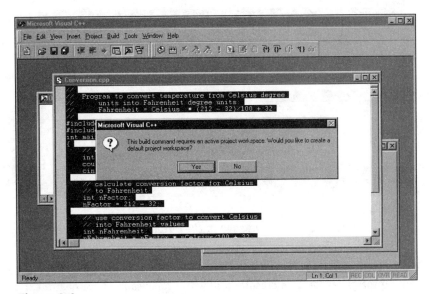

Figure 2-2
A workspace is required before Visual C++ can build your program.

Click Yes to create a Workspace file and to continue the build process.

The .cpp source code file is nothing more than a text file, similar to what you would build using Notepad. The Conversion.pdw Workspace that Visual C++ creates is a file in which Visual C++ can save special information about your program, information that will not fit anywhere in the Conversion.cpp file.

After a few minutes of frantic disk activity, Visual C++ responds with a pleasant bell ring sound, which indicates that the build process is complete. The output window should contain a message similar to that shown in Figure 2-3, indicating that Conversion.exe was created with 0 errors and 0 warnings.

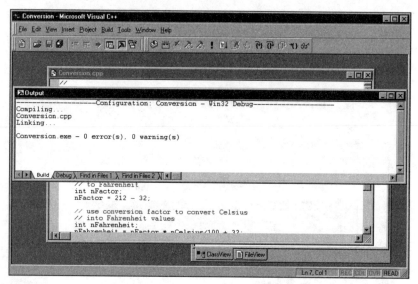

Figure 2-3
The "0 errors 0 warnings" message in the Output window indicates a successful build.

Visual C++ generates an unpleasant buzz if it detects anything wrong during the build process (at least, Microsoft thinks it's unpleasant — I've heard it so many times, it's starting to grow on me). In addition, the output window contains an explanation of what Visual C++ found wrong.

I removed a semicolon at the end of one of the lines in the program and recompiled just to demonstrate the error reporting process. The result is shown in Figure 2-4.

The error message displayed in Figure 2-4 is actually quite descriptive. It accurately describes the problem ("missing ; . . .") and the location (line 18 of the file Conversion.cpp). I replaced the semicolon and rebuilt the program to solve the problem.

Note

Not all error messages are quite as clear as this one. Many times a single error can create a number of error messages. At first, these error messages seem confusing. Over time, however, you get a feel for what Visual C++ is "thinking" during the build process and what might be confusing it.

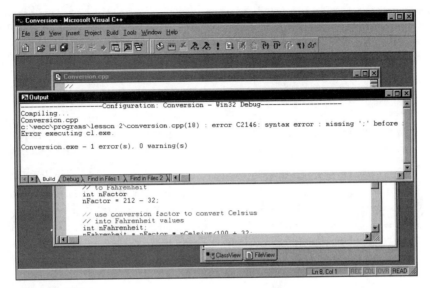

Figure 2-4
*Visual C++ reports errors found during the build process in the Output
window.*

**You will undoubtedly hear the unpleasant buzz of an error
detected by Visual C++ before you eventually get Conversion.cpp
entered correctly. Should you never get the code entered in a way
that Visual C++ approves, you may copy the Conversion.cpp file
from x:\wecc\programs\lesson02\conversion.cpp where x is your
CD drive.**

C++ Error Messages

Why are all C++ packages, including Visual C++, so picky when it comes to
C++ syntax? If Visual C++ can figure out that I left off a semicolon, why
can't it just fix the problem and go on?

The answer is simple but profound. Visual C++ *thinks* that you left off a
semicolon. I could have introduced any number of errors that Visual C++
might have misdiagnosed as a missing semicolon. Had the compiler simply
"corrected" the problem by introducing a semicolon, Visual C++ would
have masked the real problem.

Continued

C++ Error Messages
Continued

As you will see, finding an error buried in a program that builds without error is difficult and time consuming. It is far better to let the compiler find the error, if possible.

This lesson was hard in coming. Early in the days of computing, compilers tried to detect and correct any error that they could find. This sometimes reached ridiculous proportions.

My friends and I loved to torture one "friendly" compiler in particular by entering a program containing nothing but the existential question of the ages IF. (In retrospect, I guess my friends and I were nerdy.) Through a series of tortured gyrations, this particular compiler would eventually create an involved command line from this single word that would build successfully. I know that the compiler misunderstood my intent with the word IF because I didn't intend a single thing.

In my experience, almost every single time the compiler tried to "fix" my program, it was wrong. Although misguided, fixing the program was harmless if the compiler reported the error before fixing it. Compilers that corrected errors without reporting them did much more harm than good.

Executing Your Program

10 Min. To Go

You can execute the successfully built Conversion.exe by clicking Execute Conversion.exe item under the Build menu. Alternatively, you can press Ctrl+F5.

Avoid using the Go menu command or the equivalent F5 key for now.

Visual C++ opens a program window similar to that shown in Figure 2-5, requesting a temperature in degrees Celsius.

Enter a temperature, such as 100 degrees. After pressing Enter, the program responds with the equivalent measurement in degrees Fahrenheit as shown in Figure 2-6. The "Press any key to terminate" message jammed up against the temperature output is not aesthetically pleasant, but the converted temperature is unmistakable — we fix this blemish in Chapter 5.

Figure 2-5
The Conversion.exe program begins by requesting a temperature to convert.

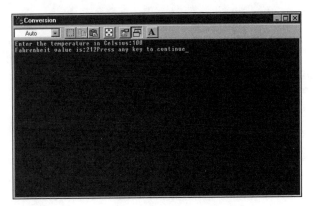

Figure 2-6
*The Conversion.exe program waits for user input after the program
terminates.*

**The "Press any key to terminate" prompt gives the user time to
read the program output before closing the window after the program terminates. This message does not appear when using the
Go command available through the F5 key.**

Congratulations! You have just entered, built, and executed your first program.

Closing Points

There are two points worth noting before continuing. First, the form of the program output from Conversion.exe might surprise you. Second, Visual C++ offers a lot more help than just build error messages.

Program output

Windows programs have a very visually oriented, windows-based output. Conversion.exe is a 32-bit program that executes under Windows, but it is not a "Windows" program in the visual sense.

 If you don't know what is meant by the phrase "32-bit program," don't worry about it.

As I pointed out in the introduction, this is not a book about writing Windows programs. The basic C++ programs that you write in this book have a command line interface executing within a DOS box.

Budding Windows programmers should not despair — you did not waste your money. Learning C++ is a prerequisite to writing Windows programs.

Visual C++ help

Visual C++ offers a help system that gives significant support to the C++ programmer. To see how this help works, double-click on the word #include until it is completely highlighted. Now press F1.

Visual C++ responds by opening the MSDN Library and displaying an entire page of information about #include as shown in Figure 2-7 (you probably don't understand all of what it's saying, but you soon will).

You can find the same information by selecting Index. . . under the Help menu. Enter #include in the index window which appears to reveal the same information.

As you grow as a C++ programmer, you will rely more and more on the MSDN Library help system.

Done!

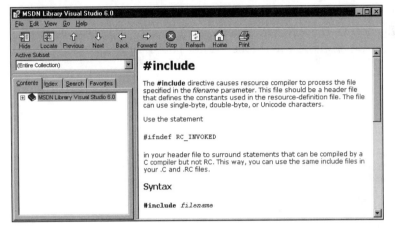

Figure 2-7
The F1 key provides significant help to the C++ programmer.

REVIEW

Visual C++ 6.0 has a user-friendly environment in which you can create and test your programs. You use the Visual C++ editor to enter your program's source code. Once entered, your C++ statements are converted into an executable file through a building process. Finally, you can execute your completed program from within Visual C++.

In the next chapter, we look at how we to create the same program using the GNU C++ compiler, which is found on the accompanying CD-ROM. If you are definitely committed to Visual C++, you may want to skip ahead to Session 4, which explains exactly how the program you just entered works.

QUIZ YOURSELF

1. What kind of file is a C++ source program? (That is, is it a Word file? An Excel spreadsheet file? A text file?) (See the first paragraph of Creating Your First Program.)

2. Does C++ care about indention? Does it care about case? (See Creating Your First Program.)

3. What does "building your program" mean? (See Building Your Program.)

4. Why does C++ generate error messages? Why can't it just try to make sense out of what I enter? (See the C++ Error Messages sidebar.)

Creating Your First C++ Program in GNU C++

Session Checklist

✔ Installing GNU C++ from the enclosed CD-ROM

✔ Creating your first C++ program using GNU C++

✔ Building your C++ source statements into an executable program

✔ Executing your program

**30 Min.
To Go**

C hapter 2 went through the steps to write, build, and execute a Visual C++ program. Many readers of *C++ Weekend Crash Course* will not have access to Visual C++. For those readers, this book includes the capable public domain GNU C++ on the enclosed CD-ROM.

"GNU" is pronounced "guh-new." GNU stands for the circular definition "GNU is Not Unix." This joke goes way back to the early days of C++ — just accept it as is. GNU is a series of tools built by the Free Software Foundation. These tools are available to the public with some restrictions but without cost.

This chapter goes through the steps necessary to turn the same Conversion.cpp program demonstrated in Chapter 2 into an executable program using GNU C++.

The Conversion program we are about to create converts a temperature entered by the user in degrees Celsius into degrees Fahrenheit.

Installing GNU C++

The CD-ROM that accompanies this book includes the most recent version of the GNU C++ environment at the time of this writing. The installation instructions are included in Appendix C; this session provides instructions for downloading and installing GNU C++ from the Web.

The GNU environment is maintained by a number of dedicated volunteer programmers. If you prefer you may download the most recent version of GNU C++ from the Web.

The GNU development environment is an extremely large package. GNU includes a number of utilities and programming languages besides C++. GNU C++ alone supports a number of computer processors and operating systems. Fortunately you don't need to download all of GNU in order to develop C++ programs. The GNU environment is broken up into a number of ZIP files. The "ZIP picker" utility, provided by Delorie Software on their Web site, calculates the ZIP files that you need to download based on the answers to a set of simple questions.

To install GNU C++ from the Web:

1. Surf the web page http://www.delorie.com/djgpp/zip-picker.html.

2. The site shows you the questionnaire reproduced below. Answer the zip-picker's questions as shown in bold to install a minimum configuration:

   FTP Site

   Select a suitable FTP site: **Pick one for me**

   Basic Functionality

   Pick one of the following: **Build and run programs with DJGPP**

   Which operating system will you be using? **<your version of Windows>**

   Do you want to be able to read the on-line documentation? : **No**

   Which programming languages will you be using? **Click C++**

   Integrated Development Environments and Tools

   Which IDE(s) would you like? **Click on RHIDE. Leave the emacs options unchecked.**

   Would you like gdb, the text-mode GNU debugger? **No**

Extra Stuff

Please check off each extra thing that you want. **Don't check anything in this list.**

3. Next, click on "Tell me what files I need". The ZIP picker responds with some simple installation instructions plus a list of the zip files that you will need. The listing below shows the files necessary to implement the minimal installation described here — the file names that you receive will differ to reflect the current version number.

```
Read the file README.1ST before you do anything else with
DJGPP! It has important installation and usage instructions.

v2/djdev202.zip      DJGPP Basic Development Kit    1.4 mb
v2/faq211b.zip       Frequently Asked Questions     551 kb

v2apps/rhide14b.zip  RHIDE                          1.6 mb

v2gnu/bnu281b.zip    Basic assembler, linker        1.8 mb
v2gnu/gcc2952b.zip   Basic GCC compiler             1.7 mb
v2gnu/gpp2952b.zip   C++ compiler                   1.6 mb
v2gnu/lgpp295b.zip   C++ libraries                  484 kb
v2gnu/mak377b.zip    Make (processes makefiles)     242 kb

Total bytes to download: 9,812,732
```

4. Create a folder named \DJGPP.

5. Download each of the ZIP files listed by the ZIP picker in the DJGPP directory by clicking on the name of the file.

6. Unzip the files into the DJGPP folder itself.

7. Add the following commands to AUTOEXEC.BAT:

    ```
    set PATH=C:\DJGPP\BIN;%PATH%
    set DJGPP=C:\DJGPP\DJGPP.ENV
    ```

    Note: the above command lines assume your DJGPP folder is directly under C:\. If you've placed your DJGPP folder somewhere else, substitute that path in the commands above.

8. Reboot to complete the installation.

The \BIN folder includes the actual GNU tool executables. The DJGPP.ENV file sets a series of options to describe the Windows GNU C++ "environment."

Before you begin using GNU C++, check the DJGPP.ENV file to make sure that Long File Name support is enabled. Disabling Long File Name support is the most common GNU C++ installation error.

Open the DJGPP.ENV file using a text file editor such as Microsoft Notebook. Don't worry if you see one long string of text punctuated by little black boxes — Unix uses a different newline character than Windows. Look for the phrase "LFN=y" or "LFN=Y" (the case is not important). If you find "LFN=n" instead (or if you don't find "LFN" at all), change the "n" to a "y". Save the file. (Make sure that you save the file as an ASCII text file and not in some other format such as a Word .DOC file.)

Creating Your First Program

20 Min. To Go

The heart of the GNU C++ package is a utility known as rhide. At its core rhide is just an editor that links to the remaining pieces of GNU C++ into an integrated Visual C++–like package.

Entering the C++ code

Open an MS-DOS window by clicking on the MS-DOS icon under the Programs menu. Create a directory where you would like your program created. I created the directory c:\wecc\programs\lesson03. In this directory, enter the command rhide at the MS-DOS prompt.

The rhide Interface

The rhide interface is fundamentally different in appearance than that of a Windows-oriented program. Windows programs "paint" their output to the screen, which gives Windows programs a more refined appearance.

By comparison, the rhide interface is based on characters. rhide uses a number of blocking characters available in the PC arsenal to simulate a Windows interface, which gives rhide a less elegant appearance. For example, rhide does not support resizing the window away from the 80×25 character display which is the standard for MS-DOS programs.

For those of you old enough to remember, the rhide **interface looks virtually identical to the interface of the now defunct Borland suite of programming tools.**

Nevertheless the rhide **interface is functional and provides convenient access to the remaining GNU C++ tools.**

Create an empty file by entering New under the File menu. Enter the following program exactly as written.

Don't worry too much about indentation or spacing — it isn't critical whether a given line is indented two spaces or three spaces, or whether there is one or two spaces between two words.

You can cheat and copy the Conversion.cpp file that is found on the enclosed CD-ROM.

```
//
//   Program to convert temperature from Celsius degree
//   units into Fahrenheit degree units:
//   Fahrenheit = Celsius  * (212 - 32)/100 + 32
//
#include <stdio.h>
#include <iostream.h>
int main(int nNumberofArgs, char* pszArgs[])
{
    // enter the temperature in Celsius
    int nCelsius;
    cout << "Enter the temperature in Celsius:";
    cin >> nCelsius;

    // calculate conversion factor for Celsius
    // to Fahrenheit
```

```
    int nFactor;
    nFactor = 212 - 32;

// use conversion factor to convert Celsius
    // into Fahrenheit values
    int nFahrenheit;
    nFahrenheit = nFactor * nCelsius/100 + 32;

    // output the results
    cout << "Fahrenheit value is:";
    cout << nFahrenheit;

    return 0;
}
```

Once you have completed, your rhide window should appear like that shown in Figure 3-1.

Figure 3-1
rhide provides a character-based user interface for creating GNU C++ programs.

Select Save As. . . under the File menu as shown in Figure 3-2 to save the file under the name Conversion.cpp.

Figure 3-2
The Save As. . . command enables the user to create C++ source files.

Building Your Program

We used a limited set of commands in Session 1 to instruct the human computer in changing the tire of a car. Although restricted, even these instructions were understandable to the average human (at least the average English-speaking human).

The Conversion.cpp program you just entered contains C++ statements, a language that doesn't look much like anything you would read in the morning paper. As cryptic and crude as these C++ commands might appear to be, the computer understands a language much more basic than even C++.

The language your computer processor understands is known as *machine language.* The C++ compiler converts your C++ program to the machine language of the microprocessor CPU in your PC. Programs that you can execute from the Programs option of the Start menu, including Visual C++ itself, are nothing more than files consisting of these machine instructions.

It is possible to write a program directly in machine language, but it is much more difficult to do than to write the same program in C++.

The primary job of your GNU C++ package is to convert your C++ program to an executable machine instruction file.

The act of creating an executable .EXE is known as *building*. The build process is also known as *compiling* or *making* in the Unix world (there is a difference between the three, but the differences are not relevant at this point). That part of the C++ package that performs the actual build process is known as the compiler.

To build your Conversion.cpp program, click Compile and then click Make or press F9. rhide opens a small window at the bottom of the current window to display the progress of the build process. If all goes well, the message "Creating Conversion.exe" followed by "no errors" appears as shown in Figure 3-3.

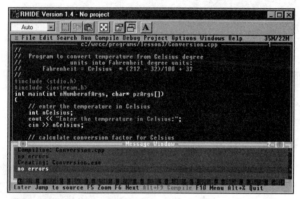

Figure 3-3
rhide displays the "no errors" message if the build process is successful.

GNU C++ Installation Errors

A number of common errors might occur during installation to spoil your "out-of-the-box" programming experience with inexplicable errors.

The message "Bad command or file name" means that MS-DOS can't find gcc.exe, the GNU C++ compiler. Either you did not install GNU C++ properly or your path does not include c:\djgpp\bin where gcc.exe resides. Try reinstalling GNU C++ and make sure that the command SET PATH=c:\djgpp\bin;%PATH% is in your autoexec.bat file. After reinstalling GNU C++, reboot your computer.

The message "gcc.exe: Conversion.cpp: No such file or directory (ENOENT)" indicates that gcc does not know that you are using long filenames (as opposed to old MS-DOS 8.3 filenames). To correct this problem, edit the file c:\djgpp\djgpp.env. Set the LFN property to Y as shown in this figure.

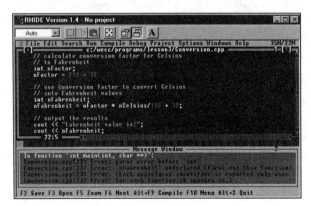

GNU C++ generates an error message if it finds an error in your C++ program. To demonstrate the error reporting process, I removed a semicolon at the end of one of the lines in the program and recompiled. The result is shown in Figure 3-4 (line 4 should read nFactor = 212 - 32; with the semicolon)

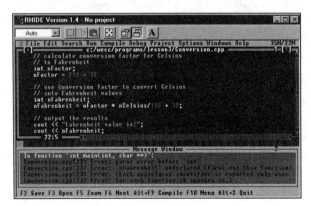

Figure 3-4
GNU C++ reports errors found during the build process in the rhide output window.

The error message that is reported in Figure 3-4 is a little imposing; however, it is reasonably descriptive, if you take one line at a time.

The first line indicates that it detected the problem while it was analyzing code contained within main(), that is, code found between the open and closed braces following the keyword main().

The second line indicates that it couldn't understand how int on line 22 fit into the scheme of things. Of course, int doesn't fit, but without the semicolon, GNU C++ thought that line 18 and 22 were one statement. The remaining errors stem from not being able to understand line 22.

To fix the problem, I first analyzed line 22 (notice the line 22:5 at the lower left of the code window — the cursor is on column 5 of line 22). Because line 22 seems to be in order, I look back up to line 18 and notice that a semicolon is missing. I add the semicolon and recompile. This time, GNU C++ completes without complaint.

C++ Error Messages

Why are all C++ packages so fussy when it comes to C++ syntax? Visual C++ was able to determine without a doubt that I had removed a semicolon in the previous example. However, if a C++ compiler can figure out that I left off a semicolon, then why doesn't it just fix the problem and go on?

The answer is simple but profound. Visual C++ *thinks* that you left off a semicolon. I could have introduced any number of errors that Visual C++ might have misdiagnosed as a missing semicolon. Had the compiler simply "corrected" the problem by introducing a semicolon, Visual C++ would have masked the real problem.

As you will see, finding an error buried in a program that builds without error is difficult and time consuming. It is far superior to let the compiler find the error, if possible.

This lesson was hard in coming. Early in the days of computing, compilers tried to detect and correct any error that they could find. This sometimes reached ridiculous proportions.

My friends and I loved to torture one of these "friendly" compilers by entering a program containing nothing but the existential question of the ages "IF." (In retrospect, I guess my friends and I were nerdy.) Through a series of tortured gyrations, this particular compiler would eventually create an involved command line from this single word that would build successfully. I know that the compiler misunderstood my intent with the word "IF" because I didn't intend a single thing.

In my experience, almost every time that the compiler tried to "fix" my program, the compiler was wrong. Although misguided, this is harmless if the compiler reports the error before fixing it. Compilers that correct errors without reporting them do much more harm than good.

Executing Your Program

**10 Min.
To Go**

To execute the Conversion program, click Run and Run again or enter Ctrl+F9 as shown in Figure 3-5.

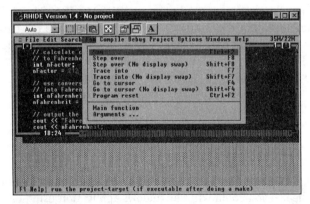

Figure 3-5
rhide opens a window in which it executes the current program.

Immediately a window opens in which the program requests a temperature in Celsius as shown in Figure 3-6.

Figure 3-6
The user screen displays the calculated temperature in Fahrenheit degrees.

Enter a known temperature such as 100 degrees. After pressing the Enter key, the program returns with the equivalent temperature of 212 degrees Fahrenheit. However, because rhide closes the window as soon as the program terminates, you are not given a chance to see the output before the window closes. rhide opens an alert box with the message that the program terminated with an error code of zero. Despite the name "error code," a zero means no error occurred.

To see the output from the now terminated program, click the User Screen menu item of the Windows menu or enter Alt+F5. This window displays the current MS-DOS window. In this window, you see the last 25 lines of output of the program including the calculated Fahrenheit temperature as shown in Figure 3-6.

Congratulations! You have just entered, built, and executed your first program using GNU C++.

Closing Points

There are two points to emphasize. First, GNU C++ is not intended for developing Windows programs. In theory, you could write a Windows application using GNU C++, but it wouldn't be easy without the help provided by the Visual C++ libraries. Second, GNU C++ provides a type of help that can be very helpful.

Program output

Windows programs have a very visually oriented, windows-based output. Conversion.exe is a 32-bit program that executes under Windows, but it is not a "Windows" program in the visual sense.

If you don't know what is meant by the phrase "32-bit program," don't worry about it.

As I pointed out in the introduction, this is not a book about writing Windows programs. The C++ programs that you write in this book have a command-line interface executing within an MS-DOS box.

Budding Windows programmers should not despair — you did not waste your money. Learning C++ is a prerequisite to writing Windows programs.

Done!

GNU C++ help

GNU C++ provides a help system through the `rhide` user interface. Place your cursor on a construct that you don't understand and press F1; a window pops up like that shown in Figure 3-7. Alternatively, click Index under Help to display a list of help topics. Click the topic of interest to display help.

Figure 3-7
rhide supports F1- and Index-type help.

The help provided by GNU C++ is not nearly as comprehensive as that provided by Visual C++. For example, place the cursor on the `int` statement and press F1. What appears is a window describing the editor, not exactly what I was looking for. The help provided by GNU C++ tends to center on library functions and compiler options. Fortunately, once you have mastered the C++ language itself, GNU C++ help is satisfactory for most applications.

REVIEW

GNU C++ provides a user-friendly environment in which you can create and test your programs in the form of the `rhide` utility. You can use `rhide` in much the same way that you would use Visual C++. You use the `rhide` editor to enter the code and the builder to convert the source code into machine code. Finally, `rhide` provides the capability to execute the final program from within the same environment.

The next chapter goes over the C++ program step by step.

QUIZ YOURSELF

1. What kind of file is a C++ source program? (That is, is it a Word file? An Excel spreadsheet file? A text file?) (See the first paragraph of "Creating Your First Program.")

2. Does C++ care about indention? Does it care about case? (See "Creating Your First Program.")

3. What does "building your program" mean? (See "Building Your Program.")

4. Why does C++ generate error messages? Why can't it just try to make sense out of what is entered? (See the "C++ Error Messages" sidebar.)

C++ Instructions

Session Checklist

✔ Reviewing the Conversion program from Sessions 2 and 3

✔ Understanding the parts of a C++ program

✔ Introducing common C++ commands

**30 Min.
To Go**

I n Sessions 2 and 3, you were asked to enter a C++ program by rote. The idea was to learn the C++ environment (whichever environment you chose) rather than learn how to program. This session analyzes the Conversion.cpp program. You will see exactly what each part of the program does and how each part contributes to the overall solution.

The Program

Listing 4-1 is the Conversion.cpp program (again) except that it is annotated by commenting features which I describe in the remainder of the lesson.

There are several aspects to this program that you have to take on faith, at least for now. Be patient. Every structure found in this program is explained in time.

This version has extra comments....

Listing 4-1
Conversion.cpp from \wecc\programs\lesson 02

```cpp
//
//   Conversion - convert temperature from Celsius
//                degree units into Fahrenheit degree
//                units:
//      Fahrenheit = Celsius  * (212 - 32)/100 + 32
//
#include <stdio.h>              // framework
#include <iostream.h>
int main(int nNumberofArgs, char* pszArgs[])
{
    // here is our first statement
    // it's a declaration
    int nCelsius;

    // our first input/output statements
    cout << "Enter the temperature in Celsius:";
    cin  >> nCelsius;

    // the assignment marks a calculation expression
    int nFactor;
    nFactor = 212 - 32;

    // an assignment using an expression containing
    // variables
    int nFahrenheit;
    nFahrenheit = nFactor * nCelsius/100 + 32;

    // output the results
```

```
    cout << "Fahrenheit value is:";
cout << nFahrenheit;

    return 0;
}
```

The C++ Program Explained

Our Human Program back in Session 1 consisted of a sequence of commands. Similarly, a C++ program consists of a sequence of C++ statements that the computer processes in order. These statements fall into a series of broad types. Each of these is described here.

The basic program framework

Every program written in C++ begins with the same basic framework:

```
#include <stdio.h>
#include <iostream.h>
int main(int nNumberofArgs, char* pzArgs[])
{
...your code goes here...
    return 0;
}
```

You don't need to worry too much about the details of this framework — these details will come later — but you should have some idea of what they're about. The first two lines are called **include statements** because they cause the contents of the named file to be included at that point in the program. We'll just consider them magic at this point.

The next statement in every framework is the int main(...) statement. This is followed by an open and closed brace. Your programs are written within these braces. Execution of the program begins at the open brace and ends at the return statement, which immediately precedes the closed brace.

Unfortunately, a more detailed explanation of this framework must be left to future chapters. Don't worry . . . we get to it before the weekend is out.

Comments

The first few lines of the program appear to be free form text. Either this "code" was meant for human eyes or the computer is a lot smarter than anyone's ever given it credit for being. These first six lines are known as comments. A **comment** is a line or portion of a line that is ignored by the C++ compiler. Comments enable the programmer to explain what he or she was doing or thinking while writing a particular segment of code.

A C++ comment begins with a double slash ("//") and ends with a newline. You can put any character you want in a comment. A comment may be as long as you want, but it is customary to keep comments to 80 characters or so, because that's all that will fit on the computer screen.

A **newline** would have been known as a "carriage return" back in the days of typewriters, when the act of entering characters into a machine was called "typing" and not "keyboarding." A newline is the character that terminates a command line.

C++ allows a second form of comment in which everything appearing after a /* and before a */ are ignored; however, this form of comment is not normally used in C++ anymore.

It may seem odd to have a command in C++, or any other programming language, which is ignored by the computer. However, all computer languages have some version of the comment. It is critical that the programmer explain what was going through her or his mind at the time that the code was written. It may not be obvious to the next person who picks up the program and uses it or modifies it. In fact, after only a few months it may not be obvious to the programmer what he or she meant.

Use comments early and often.

**20 Min.
To Go**

There's that framework again

The next four lines represent that framework I mentioned earlier. Remember that the program begins executing with the first statement after the open brace.

Statements

The first noncomment line after the brace is a C++ statement. A **statement** is a single set of commands. All statements other than comments end with a semicolon (;). (There is a reason that comments don't, but it's obscure. To my mind, comments should end in a semicolon as well, for consistency's sake if for no other reason.)

As you look through the program, you can see that spaces, tabs, and newlines appear throughout the program. In fact, I have placed a newline after every statement in this program. These characters are collectively known as white space because you can't see any of them on the monitor. A **white space** is a space, a tab, a vertical tab, or a newline. C++ ignores white space.

You may add white space anywhere you like in your program to enhance readability, except in the middle of a word.

While C++ may ignore white space, it does not ignore case. The variable `full-speed` and the variable `FullSpeed` have nothing to do with each other. While the command `int` may be understood completely, C++ has no idea what `INT` means.

Declarations

The line `int nCelcius;` is a declaration statement. A **declaration** is a statement that defines a variable. A **variable** is a "holding tank" for a value of some type. A variable contains a value, such as a number or a character.

The term *variable* stems from algebra formulae of the following type:

```
x = 10
y = 3 * x
```

In the second expression, *y* is set equal to 3 times *x*, but what is *x*? The variable *x* acts as a holding tank for a value. In this case, the value of *x* is 10, but we could have just as well set the value of *x* to 20 or 30 or –1. The second formula makes sense no matter what the value of *x*.

In algebra, it's allowed to begin with a statement such as *x = 10*. In C++, the programmer must first define the variable *x* before it can be used.

In C++, a variable has a type and a name. The line `int nCelcius;` declares an variable `nCelcius` designed to hold an integer. (Why they couldn't have just said `integer` instead of `int`, I'll never know. It's just one of those things that you learn to live with.)

The name of a variable has no particular significance to C++. A variable must begin with a letter ('A' through 'Z' or 'a' through 'z'). All subsequent characters must be a letter, a digit ('0' to '9'), or an underscore ('_'). Variable names can be as long as you want to make them within reason.

There actually is a limitation but it's much larger than the reader's. Don't exceed what the reader can comfortably remember — 20 characters or so.

By convention, variable names begin with a lowercase letter. Each new word in a variable begins with a capital as in myVariable. **I explain the significance of the** *n* **in** nCelsius **in Session 5.**

Try to make variable names short but descriptive. Avoid names like x **because** x **has no meaning. A variable name such as** lengthOfLineSegment **is much more descriptive.**

10 Min. To Go

Input/output

The lines beginning with cout and cin are known as input/output statements, often contracted to I/O statements. (Like all engineers, programmers love contractions and acronyms.)

The first I/O statement says output the phrase "Enter the temperature in Celsius:" to cout (pronounced "see-out"). cout is the name of the standard C++ output device. In this case, the standard C++ output device is your monitor.

The next line is exactly the opposite. This line says to extract a value from the C++ input device and store it in the integer variable nCelsius. The C++ input device is normally the keyboard. This is the C++ analogue to the algebra formula *x = 10* mentioned above. For the remainder of the program, the value of nCelsius is whatever the user enters here.

Expressions

In the next two lines, which are marked as a "calculation expression," the program declares a variable nFactor and assigns it the value resulting from a calculation. This command calculates the difference of 212 and 32. In C++, such a formula is called an expression.

An **operator** is a command that generates a value. The operator in this calculation is "−".

An **expression** is a command that has a value. The expression here is "212 − 32".

Assignment

The spoken language can be very ambiguous. The term *equals* is one of those ambiguities.

The word *equals* can mean that two things have the same value as in 5 cents equals a nickel. Equals can also imply assignment as in math when you say that y equals 3 times x.

To avoid ambiguity, C++ programmers call = the **assignment operator**.

The assignment operator says store the results of the expression on the right of the = in the variable to the left. Programmers say that nFactor is assigned the value 212 − 32.

Expressions (continued)

The second expression in Conversion.cpp presents a slightly more complex expression than the first. This expression uses the same mathematical symbols: * for multiplication, / for division, and + for addition. In this case, however, the calculation is performed on variables and not simply constants.

The value contained in the variable nFactor (calculated immediately prior, by the way) is multiplied by the value contained in nCelcius (which was input from the keyboard). The result is divided by 100 and summed with 32. The result of the total expression is assigned to the integer variable nFahrenheit.

The final two commands output the string "Fahrenheit value is:" to the display followed by the value of nFahrenheit.

Done!

REVIEW

You have finally seen an explanation of the Conversion program entered in Sessions 2 and 3. Of necessity, this explanation has been at a high level. Don't worry, however; the details are forthcoming.

- All programs begin with the same framework.
- C++ allows you to include comments that are explanations to yourself and others as to what different parts of a program do.

- C++ expressions look a lot like algebraic expressions, except that C++ variables have to be declared before they can be used.
- = is called assignment.
- C++ input and output statements default to the keyboard and the screen or MS-DOS window.

QUIZ YOURSELF

1. What does the following C++ statement do? (See Comments.)

```
// I'm lost
```

2. What does the following C++ statement do? (See Declarations.)

```
int nQuizYourself; // help me out here
```

3. What does the following C++ statement do? (See Input/Output.)

```
cout << "Help me out here";
```

4. What does the following C++ statement do? (See Expressions.)

```
nHelpMeOutHere = 32;
```

Friday Evening

1. Write a program to lower a car using these objects:

   ```
   car
   tire
   nut
   jack
   wrench
   ```

   Let's further assume that our processor understands these actions:

   ```
   grab
   move, move up and move down
   release
   turn
   ```

   Hints:

   a. You need to assume that the processor person understands up and down and that a jack has a handle.

   b. Not all of the nouns and verbs provided are used.

2. Remove the minus sign between the 212 and 32 and rebuild. Record and explain the error message returned.

3. Fix the "problem" in the way Visual C++ requests and rebuild.

4. Execute the program entering a known value such as 100 degrees Celsius. Record the result.

5. Explain the resulting behavior.

6. Explain why this example would highlight a very unfortunate situation were Visual C++ a self-correcting compiler.

   Hint: Believe it or not, "32;" is a valid command.

7. Remove the closing quote on line 26 of Conversion.cpp within rhide so that it appears as follows:

   ```
   cout << "Fahrenheit value is:;
   ```

   Rebuild and note any error messages.

8. Can you explain the error messages you see?

9. If GNU C++ were to attempt to automatically solve the problem, what might it do? Try performing this solution yourself and rebuild. Note the result.

10. Execute the "fixed" program. Enter a temperature of 100 degrees Celsius and note the result.

11. Consider for a moment what would happen if GNU C++ applied its "solution"? Does such an approach help? Is it harmful?

12. Any comments?

    Hints:

    a. GNU C++ thinks that a string begins when it sees a beginning quote and that the string terminates with the next quote symbol.

    b. The rhide editor highlights words depending on what it thinks they are. Strings appear in light blue.

    c. If you're confused, peek ahead to the answer for question 9 (see Appendix A). If you understand that hint, then go back and answer all the questions.

13. Which of the following are legal variable names:

    a. twoFeetOfRope

    b. 2FeetOfRope

    c. two Feet Of Rope

    d. lengthOf2Ropes

    e. &moreRope

14. Write a program that prompts the user for three numbers and then returns their sum. Extra credit: Output the average of the three numbers rather than the sum.

Hints:

a. Begin with the standard C++ framework.

b. Don't forget to declare your variables.

c. Don't forget that division has higher precedence than addition. You may need to use parentheses especially on the extra credit program.

☑ **Friday**

☑ **Saturday**

☐ **Sunday**

PART

II

Saturday Morning

Variable Types

Session Checklist

✔ Declaring variables

✔ Dealing with the limitations of an integer variable

✔ Using floating point variables

✔ Declaring and using other variable types

**30 Min.
To Go**

One problem with the Conversion program from Part I is that it deals only with integers. This integer limitation is not a problem for daily use — it is unlikely that someone would enter a fractional temperature such as 10.5___A worse problem is conversion round off. Most integer Celsius values convert to a fractional Fahrenheit reading. The Conversion program takes no heed of this — it simply lops off the fractional part without any warning.

It may not be obvious, but this program had to be carefully written to minimize the effect that the rounding off of fractions would have on the output.

This chapter examines the limitations of integer variables. It goes on to examine other variables types, including those designed to limit rounding-off error, and to look at the advantages and disadvantage of each.

Decimal Numbers

Integers are the counting numbers that you are most accustomed to: 1, 2, 3, and so on plus the negative numbers −1, −2, −3, and so on. Integers are most useful in our everyday life; however, they cannot easily express fractions. Integer fractional values such as $^2/_3$ or $^{15}/_{16}$ or $3^{111}/_{126}$ are clumsy to work with. It is difficult to compare two fractional numbers if their denominator is not the same. For example, when working on the car, I have a hard time knowing which bolt is larger — $^3/_4$ or $^{25}/_{32}$ (it's the latter).

I have been told, but I cannot prove, that the problem of integer fractions is what leads to the otherwise inexplicable prominence of 12 in everyday life. Twelve is the smallest integer that is divisible by 4, 3, and 2. One-fourth of a unit is accurate enough for most purposes.

The creation of decimal fractions proved to be a great improvement. It is clear that 0.75 is less than 0.78 (these are the same values as earlier, expressed as decimal values). In addition, floating-point math is much easier because there is no need to find least-common denominators and other such nonsense.

The limitations of int's in C++

The variable type int is the C++ version of an integer. Variables of type int suffer the same limitations that their counting integer equivalents in math do.

Integer round off

Reconsider the problem of calculating the average of three numbers. (This was the extra credit problem in Session 4.)

Given three int variables, nValue1, nValue2, and nValue3, an equation for calculating the average is the following:

```
(nValue1 + nValue2 + nValue3) / 3
```

This equation is correct and reasonable. However, let's consider the equally correct and reasonable solution:

```
nValue1/3 + nValue2/3 + nValue3/3
```

To see what affect this might have, consider the following simple averaging program which utilizes both algorithms:

```cpp
// IntAverage - average three numbers using integer
//              data type
#include <stdio.h>
#include <iostream.h>

int main(int nArg, char* pszArgs[])
{
    int nValue1;
    int nValue2;
    int nValue3;

    cout << "Integer version\n";
    cout << "Input three numbers (follow each with newline)\n";
    cout << "#1:";
    cin  >> nValue1;

    cout << "#2:";
    cin  >> nValue2;

    cout << "#3:";
    cin  >> nValue3;

    // the following solution does not suffer from round off as much
    cout << "The add before divide average is:";
    cout << (nValue1 + nValue2 + nValue3)/3;
    cout << "\n";

    // this version suffers from serious round off
    cout << "The divide before add average is:";
    cout << nValue1/3 + nValue2/3 + nValue3/3;
    cout << "\n";

    cout << "\n\n";
    return 0;
}
```

This program retrieves the three values nValue1, nValue2, and nValue3 from cin, the keyboard. It then outputs the average of the three numbers, using the add-before-divide algorithm followed by the divide-before-add algorithm.

After building and executing the program, I entered the values 1, 2, and 3 expecting to get an answer of 2 in both cases. Instead, I got the results shown in Figure 5-1.

Figure 5-1
The divide-before-add algorithm displays significant rounding-off error.

To understand the reason for this strange behavior let's enter the values of 1, 2, and 3 directly in equation 2.

```
1/3 + 2/3 + 3/3
```

Because integers cannot express fractions, the result of an integer operation is always the fraction rounded toward zero.

This rounding down of integer calculations is called *truncation*.

With integer truncation in mind, the above equation becomes

```
0 + 0 + 1
```

or 1.

The add-before-divide algorithm fairs considerably better:

```
(1 + 2 + 3)/3
```

equals 6/3 or 2.

Even the add-before-divide algorithm is not always correct. Enter the values 1, 1, and 3. The answer returned by both algorithms is 1 instead of the correct 1⅔.

You must be very careful when performing division involving integers because truncation is likely to occur.

Limited range

A second problem with the int variable type is its limited range. A normal int variable can store a maximum value of 2,147,483,647 and a minimum value of –2,147,483,648 — more or less, plus 2 billion to minus 2 billion.

Some older (actually, "very older") compilers limit the range of an int variable to the range -32,768 to 32,767.

Solving the truncation problem

Fortunately, C++ understands decimal numbers.

C++ refers to decimal numbers as *floating-point numbers,* or simply as *floats*. The term floating point stems from the decimal point being allowed to float back and forth as necessary to express the value.

Floating point variables are declared in the same way as int variables:

```
float fValue1;
```

To see how floating point numbers fix the rounding-off problem inherent with integers, I converted all of the int variables to float in the earlier IntAverage program. (The resulting program is contained on the enclosed CD-ROM under the name FloatAverage.)

FAverage converted the numbers 1, 2, and 3 to the proper average of 2 using both algorithms as shown in Figure 5-2.

**20 Min.
To Go**

If you intend to perform calculations, stick with floating-point numbers.

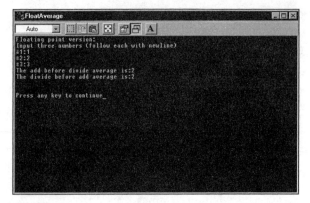

Figure 5-2
*Floating-point variables calculate the proper average for the values 1, 2,
and 3.*

Limitations of floating point

While floating-point variables can solve many calculation problems, such as truncation, they have a number of limitations.

Counting

For one thing, floating-point variables cannot be used in applications where counting is important. This includes C++ constructs that require counting capability.
This is because C++ can't be sure exactly which whole number value is meant by a
given floating-point number. For example, it's clear that 1.0 is 1, but what about
0.9 or 1.1? Should these also be considered as 1?

C++ simply avoids the problem by insisting on using int values when counting
is involved.

Calculation speed

Historically, a computer processor can process integer arithmetic quicker than it
can process floating-point arithmetic. Thus, while a processor might be capable of
adding 1000 integer numbers in a given amount of time, the same processor might
be capable of performing only 200 floating-point calculations.

Calculation speed has become less and less of a problem as microprocessors increase in capability. Most modern processors contain special calculation circuitry enabling them to perform floating-point calculations almost as fast as integer calculations.

Loss of accuracy

Further, even floating-point variables don't solve all computational problems. Floating-point variables have a limited precision: about six digits.

To see why this is a problem, consider that ⅓ is expressed as 0.333. . . in a continuing sequence. The concept of an infinite series makes sense in math, but not to a computer. The computer has finite accuracy. Thus, a floating-point version of ⅓ is roughly 0.333333. When these 6 digits are multiplied by 3 again, the processor computes a value of 0.999999 rather than the mathematically expected 1. The loss of accuracy in computations due to the limitations of the floating-point data type is called *round-off error*.

C++ can correct for many forms of round-off error. For example, in output, C++ can determine that instead of 0.999999, that the user really meant 1. In other cases, however, even C++ cannot correct for round-off error.

"Not so limited" range

The `float` data type also has a limited range, although the range of a `float` is much larger than that of an integer. The maximum value of a floating-point variable is roughly 10 to the 38th power. That's 1 followed by 38 zeroes.

Note

Only the first 6 digits have any meaning because the remaining 32 digits suffer from floating point round off error. Thus, a floating-point variable can hold the value 123,000,000 without round-off error but not the value 123,456,789.

Other Variable Types

C++ provides other variable types in addition to `int` and `float`. These are shown in Table 5-1. Each type has its advantages as well as its limitations.

Table 5-1
Other C++ Variable Types

Name	Example	Purpose
char	'c'	A single char variable can store a single alphabetic or digital character. Not suitable for arithmetic. (The single quotes indicate the single character *c*.)
string	"this is a string"	A string of characters; a sentence. This is used to contain phrases. (The double quotes indicate the string of characters *this is a string*.)
double	1.0	A larger, economy-size floating-point type with 15 significant digits and a maximum value of 10 to the 308th power.
long	10L	A larger integer type with a range of 2 billion to --2 billion.

Thus, the statement

```
// declare a variable and set it to 1
long lVariable;
lVariable = 1;

// declare a variable of type double and set it to 1.0
double dVariable;
dVariable = 1.0;
```

declares a variable lVariable to be of type long and sets it equal to the value 1, while dVariable is a double type variable set to the value 1.0.

It is possible to declare a variable and initialize it in the same statement:

```
int nVariable = 1;  // declare a variable and
                    // initialize it to 1
```

There is no particular significance of the name of the variable to the C++ compiler.

A char variable can hold a single character, whereas a string holds a string of characters. Thus, 'a' is the character *a* whereas "a" is a string containing just the letter *a*. (String is not actually a variable type, but for most purposes you can treat it as such. You will learn more details about string in Chapter14.)

The character 'a' and the string "a" are not the same thing. If an application requires a string, you cannot provide it a character, even if the string contains only the single character.

Both long and double are extended forms of int and float respectively — long stands for long integer, and double stands for double-precision floating point.

Types of constants

Notice how each data type is expressed.

In an expression such as n = 1;, the constant 1 is an int. If you really meant for 1 to be a long integer then you need to write the statement as n = 1L;. The analogy is as follows, 1 represents a single ball in the bed of a pickup truck, while 1L is a single ball in a dump truck. The ball is the same, but the capacity of its container is much larger.

Similarly 1.0 represents the value 1 but in a floating-point container. Notice, however, that the default for floating-point constants is double. Thus, 1.0 is a double number and not a float.

Special characters

In general, you can store any printable character you want in a char or string variable. There is also a set of nonprintable characters that are so important that they are allowed as well. Table 5-2 lists these characters.

You have already seen the newline character. This character breaks a string into separate lines.

Table 5-2
Nonprintable but Often Used Character Constants

Character Constant	Meaning
'\n'	new line
'\t'	tab
'\0'	null
'\\'	backslash

So far, I have only placed newlines at the end of strings. However, a newline can be placed anywhere within a string. Consider, for example, the following string:

```
cout << "This is line 1\nThis is line 2"
```

appears on the output as

```
This is line 1
This is line 2
```

Similarly, the '\t' tab character moves output to the next tab position. Exactly what that means is dependent on the type of computer you are using to run the program.

Because the backslash character is used to signify special characters, there needs to be a character pair for the backslash itself. The character '\\' represents the backslash.

C++ Collision with MS-DOS Filenames

MS-DOS uses the backslash character to separate folder names in the path to a file. Thus, Root\FolderA\File represents *File* in *FolderA*, which is a subdirectory of *Root*.

Unfortunately, MS-DOS's use of backslash conflicts with that of C++. The MS-DOS path Root\FolderA\File is represented by the C++ string "Root\\FolderA\\File". The double backslashes are necessary because of the special use of the backslash character in C++.

Mixed Mode Expressions

I almost hate to bring this up, but C++ enables you to mix variable types in a single expression. That is, you can add an integer with a double. The following expression in which nValue1 is an int is allowed:

```
// in the following expression the value of nValue1
// is converted to a double before performing the
// assignment
int nValue1 = 1;
nValue1 = nValue1 + 1.0;
```

An expression in which the two operands are not of the same type is called a *mixed mode expression*. Mixed mode expressions generate a value whose type is equal to the more capable of the two operands. In this case, nValue1 is converted to a double before the calculation proceeds.

Similarly, an expression of one type may be assigned to a variable of a different type as in the following statement

```
// in the following assignment, the whole
// number part of fVariable is stored into nVariable
fVariable = 1.0;
int nVariable;
nVariable = fVariable;
```

Precision or range may be lost if the variable on the left side of the assignment is "smaller." In the previous example, the value of *fVariable* must be truncated before being stored in *nVariable*.

Converting a "larger" size value to a "smaller" size variable is called *promotion* while converting values in the opposite direction is known as *demotion*. We say that the value of int variable nVariable1 is promoted to a double:

```
int nVariable1 = 1;
double dVariable = nVariable1;
```

Mixed mode expressions are not a good idea. You should make your own decisions instead of leaving it up to C++ — C++ may not understand what you really want.

Naming Conventions

You may have noticed that I begin the name of each variable with a special character that seems to have nothing to do with the name. These special characters are shown below. Using this convention, you can immediately recognize dVariable as being a variable of type double.

Character	Type
n	int
l	long
f	float
d	double
c	character
sz	String

These leading characters help the programmer keep track of the variable type. Thus, you can immediately identify the following as a mixed mode assignment of a long variable to an int variable.

```
nVariable = lVariable;
```

Remember, however, that although I might use some special characters in variable names, these characters have no significance to C++. I could just as soon have used q to signify *int* had I wanted to. Many programmers don't use any naming convention at all.

REVIEW

As you have seen, integer variables are both efficient in terms of machine time and easy to program. Integer variables have definite limitations when used in calculations, however. Floating-point variables are ideal for use in mathematical equations because they do not suffer from significant round off nor significant range limitation. On the downside, floating-point variables are more difficult to use and not as universally applicable as integers.

- Integer variables represent counting numbers, such as 1, 2, and so on.
- Integer variables have a range of –2 billion to +2 billion.
- Floating-point variables represent decimal fractional values.
- Floating point variables have a practically unlimited range.
- The char variable type is used to represent ANSI characters.

QUIZ YOURSELF

1. What is the range of an int variable? (See "Limited Range.")
2. Why don't float variables suffer from significant rounding off error? (See "Solving the Truncation Problem.")
3. What is the type of the constant 1? What is the type of 1.0? (See "Types of Constants.")

Mathematical Operations

Session Checklist

✔ Using the C++ mathematical operators

✔ Identifying expressions

✔ Increasing clarity with "special" mathematical operators

**30 Min.
To Go**

The Conversion and Average programs made use of simple mathematical operators such as addition, multiplication, and division. I have used these operators without describing them because they are largely intuitive. This session describes the set of mathematical operators.

The mathematical operators are listed in Table 6-1. The first column lists the precedence of the operator with those operators at the top of the table having higher precedence than those below.

Table 6-1
C++ Mathematical Operators

Operator	Meaning
+ (unary)	effectively does nothing
- (unary)	returns the negative of its argument
++ (unary)	increment
-- (unary)	decrement
*	multiplication
/	division
%	modulo
+	addition
–	subtraction
=, *=,%=,+=,-=	assignment types

Each of these operators is addressed in the following sections.

Arithmetic Operators

The multiplication, division, modulo, addition, and subtraction are the operators used to perform conventional arithmetic. Each of these operators has the conventional meaning that you studied in grammar school with the possible exception of modulo.

The modulo operator is similar to what my teachers called the remainder after division. For example, 4 goes into 15 three times with a remainder of 3. Expressed in C++ terms 15 modulo 4 is 3.

Because programmers are always trying to impress nonprogrammers with the simplest things, C++ programmers define modulo as follows:

```
IntValue % IntDivisor
```

is equal to

```
IntValue - (IntValue / IntDivisor) * IntDivisor
```

Let's try this out on our earlier example:

```
15 % 4 is equal to 15 - (15/4) * 4
                    15 - 3 * 4
                    15 - 12
                    3
```

Because modulo depends on the round off error inherent in integers, modulo is not defined for floating-point numbers.

Expressions

The most common type of statement in C++ is the expression. An *expression* is a statement that has a value. All expressions also have a type.

For example, a statement involving any of the mathematical operators is an expression because all of these operators return a value. Expressions can be complex or extremely simple. In fact, the statement "1" is an expression. There are five expressions in the following statement:

```
z = x * y + w;
1. x * y + w
2. x * y
3. x
4. y
5. w
```

An unusual aspect of C++ is that an expression is a complete statement. Thus, the following is a legal C++ statement:

```
1;
```

All expressions have a type. As we have already noted, the type of the expression 1 is int. In an assignment, the type of the expression to the right of the assignment is always the same as the type of the variable to the left — if it is not, C++ makes the necessary conversions.

Operator Precedence

Each of the C++ operators has a property which determines the order that operators are evaluated in compound expressions (expressions with more than one operator). This property is known as precedence.

The expression

```
x/100 + 32
```

divides *x* by 100 before adding 32. In a given expression, C++ performs multiplication and division before addition or subtraction. We say that multiplication and division have higher *precedence* than addition and subtraction.

What if the programmer wanted to divide *x* by 100 plus 32? The programmer can bundle expressions together using parentheses as follows:

```
x/(100 + 32)
```

This has the same effect as dividing *x* by 132. The expression within the parentheses is evaluated first. This allows the programmer to override the precedence of individual operators.

The original expression

```
x / 100 + 32
```

is identical to the expression:

```
(x/100) + 32
```

The precedence of each of the operators described in Table 6-1 is shown in Table 6-2.

Table 6-2
C++ Mathematical Operators Including Their Precedence

Precedence	Operator	Meaning
1	+ (unary)	effectively does nothing
1	- (unary)	returns the negative of its argument
2	++ (unary)	increment
2	-- (unary)	decrement

Precedence	Operator	Meaning
3	*	multiplication
3	/	division
3	%	modulo
4	+	addition
4	–	subtraction
5	=, *=,%=,+=,-=	assignment types

Operators of the same precedence are evaluated from left to right. Thus the expression

```
x / 10 / 2
```

is the same as

```
(x / 10) / 2
```

Multiple levels of parentheses are evaluated from the inside out. In the following expression:

```
(y / (2 + 3)) / x
```

the variable y is divided by 5 and the result divided by x.

Unary Operators

Unary operators are those operators that take a single argument.

A binary operator is an operator that takes two arguments. For example, consider a + b. In C++ jargon, the arguments to the addition operator are the expression to the left and the expression on the right.

The unary mathematical operators are +, -, ++, and --.

The minus operator changes the sign of its argument. Positive numbers become negative and vice versa. The plus operator does not change the sign of its argument. Effectively the plus operator has no effect at all.

The ++ and the -- operators increment and decrement their arguments by one.

10 Min. To Go

Why a Separate Increment Operator?

The authors of C++ noted that programmers add 1 more than any other constant. As a convenience factor, a special "add 1" instruction was added to the language.

In addition, most computer processors have an increment instruction that is faster than the addition instruction. When C++ was created, saving a few instructions was a big deal considering what the state of development of microprocessors was.

No matter why the increment and decrement operators were created, you will see in Session 7 that they get a lot more use than you might think.

The increment and decrement operators are limited to non-floating-point variables.

The increment and decrement operators are peculiar in that both come in two flavors: a prefix version and a postfix version.

The prefix version of increment is written ++x while the postfix appears as x++.

Consider the increment operator (the decrement is exactly analogous).

Suppose that the variable n has the value 5. Both ++n and n++ increment n to the value 6. The difference between the two is that the value of ++n in an expression is 6 while the value of n++ is 5. The following example demonstrates this:

```
// declare three integer variables
int n1, n2, n3;

// the value of both n1 and n2 is 6
n1 = 5;
n2 = ++n1;

// the value of n1 is 6 but the value of n3 is 5
```

```
n1 = 5;
n3 = n1++;
```

Thus, n2 is given the value of n1 *after* n1 has been incremented using the preincrement operator, while n3 gets the vale of n1 *before* it is incremented using the postincrement operator.

Assignment Operators

The assignment operators are binary operators that change the value of their left-hand argument.

The simple assignment operator, '=', is an absolute necessity in any programming language. This operator stores the value of the right-hand argument in the left-hand argument. The other assignment operators, however, appear to be someone's whim.

The creators of C++ noticed that assignments often follow the form:

```
variable = variable # constant
```

where '#' is some binary operator. Thus, to increment an integer operator by 2 the programmer might write:

```
nVariable = nVariable + 2;
```

This says, add 2 to the value of nVariable and store the results in nVariable.

 It is common to see the same variable on both the right-hand and left-hand sides of an assignment.

Because the same variable appeared to be showing up on both sides of the '=' sign, they decided to add the operator to the assignment operator. All of the binary operators have an assignment version. Thus, the assignment above could be written:

```
nVariable += 2;
```

Done!

Once again, this says add 2 to the value of nVariable.

 Other than assignment itself, these assignment operators are not used that often. In certain cases, however, they can actually make the resulting program easier to read.

REVIEW

The mathematical operators are used more than any other operators in C++ programs. This is hardly surprising: C++ programs are always converting temperatures back and forth from Celsius to Fahrenheit and myriad other operations that require the ability to add, subtract, and count.

- All expressions have a value and a type.
- The order of evaluation of operators within an expression is normally determined by the precedence of the operators; however, this order can be overridden through the use of parentheses.
- For many of the most common expressions, C++ provides shortcut operators. The most common is the i++ operator in place of i = i + 1.

QUIZ YOURSELF

1. What is the value of 9 % 4? (See "Arithmetic Operators.")

2. Is 9 % 4 an expression? (See "Expressions.")

3. If n = 4, what is the value of n + 10 / 2? Why is it 9 and not 7?
   (See "Operator Precedence.")

4. If n = 4, what is the difference between ++n and n++?
   (See "Unary Operators.")

5. How would I write n = n + 2 using the += operator?
   (See "Assignment Operators.")

Logical Operations

Session Checklist

✔ Using simple logical operators and variables

✔ Working with binary numbers

✔ Performing bitwise operations

✔ Creating logical assignment statements

**30 Min.
To Go**

Other than a few oddballs such as increment and decrement, the C++ mathematical operators are common operations that you encounter in everyday life. By comparison, the C++ logical operators are unknown.

It isn't that people don't deal with logical operations. If you think back to our mechanical tire changer in Session 1, the capability to express logical computations such as "if the tire is flat AND I have a lug wrench. . ." is a must. People compute AND and OR constantly; it's just that they aren't accustomed to writing them down.

Logical operators fall into two types. One type, which I call simple logical operators, are operators that are common in everyday life. The second type, the bitwise logical operators, is unique to the computer world. I consider the simple operators before jumping off into the more complex bitwise versions.

Simple Logical Operators

The simple logical operators represent the same kind of logical decisions you'd make in daily life: such as considering whether something is true or false, or comparing two things to determine whether they're the same. The simple logical operators are shown in Table 7-1.

Table 7-1
Simple Logical Operators

Operator	Meaning
==	equality; true if the left hand argument has the same value as the right
!=	inequality; opposite of equality
>, <	greater than, less than; true if the left hand argument is greater than/less than the right hand argument
>=, <=	greater than or equal to, less than or equal to; true if either > or == is true, /< or == is true
&&	AND; true if both the left and right hand arguments are true
||	OR; true if either the left or the right hand arguments are true
!	NOT; true if it's argument is false

The first six entries in Table 7-1 are the comparison operators. The equality operator is used to compare two numbers. For example, the following is true if the value of nVariable is 0.

```
nVariable == 0;
```

Don't confuse the equality operator == with the assignment operator =. Not only is this is a common mistake, but it's a mistake that the C++ compiler cannot catch.

```
nVariable = 0;    // programmer meant to say nVariable == 0
```

The greater than (>) and less than (<) operators are similarly common in every-day life. The following logical comparison expression is true:

```
int nVariable1 = 1;
int nVariable2 = 2;
nVariable1 < nVariable2;
```

The greater than or equal to (>=) and less than or equal to (<=) are similar except that they include equality, whereas the other operators do not.

The && (AND) and || (OR) are equally common. These operators are typically combined with the other logic operators:

```
// true if nV2 is greater than nV1 but smaller than nV3
(nV1 < nV2) && (nV2 < nV3);
```

Be careful when using the comparison operators on floating-point numbers. Consider the following example:

```
float fVariable1 = 10.0;
float fVariable2 = (10 / 3) * 3;
fVariable1 == fVariable2;    // are these two equal?
```

The comparison in the above example is not necessarily true. 10 / 3 is equal to 0.333.... C++ cannot represent an infinite number of digits. Stored as a float, 10/3 becomes something like 0.333333. Multiplying this number by 3 gives a result of 0.999999 which is not exactly equal to 10.

Just as `(10.0 / 3) * 3` **is not exactly identical to 10.0, the results of a floating-point calculation may be off by some normally tiny amount. Such small differences may be unnoticeable to you and me, but not to the computer. Equality means exactly that, exact equality.**

The safer comparison is as follows:

```
float fDelta = fVariable1 - fVariable2;
fDelta < 0.01 && fDelta > -0.01;
```

This comparison is true if `fVariable1` **and** `fVariable2` **are within some delta of each other. (The term "some delta" is intentionally vague — it should represent acceptable error.)**

The numerical processor in your PC goes to great pains to avoid floating round off errors such as the one above — depending on the situation, the numeric processor might provide a tiny delta for you automatically; however, you should never count on such aids.

Short circuits and C++

The && and || operators perform what is called *short circuit evaluation*. Consider the following:

```
condition1 && condition2;
```

If condition1 is not true, then the result is not true no matter what the value of condition2 (that is, condition2 could be true or false without changing the result). Similarly, in the following

```
condition1 || condition2;
```

if condition1 is true then the result is true no matter what the value of condition2.

To save time, C++ evaluates condition1 first. C++ does not evaluate condition2 if condition1 is false in the case of && or condition1 is true in the case of ||.

Logical variable types

If > and && are operators, then a comparison such as a > 10 must be an expression. Clearly, the result of such an expression must be either TRUE or FALSE.

You may have noticed already that no Boolean variable type was mentioned in Session 5. That is, there is no variable type that can have the value TRUE or FALSE and nothing else. Then what is the type of an expression such as a > 10?

C++ uses the type *int* to store Boolean values. The value 0 is taken to be FALSE. Any value other than 0 is TRUE. An expression such as a > 10 evaluates to either 0 (FALSE) or 1 (TRUE).

Microsoft Visual Basic also uses an integer to hold TRUE and FALSE values; however, in Visual Basic a comparison operation returns either a 0 (FALSE) or a –1 (TRUE).

**20 Min.
To Go**

Binary Numbers

The so-called bitwise logical operators operate on their arguments at the bit level. To understand how they work, let's first examine binary numbers, which are how computers store values.

The numbers that we are familiar with are known as decimal numbers because they are based on the number 10. A number such as 123 refers to 1×100 plus 2×10 plus 3×1. Each of these base numbers, 100, 10, and 1 are powers of 10.

$123_{10} = 1 * 100 + 2 * 10 + 3 * 1$

The use of a base number of 10 for our counting system most likely stems from the fact that humans have 10 fingers, the original counting tools. If our numbering scheme had been invented by dogs, it might well have been based on the number 8 (1 "finger" of each paw is out of sight on the back part of the leg). Such an octal system would have worked just as well:

$123_{10} = 173_8 = 1 * 64_{10} + 7 * 8_{10} + 3$

The small 10 and 8 here refer to the numbering system, 10 for decimal (base 10) and 8 for octal (base 8). A counting system may use any base other than 1.

Computers have essentially two fingers. Because of the way they are built, they prefer counting using base 2. The number 123_{10} is expressed as

$0*128 + 1*64 + 1*32 + 1*16 + 1*8 + 0*4 + 1*2 + 1*1$

or 01111011_2.

It is convention to always express binary numbers using either 4, 8, 32, or 64 binary digits even if the leading digits are zero. This is also because of the way computers are built internally.

Because the term "digit" refers to a multiple of 10, a binary digit is called a *bit*. Bit stems from *binary digit*. Eight bits make up a *byte*.

Note

With such a small base, it is necessary to use a large number of digits to express numbers. It is inconvenient to use an expression such as 01111011_2 to express such a mundane value as 123_{10}. Programmers prefer to express numbers by units of 4 bits.

A single 4-bit digit is essentially base 16, because 4 bits can express any value from 0 to 15. Base 16 is known as the hexadecimal number system. *Hexadecimal* is often contracted to *hex*.

Hexadecimal uses the same digits as decimal for the numbers 0 through 9. For the digits between 9 and 16, hexadecimal uses the first 6 letters of the alphabet: A for 10, B for 11, and so on. Thus, 123_{10} becomes $7B_{16}$.

```
7 * 16 + B (i.e. 11) * 1 = 123
```

Because programmers prefer to express numbers in 4, 8, 32, or 64 bits, they similarly prefer to express hexadecimal numbers in 1, 2, 4, or 8 hexadecimal digits, even when the leading digits are 0.

Finally, it is inconvenient to express a hexadecimal number such as $7B_{16}$ using a subscript because terminals don't support subscripts. Even on a word processor such as the one I am using now, it is inconvenient to change fonts to and from subscript mode just to type two digits. Therefore, programmers use the convention of beginning a hexadecimal number with a "0x" (the reason for such a strange convention goes back to the early days of C). Thus, 7B becomes 0x7B. Using this convention, 0x123 is most definitely not the same number as 123. (In fact, 0x123 equals 291 in decimal.)

Bitwise Logical Operations

All of the operators defined so far can be performed on hexadecimal numbers in the same way that they are applied to decimal numbers. The reason that we cannot perform a multiplication such as 0xC × 0xE in our head has to do with the multiplication tables we learned in school and not any limitations of the operators themselves.

In addition to the mathematical operators, there is a set of operations based on single-bit operators. These base operators are only defined for 1-bit numbers.

The single-bit operators

The bitwise operators perform logic operations on single bits. If you consider 0 to be false and 1 to be true (it doesn't have to be his way, but that is the common convention), then you can say things such as the following for the bitwise AND operator:

```
1 (true) AND 1 (true) is 1 (true)
1 (true) AND 0 (false) is 0 (false)
```

And similarly for the OR operator:

```
1 (true) OR 0 (false) is 1 (true)
0 (false) OR 0 (false) is 0 (false)
```

Written in tabular form it looks like Tables 7-2 and 7-3.

Table 7-2
Truth Table for the AND Operator

AND	1	0
1	1	0
0	0	0

Table 7-3
Truth Table for the OR Operator

OR	1	0
1	1	1
0	1	0

In Table 7-2, the result of 1 AND 0 is shown in row 1 (corresponding to the 1 row head) and column 2 (corresponding to the 0 column head).

One other logical operation, which is not so commonly used in day-to-day living, is the "or else" operator, which is commonly contracted to XOR. XOR is true if either argument is true, but *not true* if both are true. The truth table for XOR is shown in Table 7-4.

Table 7-4
Truth Table for the XOR Operator

XOR	1	0
1	0	1
0	1	0

Armed with these single bit operators, we can take on the C++ bitwise logical operations.

The bitwise operators

The C++ bitwise operators perform bit operations on every bit of their arguments. The individual operators are shown in Table 7-5.

Table 7-5
C++ Bitwise Operators

Operator	Function
~	NOT: toggle each bit from 1 to 0 and from 0 to 1
&	AND each bit of the left hand argument with that on the right
|	OR
^	XOR

The NOT operator is the easiest to understand: NOT converts a 1 into 0 and a 0 into 1. (That is, 0 is NOT 1 and 1 is NOT 0.)

$$\frac{\sim 0110_2 \ (0x6)}{1001_2 \ (0x9)}$$

The NOT operator is the only unary bitwise logical operator. The following calculation demonstrates the & operator:

$$
\begin{array}{l}
 0110_2 \\
\& \\
\underline{ 0011_2} \\
 0010_2
\end{array}
$$

Proceeding from left to right, 0 AND 0 is 0. In the next bit, 1 AND 0 is 0. In bit 3, 1 AND 1 is 1. In the least significant bit, 0 AND 1 is 0.

The same calculation can be performed on numbers displayed in hexadecimal by first converting the number in binary, performing the operation, and then reconverting the result to hexadecimal.

$$
\begin{array}{lcl}
0x6 & & 0110_2 \\
\underline{\ \& \ } \quad \rightarrow & & \underline{\ \& \ } \\
0x3 & & \underline{0011_2} \\
& & 0010_2 \quad \rightarrow \quad 0x2
\end{array}
$$

Such conversions back and forth are much easier to perform using hexadecimal instead of decimal numbers. Believe it or not, with practice you can perform bitwise operations in your head.

Tip

10 Min.
To Go

A simple test

We need an example program to test your ability to perform bitwise operations first on paper and, later, in your head. Listing 7-1 is a program that inputs two hex values from the keyboard and outputs the results of ANDing, ORing, and XORing.

Listing 7-1
Bitwise operator testing

```
// BitTest - input two hexadecimal values from the
//           keyboard and then output the results
//           of applying the &, | and ^ operations
#include <stdio.h>
#include <iostream.h>

int main(int nArg, char* nArgs[])
{
    // set output format to hexadecimal
    cout.setf(ios::hex);

    // input the first argument
    int nArg1;
    cout << "Enter arg1 as a four-digit hexadecimal: ";
    cin  >> nArg1;

    int nArg2;
    cout << "Enter arg2: ";
    cin  >> nArg2;

    cout << "nArg1 & nArg2 = 0x"
            << (nArg1 & nArg2) << "\n";
```

Continued

Listing 7-1 *Continued*

```
    cout << "nArg1 | nArg2 = 0x"
            << (nArg1 | nArg2) << "\n";
    cout << "nArg1 ^ nArg2 = 0x"
            << (nArg1 ^ nArg2) << "\n";

    return 0;
}
```

Output:

```
Enter arg1 as a four-digit hexadecimal: 0x1234
Enter arg2: 0x00ff
nArg1 & nArg2 = 0x34
nArg1 | nArg2 = 0x12ff
nArg1 ^ nArg2 = 0x12cb
```

The first statement, which appears as cout.setf(ios::hex);, sets the output format from the default decimal to hexadecimal (you'll have to trust me that it works for now).

The remainder of the program is straightforward. The program reads nArg1 and nArg2 from the keyboard and then outputs all combinations of bitwise calculations.

Executing the program on the values 0x1234 and x00ff results in the output shown at the end of the listing.

Hexadecimal numbers appear with a preceding 0x.

Why?

The purpose for most operators is clear. No one would quarrel with the need for the plus or minus operators. The use for the < or > operators is clear. It may not be so clear to the beginner when and why one would use the bitwise operators.

The AND operator is often used to mask out information. For example, suppose that we wanted to extract the least significant hex digit from a four-digit number:

```
0x1234        0001 0010 0011 0100
   &          → &
0x000F        0000 0000 0000 1111
              0000 0000 0000 0100   →   0x0004
```

Another use is that of setting and extracting individual bits.

Suppose that we were using a single byte to store information about a person in a database that we were building. The most significant bit might be set to 1 if the person is male, the next set to 1 if a programmer, the next set to 1 if the person is attractive, and the least significant bit set to 1 if the person has a dog.

Bit	Meaning
0	1→male
1	1→programmer
2	1→attractive
3	1→owns a dog

This byte would be encoded for each database and stored along with name, social security number, and any number of other illegal information.

An ugly male programmer who owns a dog would be coded as 1101_2. To test all records in the database by searching for unattractive programmers who don't own dogs irrespective of gender we would use the following comparison.

```
(databaseValue & 0x0110) == 0x0100
             *^^*          ^ -> 0 = not attractive
                           ^    1 = is a programmer
                     * -> no interest
                     ^ -> interested
```

Done!

In this case, the 0110 value is known as a *mask* because it masks away bit properties of no interest.

REVIEW

You learned the mathematical operators presented in Chapter 6 in grade school. You probably did not learn the simple logical operators then, but they are certainly common to everyday use. Operators such as AND and OR are understandable practically without explanation. Since C++ has no logical variable type — it uses 0 to mean FALSE and everything else to be TRUE.

By comparison, the binary operators are something new. These operators perform the same logical AND and OR type operators but on each bit separately.

QUIZ YOURSELF

1. What is the difference between the && and & operators? (See "Simple Logical Operators and Bitwise Logical Operations.")
2. What is the value of (1 && 5)? (See "Simple Logical Operators.")
3. What is the value of 1 & 5? (See "Bitwise Logical Operations.")
4. Express 215 as the sum of powers of ten. (See "Binary Numbers.")
5. Express 215 as the sum of powers of two. (See "Binary Numbers.")
6. What is 215 in hexadecimal? (See "Binary Numbers.")

8

Flow Control Commands

Session Checklist

✔ Controlling the flow through the program

✔ Executing a group of statements repetitively

✔ Avoiding "infinite loops"

**30 Min.
To Go**

The programs that have appeared so far in this book have been very simple. Each took a single set of values as input, output the result, and terminated. This is similar to instructing our computerized mechanic in how to take off a single lug nut with no option to loop around to the other lug nuts on the wheel or other wheels on the car.

What is missing in our programs is any form of flow control. We have no ability to make tests of any sort, much less make decisions based on those tests.

This chapter examines the different C++ flow control commands.

The Branch Command

The simplest form of flow control is the branch statement. This instruction enables the computer to decide which path to take through C++ instructions based on some logic condition. In C++, the branch statement is implemented using the if statement:

```
if (m > n)
{
    // instructions to be executed if
    // m is greater than n
}
else
{
    // ...instructions to be executed if not
}
```

First, the condition m > n is evaluated. If the result is true, then control passes to the instructions following the {. If m is not greater than n, then control passes to the brace immediately following the else clause.

The else clause is optional. If it is not present, C++ acts as if it is present, but empty.

 Actually the braces are optional if there is only one statement to be executed as part of the while **loop; however, it is too easy to make a mistake that the C++ compiler can't catch without the braces as a guide marker. It is much safer to always include the braces. If your friends try to entice you into not using braces, just say "NO."**

The following program demonstrates the if statement.

```
// BranchDemo - input two numbers. Go down one path of the
//              program if the first argument is greater than
//              the second or the other path if not
#include <stdio.h>
#include <iostream.h>

int main(int nArg, char* pszArgs[])
{

    // input the first argument...
```

```
int nArg1;
cout << "Enter arg1: ";
cin  >> nArg1;

// ...and the second
int nArg2;
cout << "Enter arg2: ";
cin  >> nArg2;

// now decide what to do:
if (nArg1 > nArg2)
{
    cout << "argument 1 is greater than argument 2\n";
}
else
{
    cout << "argument 1 is not greater than argument 2\n";
}

return 0;
}
```

Here the program reads to integers from the keyboard and branches accordingly. This program generates the following typical results:

```
Enter arg1: 10
Enter arg2: 8
argument 1 is greater than argument 2
```

Looping Commands

Branch statements enable you to control flow of a program's execution down one path of a program or another. This is the C++ equivalent of allowing the computerized mechanic to decide whether to use a wrench or a screwdriver depending on the problem. This still doesn't get us to the point where the mechanic can turn the wrench more than once, remove more than one lug nut, or handle more than one wheel on the car. For that, we need looping statements.

The while loop

The simplest form of looping statement is the while loop. The form of a while loop is as follows:

```
while(condition)
{
    // ...repeatedly executed as long as condition is true
}
```

The condition is tested. If it is true, then the statements within the braces are executed. Upon encountering the closed brace, control returns to the beginning and the process starts over. The net effect is that the C++ code between the braces is executed repeatedly as long as the condition is true.

 The condition is only checked at the beginning of the loop. Even if the condition ceases to be true, control does not exit the loop until the beginning of the loop.

If the condition is true the first time, then what will make it false in the future? Consider the following example program:

```
// WhileDemo - input a loop count. Loop while
//               outputting astring nArg number of times.
#include <stdio.h>
#include <iostream.h>

int main(int nArg, char* pszArgs[])
{

    // input the loop count
    int nLoopCount;
    cout << "Enter nLoopCount: ";
    cin  >> nLoopCount;

    // now loop that many times
    while (nLoopCount > 0)
    {
        nLoopCount = nLoopCount - 1;
        cout << "Only " << nLoopCount << " loops to go\n";
```

```
    }
    return 0;
}
```

WhileDemo begins by retrieving a loop count from the user that it stores in the variable nLoopCount. That done, the program continues by testing nLoopCount. If nLoopCount is greater than 0, the program decrements nLoopCount by 1 and outputs the result to the display. The program then returns to the top of the loop to test whether nLoopCount is still positive.

When executed, the program WhileDemo outputs the following results :

```
Enter nLoopCount: 5
Only 4 loops to go
Only 3 loops to go
Only 2 loops to go
Only 1 loops to go
Only 0 loops to go
```

When I enter a loop count of 5, the program loops five times, each time outputting the count down value.

If the user enters a negative loop count, the program skips the loop entirely. Because the condition is never true, control never enters the loop. In addition, if the user enters a very large number, the program loops for a long time before completing.

A separate, seldom used version of the while loop, known as the do while, is identical to the while loop except that the condition isn't tested until the bottom of the loop:

```
do
{
    // ...the inside of the loop
} while (condition);
```

**20 Min.
To Go**

Using the autodecrement feature

The program decrements the loop count by using the assignment and subtraction statements. A more compact statement would use the autodecrement feature.

The following loop is slightly simpler than the one above.

```
while (nLoopCount > 0)
{
    nLoopCount--;
```

```
    cout << "Only " << nLoopCount << " loops to go\n";
}
```

The logic in this version is the same as the original — the only difference is the way that nLoopCount is decremented.

Because autodecrement both decrements its argument and returns its value, the decrement operation can actually be combined with either of the other statements. For example, the following version is the smallest loop yet.

```
while (nLoopCount-- > 0)
{
    cout << "Only " << nLoopCount << " loops to go\n";
}
```

This is the version that most C++ programmers would use.

This is where the difference between the predecrement and postdecrement operations arises.

Both nLoopCount-- **and** --nLoopCount **decrement** nLoopCount; **however, the former returns the value of** nLoopCount **before being decremented and the latter after.**

Do you want the loop to be executed when the user enters a loop count of 1? If you use the predecrement version, the value of --nLoopCount is 0 and the body of the loop is never entered. With the postdecrement version, the value of nLoopCount-- is 1 and control enters the loop.

The dreaded infinite loop

Suppose that because of a coding error, the programmer forgot to decrement the variable nLoopCount, as in the loop example below. The result would be a loop counter that never changed. The test condition would either be always false or always true.

```
while (nLoopCount > 0)
{
    cout << "Only " << nLoopCount << " loops to go\n";
}
```

Because the value of nLoopCount never changes, the program executes in a never-ending or infinite loop. An execution path that continues forever is known as an *infinite loop*. An infinite loop occurs when the condition that would otherwise terminate the loop cannot occur — usually due to some coding error.

There are many ways of creating an infinite loop, most of which are much more difficult to spot than this one.

The for loop

A second form of loop is the for loop. The for loop has this format:

```
for (initialization; conditional; increment)
{
    // ...body of the loop
}
```

Execution of the for loop begins with the initialization clause. The initialization clause got this name because this is normally where counting variables are initialized. The initialization clause is only executed once, when the for loop is first encountered.

Execution continues to the conditional clause. In similar fashion to the while loop, the for loop continues to execute as long as the conditional clause is true.

After completing execution of the code in the body of the loop, control passes to the increment clause before returning to check the conditional clause, thereby repeating the process. The increment clause normally houses the autoincrement or autodecrement statements used to update the counting variables.

All three clauses are optional. If the initialization or increment clauses are missing, C++ ignores them. If the conditional clause is missing, C++ performs the for loop forever (or until something else breaks control outside of the loop).

The for loop is better understood by example. The following ForDemo program is nothing more than the WhileDemo program converted to use the for loop construct.

```
// ForDemo - input a loop count. Loop while
//           outputting a string nArg number of times.
#include <stdio.h>
#include <iostream.h>

int main(int nArg, char* pszArgs[])
{
```

```
    // input the loop count
    int nLoopCount;
    cout << "Enter nLoopCount: ";
    cin  >> nLoopCount;

// count up to the loop count limit
for (int i = 1; i <= nLoopCount; i++)
{
    cout << "We've finished " << i << " loops\n";
}
```

This version loops the same as before; however, instead of modifying the value of nLoopCount, this version uses a counter variable.

Control begins by declaring a variable i and initializing it to t1. The for loop then checks the variable i to make sure that it is less than or equal to the value of nLoopCount. If this is true, the program executes the output statement, increments i, and starts over.

The for loop is also convenient when you need to count from 0 up to the loop count value rather than from the loop count down to 0. This is implemented by a simple change to the for loop:

```
// ForDemo - input a loop count. Loop while
//           outputting a string nArg number of times.
#include <stdio.h>
#include <iostream.h>

int main(int nArg, char* pszArgs[])
{

    // input the loop count
    int nLoopCount;
    cout << "Enter nLoopCount: ";
    cin  >> nLoopCount;

    // count up to the loop count limit
    for (int i = 1; i <= nLoopCount; i++)
    {
        cout << "We've finished " << i << " loops\n";
    }
    return 0;
}
```

Rather than begin with the loop count, this version starts with 1 and "loops up" to the value entered by the user.

The use of the variable i **for** for **loop increments is historical (stemming from the early days of the Fortran programming language). It is for this reason that such loop variables don't follow the standard naming convention.**

When declared within the initialization portion of the for **loop, the index variable is only known within the** for **loop itself. Nerdy C++ programmers say that the scope of the variable is the** for **loop. In the example above, the variable** i **is not accessible from the** return **statement because that statement is not in the loop.**

Special loop controls

It can happen that the condition for terminating the loop occurs neither at the beginning nor at the end of the loop. Consider the following program, which accumulates a number of values entered by the user. The loop terminates when the user enters a negative number.

The challenge with this problem is that the program can't exit the loop until after the user has entered a value, yet it has to exit the loop before the value is added to the sum.

For these cases, C++ defines the break command. When encountered, the break causes control to exit the current loop immediately; that is, control passes from the break statement to the statement immediately following the closed brace.

The format of the break commands is as follows:

```
while(condition) // break works equally well in for loop
{
    if (some other condition)
    {
        break;   // exit the loop
    }
}                // control passes here when the
                 // program encounters the break
```

Armed with this new break command, my solution to the accumulator problem appears as the program BreakDemo.

```
// BreakDemo - input a series of numbers.
//            Continue to accumulate the sum
//            of these numbers until the user
//            enters a 0.
#include <stdio.h>
#include <iostream.h>

int main(int nArg, char* pszArgs[])
{

    // input the loop count
    int nAccumulator = 0;
    cout << "This program sums values entered "
         << "by the user\n";
    cout << "Terminate the loop by entering "
         << "a negative number\n";

    // loop "forever"
    for(;;)
    {
        // fetch another number
        int nValue = 0;
        cout << "Enter next number: ";
        cin  >> nValue;

        // if it's negative...
        if (nValue < 0)
        {
            // ...then exit
            break;
        }

        // ...otherwise add the number to the accumulator
        nAccumulator = nAccumulator + nValue;
    }

    // now that we've exited the loop
    // output the accumulated result
    cout << "\nThe total is "
         << nAccumulator
```

```
        << "\n";

    return 0;
}
```

After explaining the rules to the user (entering negative number to terminate, and so forth), the program enters an infinite `for` loop.

A `for` loop with no condition loops forever.

The loop is not truly infinite because it contains a `break` internally; however, the loop command is still referred to as infinite because the break condition doesn't exist in the command itself.

Once in the loop, BreakDemo retrieves a number from the keyboard. Only after the program has read a number can it test to determine whether the number read matches the exit criteria. If the input number is negative, control passes to the `break`, causing the program to exit the loop. If the input number is not negative, control skips over the `break` command to the expression that sums the new value to the accumulator.

Once the program exits the loop, it outputs the accumulated value and exits. Here's the output of a sample session:

```
This program sums values entered by the user
Terminate the loop by entering a negative number
Enter next number: 1
Enter next number: 2
Enter next number: 3
Enter next number: 4
Enter next number: -1

The total is 10
```

When performing an operation on a variable repeatedly in a loop, make sure that the variable was initialized properly before entering the loop. In this case, the program zeros `nAccumulator` before entering the loop where `nValue` is added to it.

Nested Control Commands

The three loop programs in this chapter are the moral equivalent of instructing the mechanic in how to remove a lug nut: continue to turn the wrench until the nut falls off. What about instructing the mechanic to continue removing lug nuts until the wheel falls off? For this we need to implement nested loops.

A loop command within another loop command is known as a **nested loop**.

As an example, let's modify the BreakDemo program into a program that accumulates any number of sequences. In this NestedDemo program, the inner loop sums numbers entered from the keyboard until the user enters a negative number. The outer loop continues accumulating sequences until the sum is 0.

```cpp
// NestedDemo - input a series of numbers.
//              Continue to accumulate the sum
//              of these numbers until the user
//              enters a 0. Repeat the process
//              until the sum is 0.
#include <stdio.h>
#include <iostream.h>

int main(int nArg, char* pszArgs[])
{
    // the outer loop
    cout << "This program sums multiple series\n"
         << "of numbers. Terminate each sequence\n"
         << "by entering a negative number.\n"
         << "Terminate the series by entering two\n"
         << "negative numbers in a row\n";

    // continue to accumulate sequences
    int nAccumulator;
    do
    {
        // start entering the next sequence
        // of numbers
        nAccumulator = 0;
        cout << "\nEnter next sequence\n";

        // loop forever
        for(;;)
```

```
    {
        // fetch another number
        int nValue = 0;
        cout << "Enter next number: ";
        cin  >> nValue;

        // if it's negative...
        if (nValue < 0)
        {
            // ...then exit
            break;
        }

        // ...otherwise add the number to the accumulator
        nAccumulator = nAccumulator + nValue;
    }

    // output the accumulated result...
    cout << "\nThe total is "
        << nAccumulator
        << "\n";

    // ...and start over with a new sequence
    // if the accumulated sequence was not zero
    } while (nAccumulator != 0);
    cout << "Program terminating\n";
    return 0;
}
```

Can We switch to a Different Subject?

One last control statement is useful in a limited number of cases. The switch statement is like a compound if statement in that it includes a number of different possibilities rather than a single test:

```
switch(expression)
{
    case c1:
```

```
        // go here if the expression == c1
        break;
    case c2:
        // go here if expression == c2
        break;
    else
        // go here if there is no match
}
```

Done!

The value of expression must be an integer (int, long, or char). The case values c1, c2, and c3 must be constants. When the switch statement is encountered, the expression is evaluated and compared to the various case constants. Control branches to the case that matches. If none of the cases match, control passes to the else clause.

The break **statements are necessary to exit the** switch **command. Without the** break **statements, control "falls through" from one case to the next.**

REVIEW

The simple if statement enables the programmer to send the flow of control down one path or another based on the value of an expression. The looping commands add the capability to execute a block of code repeatedly until an expression is false. Finally, the break commands provide an extra level of control by allowing program control to exit a loop at any point.

- The if statement evaluates an expression. If the expression is not 0 (that is, it is true), control passes to the block immediately following the if clause. If not, control passes to the block of code following the else clause. If there is no else clause, control passes directly to the statement following the if.

- The looping commands, while, do while, and for execute a block of code repetitively until a condition is no longer true.

- The break statement allows control to pass out of a loop prematurely.

In Session 9, we look at ways to simplify C++ programs by using functions.

Quiz Yourself

1. Is it an error to leave the else off of an if command? What happens?
   (See "The Branch Command.")
2. What are the three types of loop commands? (See "Looping Commands.")
3. What is an infinite loop? (See "The Dreaded Infinite Loop.")
4. What are the three "clauses" that make up a for loop?
   (See "The for Loop.")

Session Checklist

✔ Writing void functions

✔ Writing functions with multiple arguments

✔ Overloading functions

✔ Creating function templates

✔ Determining variable storage class

**_30 Min.
To Go_**

Some of the example programs in Session 8 are already becoming a bit involved and we have a lot more C++ to learn. Programs with multiple levels of nesting of flow control can be difficult to follow. Add the numerous and complicated branching that a "real-world" application requires and programs would become virtually impossible to follow.

Fortunately, C++ provides a means for separating a stand-alone block of code into a stand-alone entity known as a function. In this Session, I delve into how to declare, create, and use C++ functions.

Sample Function Code

Like so many things, functions are best understood by example. This section starts with an example program, FunctionDemo, which simplifies the NestedDemo program in Session 8 by defining a function to contain part of the logic. This section then explains how the function is defined and how it is invoked using the example code as a pattern.

Sample code

The NestedDemo in Session 8 involves an inner loop that accumulates a sequence of numbers and an outer loop that repeats the process until the user decides to quit. Logically we could separate the inner loop, the part that adds a sequence of numbers, from the outer loop that repeats the process.

The following code example shows the NestedDemo is simplified by creating the function sumSequence().

 The names of functions are normally written with a set of parentheses immediately following.

```
// FunctionDemo - demonstrate the use of functions
//                by breaking the inner loop of the
//                NestedDemo program off into its own
//                function

#include <stdio.h>
#include <iostream.h>

// sumSequence - add a sequence of numbers entered from
//               the keyboard until the user enters a
//               negative number.
//               return - the summation of numbers entered
int sumSequence(void)
{
    // loop forever
    int nAccumulator = 0;
    for(;;)
    {
```

```
        // fetch another number
        int nValue = 0;
        cout << "Enter next number: ";
        cin  >> nValue;

        // if it's negative...
        if (nValue < 0)
        {
            // ...then exit from the loop
            break;
        }

        // ...otherwise add the number to the
        // accumulator
        nAccumulator = nAccumulator + nValue;
    }

    // return the accumulated value
    return nAccumulator;
}

int main(int nArg, char* pszArgs[])
{                                   // Begin Main
    cout << "This program sums multiple series\n"
         << "of numbers. Terminate each sequence\n"
         << "by entering a negative number.\n"
         << "Terminate the series by entering two\n"
         << "negative numbers in a row\n";

    // accumulate sequences of numbers...
    int nAccumulatedValue;
    do
    {
        // sum a sequence of numbers entered from
        // the keyboard
        cout << "\nEnter next sequence\n";
        nAccumulatedValue = sumSequence();

        // now output the accumulated result
        cout << "\nThe total is "
```

```
                    << nAccumulatedValue
                    << "\n";

        // ...until the sum returned is 0
        } while (nAccumulatedValue != 0);
        cout << "Program terminating\n";
        return 0;
    }                                           // End Main
```

Calling the function sumSequence()

Let's first concentrate on the main program contained within the open and closed braces marked with the comments Begin Main and End Main. This section of code looks identical to programs that we wrote previously.

The line

```
nAccumulatedValue = sumSequence();
```

calls the function sumSequence() and stores the value returned in the variable nAccumulatedValue. This value is subsequently output to the standard output on the following three lines. The main program continues to loop until the sum returned by the inner function is 0, indicating that the user has finished calculating sums.

Defining the sumSequence() function

The block of code that begins on line 13 and continues through line 38 makes up the function sumSequence().

When the main program invokes the function sumSequence() on line 55, control passes from the call to the beginning of the function on line 14. Program execution continues from that point.

Lines 16 through 34 are identical to that found in the inner loop of NestedDemo. After the program exits that loop, control passes to the return statement on line 37. At this point, control passes back to the call statement on line 55 along with the value contained in nAccumulator. On line 55, the main program stores the int returned in the local variable nAccumulatedValue and continues execution.

20 Min. To Go

In this case, the call to sumSequence() **is an expression, because it has a value. Such a call can be used anywhere an expression is allowed.**

Function

The FunctionDemo program demonstrates the definition and use of a simple function.

SYNTAX ▶ A **function** is a logically separate block of C++ code. The function construct has the form:

```
<return type> name(<arguments to the function>)
{
    // ...
    return <expression>;
}
```

The arguments to a function are values that can be passed for the function to use as input. The return value is a value that the function returns. For example, in the call to the function square(10), the value 10 is an argument to the function square(). The returned value is 100.

Both the arguments and the return value are optional. If either is absent, the keyword void is used instead. That is, if a function has a void argument list, the function does not take any arguments when called. If the return type is void, then the function does not return a value to the caller.

In the example FunctionDemo program, the name of the function is sumSequence(), the return type is int, and there are no arguments.

The default argument type to a function is void**. Thus, a function** int fn(void) **may be declared as** int fn().

Why use functions?

The advantage of a function over other C++ control commands is that it cordons off a set of code with a particular purpose from other code in the program. By being separate, the programmer can concentrate on the one function when writing it.

A good function can be described using a single sentence that contains a minimum number of ors and ands. For example, "the function sumSequence **accumulates a sequence of integer values entered by the user." This definition is concise and clear.**

The function construct made it possible for me to write essentially two distinct parts of the FunctionDemo program. I concentrated on creating the sum of a sequence of numbers when writing the sumSequence() function. I didn't think at all about other code that might call the function.

Likewise, when writing main(), I could concentrate on handling the summation returned by sumSequence(), while thinking only of what the function did, and not about how it worked.

Simple functions

The simple function sumSequence() returns an integer value which it calculates. Functions may return any of the regular types of variables. For example, a function might return a double or a char.

If a function returns no value, then the return type of the function is labeled void.

A function may be labeled by its return type. Thus, a function that returns an int is often known as an *integer* function. A function that returns no value is known as a *void* function.

For example, the following void function performs an operation but returns no value:

```
void echoSquare()
{
    int nValue;
    cout << "Enter a value:";
cin >> nValue;
cout << "\n The square is:" << nValue * nValue << "\n";
    return;
}
```

Control begins at the open brace and continues through to the return statement. The return statement in a void function is not followed by a value.

The return statement in a void function is optional. If it is not present, then execution returns to the calling function when control encounters the close brace.

Functions with arguments

Simple functions are of limited use because the communication from such functions is one-way, through the return value. Two-way communication is preferred. Such communication is through function arguments. A *function argument* is a variable whose value is passed to the calling function during the call operation.

Example function with arguments

The following example defines and uses a `square()` function which returns the square of a double-precision float passed to it:

```
// SquareDemo - demonstrate the use of a function
//              which processes arguments

#include <stdio.h>
#include <iostream.h>

// square - returns the square of its argument
//          dVar - the value to be squared
//          returns - sqare of dVar
double square(double dVar)
{
    return dVar * dVar;
}

int sumSequence(void)
{
    // loop forever
    int nAccumulator = 0;
     for(;;)
     {
        // fetch another number
        double dValue = 0;
        cout << "Enter next number: ";
        cin  >> dValue;

        // if it's negative...

        if (dValue < 0)
        {
```

```
            // ...then exit from the loop
            break;
        }

        // ...otherwise calculate the square
        int nValue = (int)square(dValue);

        // now add the square to the
        // accumulator
        nAccumulator = nAccumulator + nValue;
    }

    // return the accumulated value
    return nAccumulator;
}

int main(int nArg, char* pszArgs[])
{
    cout << "This program sums multiple series\n"
         << "of numbers. Terminate each sequence\n"
         << "by entering a negative number.\n"
         << "Terminate the series by entering two\n"
         << "negative numbers in a row\n";

    // Continue to accumulate numbers...
    int nAccumulatedValue;
    do
    {
        // sum a sequence of numbers entered from
        // the keyboard
        cout << "\nEnter next sequence\n";
        nAccumulatedValue = sumSequence();

        // now output the accumulated result
        cout << "\nThe total is "
             << nAccumulatedValue
             << "\n";

    // ...until the sum returned is 0
    } while (nAccumulatedValue != 0);
```

```
        cout << "Program terminating\n";
        return 0;
}
```

This is the same FunctionDemo program except that SquareDemo adds the square of the values entered.

The value of dValue is passed to the function square() on the line

```
int nValue = (int)square(dValue);
```

contained within the function sumSequence(). The function square() multiplies the value passed to it on line 12 and returns the result. The returned value is stored in the variable dSquare, which is added to the accumulator value on line 38.

Functions with multiple arguments

Functions may have multiple arguments separated by commas. The following function returns the product of its two arguments:

```
int product(int nArg1, int nArg2)
{
    return nArg1 * nArg2;
}
```

Casting Values

Line 38 of the SquareDemo program contains an operator that we have not seen before:

```
nAccumulator = nAccumulator + (int)dValue;
```

The (int) in front of the dValue indicates that the programmer wants to convert the dValue variable from its current type, in this case double, into an int.

A *cast* is an explicit conversion from one type to another. Any numeric type may be cast into any other numeric type. Without such a cast, C++ would have converted the types anyway, but would have generated a warning.

main() exposed

It should be clear that main() is nothing more than a function, albeit, a function with strange arguments.

When a program is built, C++ adds some boilerplate code that executes before your program ever starts. This code sets up the environment in which your program operates. For example, this boilerplate code opens the cin and cout input and output objects.

Once the environment has been established, the C++ boilerplate code calls the function main() thereby beginning execution of your code. When your program is complete, it exits from main(). This enables the C++ boilerplate to clean up a few things before turning over control to the operating system which kills the program.

**10 Min.
To Go**

Multiple functions with the same nickname

Two functions in a single program cannot share the same name. If they did, C++ would have no way to distinguish them when they are called. However, in C++ the name of the function includes the number and type of its arguments. Thus, the following are not the same functions:

```
void someFunction(void)
{
    // ....perform some function
}
void someFunction(int n)
{
    // ...perform some different function
}
void someFunction(double d)
{
    // ...perform some very different function
}
void someFunction(int n1, int n2)
{
    // ....do something different yet
}
```

someFunction() is a shorthand name, or nickname, for both functions, in the same way that Stephen is shorthand for my name. Whether I use the short-hand name when describing the function or not, C++ still knows the functions as someFunction(void), someFunction(int), someFunction(double), and someFunction(int, int).

void **as an argument type is optional;** sumFunction(void) **and** sumFunction() **are the same function.**

A typical application might appear as follows:

```
int nVariable1, nVariable2;     // equivalent to
                                // int Variable1;
                                // int Variable2;
double dVariable;

// functions are distinguished by the type of
// the argument passed
someFunction();                 // calls someFunction(void)
someFunction(nVariable1);       // calls someFunction(int)
someFunction(dVariable);        // calls someFunction(double)
someFunction(nVariable1, nVariable2); // calls
                                // someFunction(int, int)

// this works for constants as well
someFunction(1);                // calls someFunction(int)
someFunction(1.0);              // calls someFunction(double)
someFunction(1, 2);             // calls someFunction(int, int)
```

In each case, the type of the arguments matches the full name of the three functions.

The return type is not part of the name of the function. Thus, the following two functions have the same name and cannot be part of the same program:

```
int someFunction(int n);     // full name of the function
                             // is someFunction(int)
double someFunction(int n);  // same name
```

Function Prototypes

In the example programs so far, the target functions sumSequence() and square()
were both defined in code that appeared before the actual call. This doesn't have to
be the case: a function may be defined anywhere in the module. A *module* is another
name for a C++ source file.

However, something has to tell main() the full name of the function before it
can be called. Consider the following code snippet:

```
int main(int argc, char* pArgs[])
{
    someFunc(1, 2);
}
int someFunc(double dArg1, int nArg2)
{
    // ...do something
}
```

The call to someFunc() from within main() doesn't know the full name of the
function. It might surmise from the arguments that the name is someFunc(int,
int) and that its return type is void; however, as you can see, this is wrong.

What is needed is some way to inform main() of the full name of someFunc()
before it is used. What is needed is a function declaration. A *function declaration*
or *prototype* appears the same as a function with no body. In use, a prototype
appears as follows:

```
int someFunc(double, int);
int main(int argc, char* pArgs[])
{
    someFunc(1, 2);
}
int someFunc(double dArg1, int nArg2)
{
    // ...do something
}
```

The call in main() now knows to cast the 1 to a double before making the call. In addition, main() knows that the function someFunc() returns an int; however, main() doesn't do anything with the result.

C++ allows the programmer to throw away the value returned by a function.

Variable Storage Types

There are three different places that function variables can be stored. Variables declared within a function are said to be local. In the following example, the variable nLocal is local to the function fn():

```
int nGlobal;
void fn()
{
    int nLocal;
    static int nStatic;
}
```

The variable nLocal doesn't "exist" until the function fn() is called. In addition, only fn() has access to nLocal — other functions cannot "reach into" the function to access it.

By comparison, the variable nGlobal exists as long as the program is running. All variables have access to nGlobal all of the time.

Done!

The static variable nStatic is something of a mix between a local and a global variable. The variable nStatic is created when execution first reaches the declaration (roughly, when the function fn() is called). In addition, nStatic is only accessible within fn(). Unlike nLocal, however, nStatic continues to exist even after the program exits fn(). If fn() assigns a value to nStatic once, it will still be there the next time that fn() is called.

There is a fourth variable type, auto, but today it has the same meaning as local.

REVIEW

By this time, you should have some idea of how complex a program can become and how creating small functions can simplify program logic. Well-conceived functions are small, ideally less than 50 lines and with fewer than 7 if or looping commands. Such functions are easier to grasp and, therefore, easier to write and debug. After all, isn't that the idea?

- C++ functions are a means for dividing code into bite-sized chunks.
- Functions may have any number of arguments, which are values passed to the function.
- Functions may return a single value to the caller.
- Function names may be overloaded as long as they can be distinguished by the number and types of their arguments.

It's all very nice to outfit your programs with numerous expressions in multiple variables that are divided into functions, but it isn't of much use if you can't get your programs to work. In Session 10, you will see some of the most basic techniques for finding coding errors in your programs.

QUIZ YOURSELF

1. How do you call a function? (See "Calling the Function sumSequence().")
2. What does a return type of void mean? (See "Function.")
3. Why write functions? (See "Why Use Functions?")
4. What is the difference between a local variable and a global variable? (See "Variable Storage Types.")

Debugging I

Session Checklist

✔ Differentiating types of errors

✔ Understanding the "crash messages" returned by C++ environment

✔ Mastering the write-statement technique of debugging

✔ Debugging both Visual C++ and the GNU/C++

**30 Min.
To Go**

Y ou may have noticed that the programs that you write as part of the exercises in earlier chapters often don't work the first time. In fact, I have seldom, if ever written, a nontrivial C++ program that didn't have some type of mistake the first time I tried to execute it.

A program that works the first time you try to execute it is known as a *gold-star program.*

Types of Errors

There are two different types of errors. Those errors that the C++ compiler can catch are relatively easy to fix. The compiler generally points you to the problem. Sometimes the description of the problem is not quite correct — it's easy to confuse a compiler — but once you learn the quirks of your own C++ package, it isn't too difficult.

A second set of errors is comprised of those errors that the compiler can't catch. These errors first show up as you try to execute the program. Errors that are first noticed when you execute the program are known as *run-time errors*. Those errors that C++ can catch are known as *compile-time errors*.

Run-time errors are much more difficult to find, because you have no hint of what's gone wrong except for whatever errant output the program might generate.

There are two different techniques for finding bugs. You can add output statements at key points and rebuild the program. You can get an idea of what's gone wrong with your program as these different output statements are executed. A second approach that is more powerful is to use a separate program called a debugger. A debugger enables you to control your program as it executes. This session examines the "output statement" technique. In Session 16, you learn to use the debugger that is built in Visual C++ and GNU C++.

The Output-Statement Technique

The approach of adding output statements to the code to debug is known as the outputstatement approach.

This technique is often called the writestatement approach. It gained this name back in the days of early programs, which were written in FORTRAN. FORTRAN's output is through its WRITE statement.

To see how this might work, let's fix the following buggy program.

```
// ErrorProgram - this program averages a series
//                of numbers, except that it contains
//                at least one fatal bug
#include <stdio.h>
#include <iostream.h>

int main(int argc, char* pszArgs[])
{
    cout << "This program is designed to crash!\n";

    // accumulate input numbers until the
    // user enters a negative number, then
    // return the average
```

```
int nSum;
for (int nNums = 0; ;)
{
    // enter another number to add
    int nValue;
    cout << "\nEnter another number:";
    cin  >> nValue;

    // if the input number is negative...
    if (nValue < 0)
    {
        // ...then output the average
        cout << "\nAverage is: "
             << nSum/nNums
             << "\n";
        break;

    }

    // not negative, add the value to
    // the accumulator
    nSum += nValue;
}
return 0;
}
```

After entering this program, I build the program to generate the executable
ErrorProgram.exe like usual. Impatiently, I guide the Window Explorer to the folder
containing the program and confidently double-click ErrorProgram to begin executing it. I enter the usual values of 1, 2, and 3 followed by –1 to terminate input.
Instead of producing the much-anticipated value of 2, the program terminates
with the not very friendly error message shown in Figure 10-1 and without any
output message at all.

Don't execute ErrorProgram from the C++ environment just yet.

Figure 10-1
*The initial version of ErrorProgram terminates suddenly instead
of generating the expected output.*

Catching Bug #1

**20 Min.
To Go**

The error message shown in Figure 10-1 displays the ubiquitous "This program has
performed an illegal operation. . ." error message. Even with the Registers information, you have nothing to start debugging with.

**Actually there is one little tidbit of information: at the top of
the error display appears the message "ERRORPROGRAM caused
a divide error." This wouldn't normally be much help except that
there's only one divide in the entire program, but let's ignore
that for the sake of argument.**

Hoping to get more information, I return to execute ErrorProgram from within
the C++ environment. What happens next is slightly different in Visual C++ than
GNU C++.

Visual C++

I enter the same 1, 2, 3, and –1 values as I did before in order to force the program
to crash.

**One of the first things you would like to do when tracking down
a problem is to find the set of operations that cause the program
to fail. By reproducing the problem, you know not only how to
recreate it for debug purposes, but you also know when it's fixed.**

Visual C++ generates the output shown in Figure 10-2. This window indicates that the program has terminated abnormally (that's the Unhandled exception part) because of a Divide by Zero error.

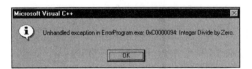

Figure 10-2
The error message from Visual C++ is slightly better than the Windows error message.

The Divide by Zero error message is only slightly better than the division error message shown in Figure 10-1; however, when I click OK, Visual C++ displays the ErrorProgram program with a yellow arrow pointing squarely at the division as shown in Figure 10-3. This is the C++ line of code on which the error originated.

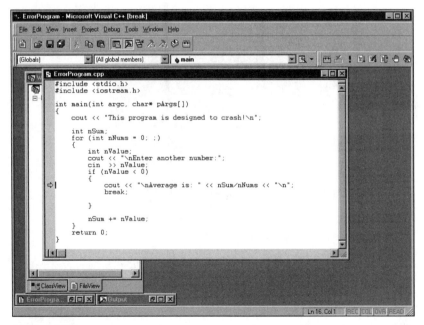

Figure 10-3
Visual C++ points the blame clearly at the division using nNums.

Now I know that at the time of the division, nNums must have been equal to 0. (Otherwise, I wouldn't have gotten a Divide by Zero error.) I can see where nNums is initialized to 0, but where is it incremented? It isn't, and this is the bug. Clearly nNums should have been incremented in the increment clause of the for loop.

To fix the problem, I replace the original for with the following:

```
for (int nNums = 0; ;nNums++)
```

GNU C++

Tracking the crash from using the GNU C++ suite is similar. From within rhide, I run the program. In response to the 1, 2, 3, and –1 input, ErrorProgram terminates with the message shown in Figure 10-4. Instead of the normal exit code of 0x00 (0 decimal), I now see the abnormal exit code of 0xff (or 255 decimal). This doesn't tell me anything other than that there was an error of some type encountered when executing the program (that much I knew already).

Figure 10-4
The exit code for the ErrorProgram in rhide is 0xff.

After clicking OK, however, I notice that rhide has opened a small window at the bottom of the display. This window, shown in Figure 10-5, tells me that the error was generated at ErrorProgram.cpp(16) in function main. This slightly cryptic message indicates that the error occurred on line 16 of ErrorProgram.cpp and that this line is in the function main() (the latter I could tell by looking at the listing, but it's nice information anyway).

From this I know all that I need to know to solve the problem the same way I did in the Visual C++ case.

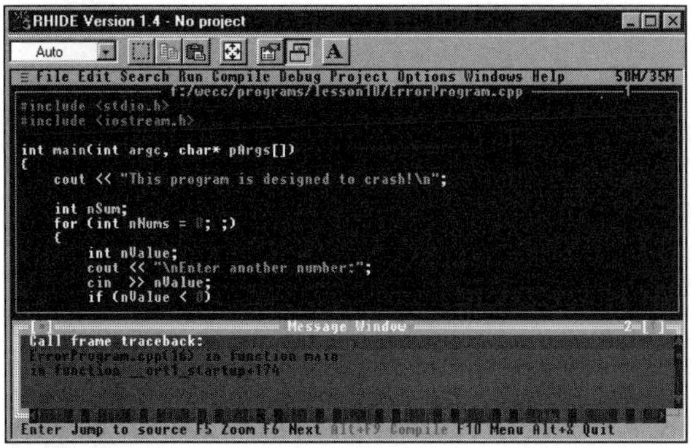

Figure 10-5
*The error message from rhide is just as informative as that from Visual C++,
albeit slightly cryptic.*

How Can C++ Tie an Error Message Back to the Source Code?

The information I received when executing the program directly from Windows or from an MS-DOS window was not very informative. By comparison, both Visual C++ and rhide were able to direct me to the line from whence the problem originated. How did they do that?

C++ has two modes when building a program. By default, C++ builds the program in what is called debug mode. In debug mode, C++ adds line-number information that maps the lines of C++ code to the corresponding lines of machine code. For example, this map might say that line 200 of machine code in the executable code was created from the C++ source code on line 16.

When the Divide by Zero error occurred, the operating system knows that the error occurred on offset 0x200 of the executable machine code. C++ tracks this back to line 16 using the debug information.

As you might imagine, this debug information takes a lot of space. This makes the executable file larger and slower. To address this problem, both GNU and Visual C++ support a build mode called release mode in which the debug information is stripped out.

**10 Min.
To Go**

Catching Bug #2

Flush with success and pride, I confidently execute the program using the same 1, 2, 3, and –1 input that caused the program to crash earlier. This time, the program doesn't crash, but it doesn't work either. The output shown below is ridiculous:

```
This program is designed to crash!

Enter another number:1

Enter another number:2

Enter another number:3

Enter another number:-1

Average is: -286331151
Press any key to continue
```

Apparently, either nSum or nNums (or both) is not being calculated properly. To proceed, I need to know the value of these variables. In fact, it would help if I knew the value of nValue as well, because nValue is used to calculate nSum.

To learn the values of the nSum, nNums and nValue, I modify the for loop as follows:

```
for (int nNums = 0; ;nNums++)
{
    int nValue;
    cout << "\nEnter another number:";
    cin  >> nValue;
    if (nValue < 0)
    {
        cout << "\nAverage is: " << nSum/nNums << "\n";
        break;

    }

    // output critical information
```

```
cout << "nSum = " << nSum   << "\n";
cout << "nNums= " << nNums   << "\n";
cout << "nValue= "<< nValue << "\n";
cout << "\n";

nSum += nValue;
}
```

Notice the addition of the output statements. These three lines display the value of nSum, nNums, and nValue on each iteration through the loop.

The results of executing the program with the now standard 1, 2, 3, and –1 input sequence are shown below. Even on the first loop, the value of nSum seems unreasonable. In fact, at this point during the first loop, the program has yet to add a new value to nSum. At this point, I would think that the value of nSum should be 0. That appears to be the problem.

```
This program is designed to crash!

Enter another number:1
nSum = -858993460
nNums= 0
nValue= 1

Enter another number:2
nSum = -858993459
nNums= 1
nValue= 2

Enter another number:3
nSum = -858993457
nNums= 2
nValue= 3

Enter another number:
```

On careful examination of the program, nSum is declared but it is not initialized to anything. The solution to is change the declaration of nSum to the following:

```
int nSum = 0;
```

Until a variable has been initialized, the value of that variable is indeterminate.

Once I have convinced myself that the result is correct, I "clean up" the program as follows:

```cpp
// ErrorProgram - this program averages a series
//                of numbers
//                (This version has been fixed.)
#include <stdio.h>
#include <iostream.h>

int main(int argc, char* pszArgs[])
{
    cout << "This program works!\n";

    // accumulate input numbers until the
    // user enters a negative number, then
    // return the average
    int nSum = 0;
    for (int nNums = 0; ;nNums++)
    {
        // enter another number to add
        int nValue;
        cout << "\nEnter another number:";
        cin  >> nValue;

        // if the input number is negative...
        if (nValue < 0)
        {
            // ...then output the average
            cout << "\nAverage is: " << nSum/nNums << "\n";
            break;
        }

        // not negative, add the value to
        // the accumulator
```

```
        nSum += nValue;
    }
    return 0;
}
```

I rebuild the program and retest with the 1, 2, 3, and –1 sequence. This time I see the expected average value of 2:

```
This program works!

Enter another number:1

Enter another number:2

Enter another number:3

Enter another number:-1

Average is: 2
```

Done!

After testing the program with a number of other inputs, I convince myself that the program is now executing properly. I remove the extra output statements and rebuild the program to complete the debugging of the program.

REVIEW

There are two basic types of errors: compile-time errors generated by the C++ compiler when it encounters an illogical coding construct, and run-time errors created when the program executes some illogical sequence of legal instructions.

Compile-time errors are relatively easy to track down because the C++ compiler is good at pointing you right to the error. Run-time errors are more difficult. The Visual C++ and GNU/C++ environments try to give you as much help as possible. In the example program in this session, they actually do a good job at pointing to the problem.

When the run-time error messages generated by the C++ environment are not enough, it's left to the programmer to find the problem by debugging the code. In this session, we used the so-called write-statement technique.

- C++ compilers are very fussy in what they accept in order to be capable of rooting out programmer errors during the build process where things are easier to fix.

- The operating system tries to catch run-time errors as well. When these errors call the program to crash, the operating system returns error information that the Visual C++ and GNU/C++ environments try to interpret.

- Output statements generated at critical points in the program can vector the programmer to the source of run-time errors.

Although crude, the write-statement technique is effective on small programs. Session 16 demonstrates more effective debugging techniques.

QUIZ YOURSELF

1. What are the two basic types of errors? (See "Types of Errors.")

2. How can output statements be used to help find run-time errors? (See "The Output-Statement Technique.")

3. What is debug mode? (See "How Can C++ Tie an Error Message Back to the Source Code?")

PART

II

Saturday Morning

1. I execute the following function to convert short tons to kilograms. When I pass it the value 2 I get the wrong results:

```
int ton2kg(int nTons)
{
    int nLongTons = nTons / 1.1;
    return 1000 * nLongTons;
}
```

   a. What is wrong with my program?

   b. What results do I get?

Bonus: What warning do I get?

2. Make sure that you know the answer to assignment 1 (you can peek if you need to). Now, what can I do to fix the problem noted in assignment 1?

3. I wrote the following little brother to the *ton2kg()* function:

```
int ton2g(int nTon)
{
    return ton2kg * 1000;
}
```

Because I am working with large boats, I pass the function a value of 5000 tons displacement. The value I get back is obviously wrong.

   a. What happened?

   b. What can I do to fix the problem?

4. Which of the following is true?

    ```
    int n1 = 1, n2 = -3, n3 = 10, n4 = 4
    ```

    a. n1 < n2

    b. (n1 + n4) == 5

    c. (n3 > n2) && (n4 > n1)

    d. (n3 / 4.0) == 2.5

    e. (n1 > n3) && (--n4 > n2)

    What is the value of n4 after this calculation?

5. Given that n1 = 0101 1101$_2$

    a. What is the hexadecimal value of n1?

    b. What is the decimal value of n1?

    c. What is the value of n1 * 2 in binary?

    Bonus: What is the difference in the bit pattern between n1 and 2 * n1?

    d. What is the value of n1 | 2?

    e. What is the value of (n1 & 2) == 0?

6. (This is a toughie!) What is the final value of n1?

    ```
    int n1 = 10;
    if (n1 > 11)
    {
        if (n1 > 12)
        {
            n1 = 0;
        }
    }
    else
    {
        n1 = 1;
    }
    }
    ```

7. What is the difference between the while() and the do...while() clauses in the following sample code?

    ```
    int n1 = 10;
    while(n1 < 5)
    ```

```
{
    n1++;
}

do
{
    n1++;
} while(n1 < 5);
```

8. Write a second function `double cube(double d)` in addition to the first function.

9. Now what happens in the following expression with the two functions present?

   ```
   int n = cube(3.0);
   ```

10. Finally, add the function `double cube(int n)` to the previous two functions. What happens?

    Hint: Write the prototype declarations of the three `cube()` functions.

PART

III

Saturday Afternoon

Session Checklist

✔ Introducing the array data type

✔ Using arrays

✔ Initializing an array

✔ Using the most common type of array — the character string

**30 Min.
To Go**

The programs written so far dealt with numbers one at a time. The summing programs input a value from the keyboard and then add it to some total contained in a single variable before reading the next number. If we return to our first analogy, the human program, these programs address one lug nut at a time. However, there are times when we want to hold all of the lug nuts at one time before operating on them.

This session examines how to store a set of values, much like the mechanic can hold or store a number of lug nuts at one time.

What Is an Array?

Let's begin by examining the whys and what fors of arrays. An *array* is a sequence of objects, usually numbers, each of which is referenced by an offset.

Consider the following problem. I need a program that can read a sequence of numbers from the keyboard. I'll use the now-standard rule that a negative number terminates input. After the numbers are read in, and only then, should the program display them on the standard output device.

I could attempt to store numbers in subsequent variables as in:

```
cin >> nV1;
if (nV1 >= 0)
{
    cin >> nV2;
    if (nV2 >= 0)
    {
        ...
```

You can see that this approach can't handle sequences involving more than just a few numbers.

An array solves the problem nicely:

```
int nV;
int nValues[128];
for (int i = 0; ; i++)
{
    cin >> nV;
    if (nV < 0)
    {
        break;
    }
    nValues[i] = nV;
}
```

The second line of this snippet declares an array nValues. Array declarations begin with the type of the array members, in this case int, followed by the name of the array. The last element of an array declaration is an open and closed bracket containing the maximum number of elements that the array can hold. In this code snippet, nValues is declared as a sequence of 128 integers.

This snippet reads a number from the keyboard and stores it in a member of the array nValues. An individual element of an array is accessed by providing the name of the array followed by brackets containing an index. The first integer in the array is nValues[0], the second is nValues[1], and so on.

In use, nValues[i] **represents the** ith **element in the array. The index variable** *i* **must be a counting variable; that is,** i **must be an** int **or a** long. **If** nValues **is an array of** ints, **then** nValues[i] **is an** int.

Accessing too far into an array

Mathematicians start counting their arrays with 1. The first member of a mathematical array x is x(1). Most programming languages also start with an offset of 1. C++ arrays begin counting at 0. The first member of a C++ array is nValues[0].

There is a good reason why C++ begins counting from 0, but you have to wait until Session 12 to learn what it is.

Because indexing in a C++ array begins with 0, the last element of a 128-integer array is nArray[127].

Unfortunately for the programmer, C++ does not check whether the index you are using is within the range of the array. C++ is perfectly happy to give you access to nArray[200]. In fact, C++ will even let you access nArray[-15].

As an analogy, suppose that distances on a highway were measured by equally spaced power line poles. (In western Texas this isn't too far from the truth.) Let's call this unit of measure a pole-length. The road to my house begins at the turn off from the main highway and continues to my house in a straight line. The length of this road is exactly 9 pole-lengths.

If we begin numbering poles with the telephone pole at the highway, then the telephone pole next to my house is pole number 10. This is shown in Figure 11-1.

I can access any position along the road by counting poles from the highway. If we measure from the highway to the highway, we calculate a distance of 0 pole-length. The next discrete point is 1 pole-length, and so on, until we get to my house at 9 pole-lengths distance.

I can measure a distance 20 pole-lengths away from the highway. Of course, this location is not on the road. (Remember that the road stops at my house.) In fact, I have no idea what you might find there. You might be on the next highway, you might be out in a field, you might even land in my neighbor's living room. Examining that location is bad enough, but storing something there could be a lot worse. Storing something in a field is one thing, but crashing through my neighbor's living room could get you in trouble.

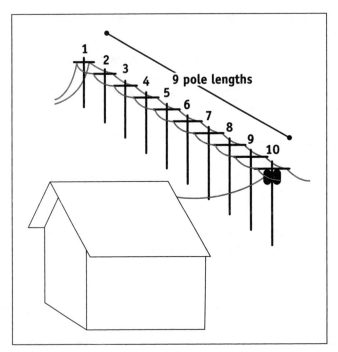

Figure 11-1
It takes 10 telephone poles to measure off a distance of 9 pole-lengths.

By analogy, reading array[20] of a 10-element array returns a more or less random value. Writing to array[20] has unpredictable results. It may do nothing, it may lead to erratic behavior, or it may crash the program.

 The most common incorrect location to access in the 128-element nArray, **is** nArray[128]. **While only one element beyond the end of the array, reading or writing this location is just as dangerous as any other incorrect address.**

**20 Min.
To Go**

An array in practice

The following program solves the initial problem posed. This program inputs a sequence of integer values from the keyboard until the user enters a –1. The program then displays the numbers input and reports their sum.

```
// ArrayDemo - demonstrate the use of arrays
//             by reading a sequence of integers
```

```
//              and then displaying them in order
#include <stdio.h>
#include <iostream.h>

// prototype declarations
int sumArray(int nArray[], int nSize);
void displayArray(int nArray[], int nSize);

int main(int nArg, char* pszArgs[])
{
    // input the loop count
    int nAccumulator = 0;
    cout << "This program sums values entered"
         << "by the user\n";
    cout << "Terminate the loop by entering "
         << "a negative number\n";

    // store numbers into an array
    int nInputValues[128];
    int nNumValues = 0;
    do
    {
        // fetch another number
        int nValue;
        cout << "Enter next number: ";
        cin  >> nValue;

        // if it's negative...
        if (nValue < 0)      // Comment A
        {
            // ...then exit
            break;
        }

        // ...otherwise store the number
        // into the storage array
        nInputValues[nNumValues++] = nValue;
    } while(nNumValues < 128); // Comment B
    // now output the values and the sum of the values
    displayArray(nInputValues, nNumValues);
```

```
    cout << "The sum is "
         << sumArray(nInputValues, nNumValues)
         << "\n";
    return 0;
}

// displayArray - display the members of an
//                array of length nSize
void displayArray(int nArray[], int nSize)
{
    cout << "The value of the array is:\n";
    for (int i = 0; i < nSize; i++)
    {
        cout.width(3);
        cout << i << ": " << nArray[i] << "\n";
    }
    cout << "\n";
}

// sumArray - return the sum of the members of an
//            integer array
int sumArray(int nArray[], int nSize)
{
    int nSum = 0;
    for (int i = 0; i < nSize; i++)
    {
        nSum += nArray[i];
    }
    return nSum;
}
```

The program ArrayDemo begins with a prototype declaration of the functions sumArray() and displayArray(). The main body of the program contains the typical input loop. This time, however, the values are stored in the array nInputValues, with the variable nNumValues storing a count of the number of values stored in the array. The program stops reading values if the user inputs a negative number (Comment A), or if the number of elements in the array is exhausted (that's the test near Comment B).

The array nInputValues **is declared as 128 integers long. You might think that this should be enough for anyone, but don't count on it. Writing more data than an array's limit permits causes your program to perform erratically, and often to crash. No matter how large you make the array, always put a check to make sure that you do not exceed the limits of the array.**

The main function ends by displaying the contents of the array and the sum.

The displayArray() function contains the typical for loop used to traverse an array. Notice again, that the index is initialized to 0 and not to 1. In addition, notice how the for loop that terminates before i is equal to nSize.

In a similar fashion, the sumArray() function loops through the array, adding each member to the total contained in nSum. Just to keep nonprogrammers guessing, the term *iterate* is used to mean traverse through a set of objects, such as an array. We say that "the sumArray() function iterates through the array."

Initializing an array

An array may be initialized at the time it is declared.

An uninitialized variable initially contains random values.

The following code snippet demonstrates how this is done:

```
float fArray[5] = {0.0, 1.0, 2.0, 3.0, 4.0};
```

This initializes fArray[0] to 0, fArray[1] to 1, fArray[2] to 2, and so on.

The number of initialization constants can determine the size of the array. For example, we could have determined that fArray has five elements just by counting the values within the braces. C++ can count as well. The following declaration is identical to the one above:

```
float fArray[] = {0.0, 1.0, 2.0, 3.0, 4.0};
```

It is not necessary to repeat the same value over and over to initialize a large a array. For example, the following initializes all 25 locations in fArray to 1.0:

```
float fArray[25] = {1.0};
```

Why use arrays?

On the surface, the ArrayDemo program doesn't do anything more than our earlier, nonarray-based programs did. True, this version can replay its input by displaying the numbers input before calculating the sum, but this hardly seems earth shattering.

Yet, the capability to redisplay the input values hints at a significant advantage to using arrays. Arrays enable the program to process a series of numbers multiple times. The main program was capable of passing the array of input values to displayArray() for display and then repass the same numbers to sumArray() for addition.

Arrays of arrays

Arrays are adept at storing sequences of numbers. Some applications require sequences of sequences. A classic example of this matrix configuration is the spreadsheet. Laid out like a chessboard, each element in the spreadsheet has both an x and a y offset.

C++ implements the matrix as follows:

```
int nMatrix[2][3];
```

This matrix is 2 elements in one dimension and 3 elements in another dimension, equalling 6 elements. As you might expect, one corner of the matrix is nMatrix[0][0], while the other corner is nMatrix[1][2].

Whether you consider nMatrix **to be 10 elements long in the** *x* **dimension or in the** *y* **dimension is a matter of taste.**

A matrix may be initialized in the same way that an array is:

```
int nMatrix[2][3] = {{1, 2, 3}, {4, 5, 6}};
```

This initializes the three-element array nMatrix[0] to 1, 2, and 3 and the three-element array nMatrix[1] to 4, 5, and 6, respectively.

Arrays of Characters

The elements of an array can be of any C++ variable type. Arrays of floats, doubles, and longs are all possible; however, arrays of characters have particular significance.

An array of characters containing my first name would appear as:

```
char sMyName[] = {'S', 't', 'e', 'p', 'h', 'e', 'n'};
```

The following small program displays my name to the MS-DOS window, the standard output device.

```
// DisplayCharArray - output a character array to
//                    standard output, the MS-DOS window
#include <stdio.h>
#include <iostream.h>

// prototype declarations
void displayCharArray(char sArray[], int nSize);

int main(int nArg, char* pszArgs[])
{
    char cMyName[] = {'S', 't', 'e', 'p', 'h', 'e', 'n'};
    displayCharArray(cMyName, 7);
    cout << "\n";
    return 0;
}

// displayCharArray - display an array of characters
//                    by outputing one character at
//                    a time
void displayCharArray(char sArray[], int nSize)
{
    for(int i = 0; i< nSize; i++)
```

```
        {
            cout << sArray[i];
        }
    }
```

This program works fine, but it is inconvenient to pass the length of the array around with the array itself. We avoided this problem when inputting integers from the keyboard by making up the rule that a negative number terminated input. If we could make the same rule here, we wouldn't need to pass the size of the array — we would know that the array was complete when we encountered the special code character.

Let's use the code 0 to mark the end of a character array.

 The character whose value is 0 is not the same thing as 0. The value of 0 is 0x30. The character whose value is 0 is often written as \0 just to make the distinction clear. Similarly, the character \y'is the character whose numeric value is y. The character \0 is known as the null character.

Using that rule, the previous small program becomes:

```
// DisplayString - output a character array to
//                  standard output, the MS-DOS window
#include <stdio.h>
#include <iostream.h>

// prototype declarations
void displayString(char sArray[]);

int main(int nArg, char* pszArgs[])
{
    char cMyName[] =
            {'S', 't', 'e', 'p', 'h', 'e', 'n', '\0'};
    displayString(cMyName);
    cout << "\n";
    return 0;
}

// displayString - display a character string
//                  one character at a time
void displayString(char sArray[])
```

```
{
    for(int i = 0; sArray[i] != 0; i++)
    {
        cout << sArray[i];
    }
}
```

The bolded declaration of `cMyName` declares the character array with the extra character '\0' on the end. The displayString program iterates through the character array until a null character is encountered.

The function `displayString()` is simpler to use than its `displayCharArray()` predecessor. It is no longer necessary to pass along the length of the character array. Further, `displayString()` works when the size of the character string is not known at compile time. For example, this would be the case if the user were entering a string of characters from the keyboard.

I have been using the term *string* as if it were a fundamental type, such as `int` or `float`. At the time of its introduction, I mentioned that *string* is actually a variation of an existing type. As you see here, a *string* is a null-terminated character array.

C++ provides an optional, more convenient means of initializing a string by using double quotes rather than the single quotes used for characters. The line

```
char szMyName[] = "Stephen";
```

is exactly equivalent to the line

```
char cMyName[] = {'S', 't', 'e', 'p', 'h', 'e', 'n', '\0'};
```

in the previous example.

The naming convention used here is exactly that: a convention. C++ does not care; however, the prefix sz stands for zero-terminated string.

The string "Stephen" is eight characters long, not seven —the null character after the n is assumed.

**10 Min.
To Go**

Manipulating Strings

The C++ programmer is often required to manipulate strings.

Although C++ provides a number of string manipulation functions, let's write our own to get an idea of how these functions might work.

Our own concatenate function

Let's begin with a simple, if somewhat lengthy, C++ program to concatenate two strings.

```
// Concatenate - concatenate two strings
//               with a " - " in the middle
#include <stdio.h>
#include <iostream.h>

// the following include file is required for the
// str functions
#include <string.h>

// prototype declarations
void concatString(char szTarget[], char szSource[]);

int main(int nArg, char* pszArgs[])
{
    // read first string...
    char szString1[256];
    cout << "Enter string #1:";
    cin.getline(szString1, 128);

    // ...now the second string...
    char szString2[128];
    cout << "Enter string #2:";
    cin.getline(szString2, 128);

    // ...concatenate a " - " onto the first...
    concatString(szString1, " - ");
    // strcat(szString1, " - ");
    // ...now add the second string...
```

```
    concatString(szString1, szString2);
    // strcat(szString1, szString2);

    // ...and display the result
    cout << "\n" << szString1 << "\n";

    return 0;
}

// concatString - concatenate the szSource string
//                 to the end of the szTarget string
void concatString(char szTarget[], char szSource[])
{
    // find the end of the first string
    int nTargetIndex = 0;
    while(szTarget[nTargetIndex])
    {
        nTargetIndex++;
    }

    // tack the second to the end of the first
    int nSourceIndex = 0;
    while(szSource[nSourceIndex])
    {
        szTarget[nTargetIndex] =
            szSource[nSourceIndex];
        nTargetIndex++;
        nSourceIndex++;
    }

    // tack on the terminating null
    szTarget[nTargetIndex] = '\0';
}
```

The function `main()` reads two strings using the `getline()` function.

The alternate cin >> szString reads up to the first space. Here we want to read until the end of the line.

Function `main()` concatenates the two strings using the `concatString()` function before outputting the result.

The `concatString()` concatenates the second argument, `szSource`, onto the end of the first argument, `szTarget`.

The first loop within `concatString()` iterates through the string `szTarget` until `nTargetIndex` references the null at the end of the string.

The loop `while(value == 0)` **is the same as** `while(value)` **because** `value` **is considered false if it's equal to 0, and true if equal to anything other than 0.**

The second loop iterates through the `szSource` string, copying elements from that string to `szTarget` starting with the first character in `szSource` and the null character in `szTarget`. The loop stops when `nSourceIndex` references the null character in `szSource`.

The `concatString()` function tacks a final null character to the resulting target string before returning.

Don't forget to terminate the strings that you construct programmatically. You will generally know that you forgot to terminate your string if the string appears to contain "garbage" at the end when displayed or if the program crashes when you next try to manipulate the string.

The result of executing the program is shown below.

```
Enter string #1:This is the first string
Enter string #2:THIS IS THE SECOND STRING

This is the first string - THIS IS THE SECOND STRING
Press any key to continue
```

It is very tempting to write C++ statements such as the following:

```
char dash[] = " - ";
concatString(dash, szMyName);
```

This doesn't work because dash **is given just enough room to store four characters. The function will undoubtedly overrun the end of the** dash **array.**

C++ string-handling functions

C++ provides significant string capability in the >> and << stream functions. You will see some of this capability in Session 28. At a more basic level, C++ provides a set of simple functions shown in Table 11-1.

Table 11-1
C++ Library Functions for Manipulating Strings

Name	Operation
`int strlen(`*string*`)`	Returns the number of characters in a string
`void strcat(`*target, source*`)`	Concatenates the source string to the end of the target string
`void strcpy(`*target, source*`)`	Copies a string to a buffer
`int strstr`	Finds the first occurrence of one string in another
`int strcmp(`*source1, source2*`)`	Compares two strings
`int stricmp(`*source1, source2*`)`	Compares two strings without regard to case

In the Concatenate program, the call to concatString() could have been replaced with a call to strcat(), which would have saved us the need to write our own version:

```
strcat(szString1, " - ");
```

You need to add the statement #include <string.h> **to the beginning of any program that uses the** str. . . **functions.**

Wide characters

The standard C++ char type is an 8-bit field capable of representing the values from 0 to 255. There are 10 digits, plus 26 lowercase letters, plus 26 uppercase letters. Even if various umlauted and accented characters are added, there is still more than enough range to represent the Roman alphabet set plus the Cyrillic alphabet.

Problems with the char type don't arise until you begin to include the Asian character sets, in particular the Chinese and Japanese kanjis. There are literally thousands of these symbols — many more than the lowly 8-bit character set.

C++ includes support for a newer character type called wchar or wide characters. While this is not an intrinsic type like char, numerous C++ functions treat it as if it were. For example, wstrstr() compares two wide character sets. If you are writing international applications and need access to Asian languages, you will need to use these wide character functions.

Obsolescent Output Functions

C++ also provides a set of lower-level input and output functions. The most useful is the printf() output function.

These are the original C input and output functions. Stream input and output didn't come along until after the introduction of C++.

In its most basic form, printf() outputs a string to cout.

```
printf("This string is output to cout");
```

The printf() function performs output using a set of embedded format control commands, each of which begins with a % sign. For example, the following prints out the value of an integer and a double variable.

```
int nInt = 1;
double dDouble = 3.5;
printf("The int value is %i; the float value is %f",
       nInt, dDouble);
```

The integer value is inserted at the point of the %i, whereas the double appears at the location of the %f:

```
The int value is 1; the float value is 3.5
```

Done!

Although difficult to use, the printf() function provides a level of output control that is difficult to achieve using stream functions.

REVIEW

The array is nothing more than a sequence of variables. Each identical-type variable is accessed by an index to the array — much like the number portion of a house address identifies the houses on a street. The combination of arrays and loop commands, such as for and while loops, enable a program to easily process a number of elements. By far the most common C++ array type is the zero-terminated character array, common-ly known as the character string.

- Arrays enable the program to loop through a number of entries quickly and efficiently using one of C++'s loop commands. For example, the increment portion of the for loop is designed to increment an index, while the con-dition portion is set up to detect the end of the array.

- Accessing elements outside the boundaries of an array is both common and dangerous. It is tempting to access element 128 of an array declared as 128 bytes long; however, because array indices start at 0, the final element is at offset 127, not 128.

- Terminating a character array with a special character enables a function to know where the array ends without the need to carry a character-length field. To facilitate this, C++ considers the character '\0', the character whose bit value is 0, an illegal, terminating, noncharacter. Programmers use the term *character string* or *ASCIIZ strings* for a null-terminated charac-ter array.

- Built in an Occidental world, the 8-bit C++ char types cannot handle the thousands of special characters required in some Asian languages. To han-dle these characters, C++ supports a special wide character, often referred to as wchar. C++ includes special functions to handle wchar strings in the standard C++ library of routines.

QUIZ YOURSELF

1. What is the definition of an array? (See "What Is an Array?")

2. What is the offset of the first and last elements of an array declared as `myArray[128]`? (See "Accessing Too Far into an Array.")

3. What is a character string? What is the type of a character string? What terminates a string? (See "Arrays of Characters.")

Intro to Classes

Session Checklist

✔ Using the class structure to group different types of variables into one object

✔ Writing programs using the class structure

***30 Min.
To Go***

Arrays are great at handling sequences of objects of the same type such as ints or doubles. Arrays do not work well, however, when grouping different types of data such as when we try to combine a social security number with the name of a person into a single record. C++ provides a structure called a class to handle this problem.

Grouping Data

Many of the programs in earlier sessions read a series of numbers, sometimes into arrays, before processing. A simple array is great for stand-alone values. However, many times (if not most of the time) data comes in groups of information. For example, a program may ask the user for her first name, last name, and social security number. Alone any one of these values is not sufficient — only in the aggregate do the values make any sense. For reasons that become clear shortly, I call such a grouping of data an *object*.

One way to describe an object is by what I call *parallel arrays*. In this approach, the programmer defines one array of strings for the first names, another for the second, and a third for the social security numbers. The three different values are coordinated through the array index.

An example

The following program uses the parallel array approach to input and display a series of names and social security numbers. szFirstName[i], szLastName[i], and nSocialSecurity[i] to combine to form a single object.

```
// ParallelData - store associated data in
//                parallel arrays
#include <stdio.h>
#include <iostream.h>
#include <string.h>

// "parallel arrays" store associated data
// (make arrays global to give all functions
// access)
char szFirstName[25][128];
char szLastName [25][128];
int  nSocialSecurity[25];

// getData - read a name and social security
//           number; return 0 if no more to
//           read
int getData(int index)
{
    cout << "\nEnter first name:";
    cin  >> szFirstName[index];

    // if the first name is 'exit' or 'EXIT'...
    if ((strcmp(szFirstName[index], "exit") == 0)
        ||
        (strcmp(szFirstName[index], "EXIT") == 0))
    {
        // ...return with a "let's quit" indicator
```

```
            return 0;
        }

    // load the remainder of the object
    cout << "Enter last name:";
    cin  >> szLastName[index];

    cout << "Enter social security number:";
    cin  >> nSocialSecurity[index];

    return 1;
}

// displayData - output the index'th data set
void displayData(int index)
{
    cout << szFirstName[index]
         << " "
         << szLastName[index]
         << "/"
         << nSocialSecurity[index]
         << "\n";
}

int main(int nArg, char* pszArgs[])
{
    // load first names, last names, and social
    // security numbers
    cout << "Read name/social security information\n"
         << "Enter 'exit' for first name to exit\n\n";
    int index = 0;
    while (getData(index))
    {
        index++;
    }

    cout << "\nEntries:\n";
    for (int i = 0; i < index; i++)
    {
        displayData(i);
```

```
    }
    return 0;
}
```

The three coordinated arrays are declared as follows:

```
char szFirstName[25][128];
char szLastName [25][128];
int  nSocialSecurity[25];
```

The three have sufficient room to handle 25 entries. The first and last names of each entry are limited to 128 characters.

No checks are made to insure that the 128-character limits are exceeded. In a real-world application, failing to make the check is unacceptable.

The main() function first reads in the objects in the loop beginning with while (getData(index)) in the function main(). The call to getData() reads the next entry. The loop exits when getData() returns a zero indicating that entry is complete.

The program then calls displayData() to display the objects entered.

The getData() function reads data from cin to the three arrays. The function returns a 0 if the user enters a first name of exit or EXIT. If the first name is not exit the function reads the remaining data and returns a 1 to indicate that there are more data objects to read.

The following output is from a sample run of the ParallelData program.

```
Read name/social security information
Enter 'exit' for first name to exit

Enter first name:Stephen
Enter last name:Davis
Enter social security number:1234

Enter first name:Scooter
Enter last name:Dog
Enter social security number:3456

Enter first name:Valentine
Enter last name:Puppy
```

```
Enter social security number:5678

Enter first name:exit

Entries:
Stephen Davis/1234
Scooter Dog/3456
```

The problem

The parallel-array approach is one solution to the data-grouping problem. In many older programming languages, there were no other options. For large amounts of data, keeping the potentially large number of arrays in synchronization becomes quite a problem.

The simple ParallelData program has only three arrays to keep track of. Consider the amount of data that a credit card might keep on each entry. Potentially dozens of arrays would be needed.

A secondary problem is that it isn't obvious to the maintenance programmer that the numerous arrays belong to each other. If the programmer updates any combination of the arrays without updating them all, the data becomes corrupted.

The Class

What is needed is a structure that can hold all of the data needed to describe a single object. A single object would hold both the first name and last name along with the social security number. C++ uses a structure known as a class.

The format of a class

A class used to describe a name and social security number grouping might appear as follows:

```
// the dataset class
class NameDataSet
{
    public:
        char szFirstName[128];
        char szLastName [128];
```

```
int  nSocialSecurity;
};
```

```
// a single instance of a dataset
NameDataSet nds;
```

A class definition starts with the keyword `class` followed by the name of
the class and an open-closed brace pair.

**The alternative keyword `struct` may be used. The keywords `struct`
and `class` are identical except that the `public` declaration is
assumed in the `struct`.**

The first line within the braces is the keyword `public`.

**Later sessions show what other keywords C++ allows
besides `public`.**

Following the `public` keyword are the entries it takes to describe the object.
The `NameDataSet` class contains the first and last name entries along with the
social security number. Remember that a class declaration includes the data
necessary to describe one object.

The last line declares the variable `nds` as a single entry of class `NameDataSet`.
Programmers say that `nds` is an *instance* of the class `NameDataSet`. You *instantiate*
the class `NameDataSet` to create `nds`. Finally, programmers say that `szFirstName`
and the others are *members* or *properties* of the class.

The following syntax is used to access the property of a particular object:

```
NameDataSet nds;
nds.nSocialSecurity = 10;
cin >> nds.szFirstName;
```

Here, `nds` is an instance of the class `NameDataSet` (that is, a particular
`NameDataSet` object). The integer `nds.nSocialSecurity` is a property of
the `nds` object. The type of `nds.nSocialSecurity` is `int`, while the type
of `nds.szFirstName` is `char[]`.

A class object can be initialized when it is created as follows:

```
NameDataSet nds = {"FirstName", "LastName", 1234};
```

In addition, the programmer may declare and initialize an array of objects as follows:

```
NameDataSet ndsArray[2] = {{ "FirstFN",  "FirstLN", 1234}
                           {"SecondFN", "SecondLN", 5678}};
```

Only the assignment operator is defined for class objects by default. The assignment operator performs a binary copy of the source object to the target object. Both source and target must be of exactly the same type.

Example program

The class-based version of the ParallelData program appears below:

```
// ClassData - store associated data in
//             an array of objects
#include <stdio.h>
#include <iostream.h>
#include <string.h>

// NameDataSet - stores name and social security
//               information
class NameDataSet
{
    public:
        char szFirstName[128];
        char szLastName [128];
        int  nSocialSecurity;
};

// getData - read a name and social security
//           number; return 0 if no more to
//           read
int getData(NameDataSet& nds)
{
    cout << "\nEnter first name:";
    cin  >> nds.szFirstName;

    if ((strcmp(nds.szFirstName, "exit") == 0)
        ||
        (strcmp(nds.szFirstName, "EXIT") == 0))
```

```
    {
        return 0;
    }

    cout << "Enter last name:";
    cin  >> nds.szLastName;

    cout << "Enter social security number:";
    cin  >> nds.nSocialSecurity;

    return 1;
}

// displayData - output the index'th data set
void displayData(NameDataSet& nds)
{
    cout << nds.szFirstName
         << " "
         << nds.szLastName
         << "/"
         << nds.nSocialSecurity
         << "\n";
}

int main(int nArg, char* pszArgs[])
{
    // allocate 25 name data sets
    NameDataSet nds[25];

    // load first names, last names, and social
    // security numbers
    cout << "Read name/social security information\n"
         << "Enter 'exit' for first name to exit\n";
    int index = 0;
    while (getData(nds[index]))
    {
        index++;
    }
```

```
cout << "\nEntries:\n";
for (int i = 0; i < index; i++)
{
    displayData(nds[i]);
}
return 0;
}
```

In this case, the main() function allocates 25 objects of class NameDataSet. As before, main() enters a loop in which entries are read from the keyboard using the function getData(). Rather than passing a simple index (or an index plus three arrays), main() passes the object that getData(NameDataSet) is to populate. Similarly, main() uses the displayData(NameDataSet) function to display each NameDataSet object.

The getData() function reads the object information into the NameDataSet object passed, which it calls nds.

The meaning of the ampersand added to the argument type getData() **is fully explained in Session 13. Suffice it to say for now that the ampersand insures that changes made in** getData() **are retained in** main().

Advantages

Done!

The basic structure of the ClassData program is the same as that of the ParallelData program; however, the ClassData program does not track multiple arrays. In an object as simple as NameDataSet, it isn't obvious that this is a significant advantage. Consider what both programs would look like if NameDataSet included the number of entries required by a credit card company, for example. The larger the object, the greater the advantage.

As we continue developing the NameDataSet **class in later chapters, the advantage increases.**

REVIEW

Arrays can only handle sequences of the same types of objects; for example, an array of ints or doubles. The class enables the programmer to group varied variable types in one object. For example, a Student class may contain a character string for the student name, an integer variable for the student identification, and a floating-point variable to hold the grade-point average. The combination into arrays of class objects combines the advantages of each in a single data structure.

- The elements of a class object do not have to be of the same type; however, because they are of different types, these elements must be addressed by name and not by index.

- The keyword struct can be used in place of the keyword class. struct is a holdover from the days of C.

QUIZ YOURSELF

1. What is an object? (See "Grouping Data.")

2. What is the older term for the C++ keyword class?
   (See "The Format of a Class.")

3. What do the following italicized words mean?
   (See "The Format of a Class.")

   a. *Instance* of a class

   b. *Instantiate* a class

   c. *Member* of a class

A Few C++ Pointers

Session Checklist

✔ Addressing variables in memory

✔ Introducing the pointer data type

✔ Recognizing the inherent dangers of pointers

✔ Passing pointers to functions

✔ Allocating objects off the free store, which is commonly known as the heap

*30 Min.
To Go*

Part II introduced the C++ operators. Operations such as addition, multiplication, bitwise AND, and logical OR were performed on intrinsic variable types such as int and float. There is another intrinsic variable type that we have yet to cover — pointers.

To anyone familiar with other programming languages, C++ seems like a conventional language, so far. Many languages don't include the logical operators presented and C++ presents its own unique semantics, but there are no concepts present in C++ that other languages do not offer. The introduction of pointers to the language is the initial departure of C++ from other, more conventional languages.

Pointers were actually introduced in the predecessor to C++, the C programming language. Everything described in this chapter works the same way in C.

Pointers are a mixed blessing. While pointers provide capabilities unique to C++, they can be syntactically difficult and they provide many opportunities to screw up.

This chapter introduces the pointer variable type. It begins with some concept definitions, flows through pointer syntax, and then introduces some of the reasons for the pointer mania that grips C++ programmers.

What's Your Address?

Just as in the saying "everyone has to be somewhere," every variable is stored somewhere in the computer's memory. Memory is divided into individual bytes, with each byte carrying its own address numbered 0, 1, 2, and so forth.

By convention, memory addresses are expressed in hexadecimal.

Different variable types require a different number of bytes of storage. Table 13-1 shows the memory that each variable type consumes in Visual C++ 6 and GNU C++ on a Pentium processor.

Table 13-1
Memory Requirements for Different Variable Types

Variable Type	Memory Consumed [bytes]
int	4
long	4
float	4
double	8

Consider the following Layout test program, which demonstrates the layout of variables in memory. (Ignore the new & operator — suffice it to say that &n returns the address of the variable n.)

```
// Layout - this program tries to give the
//          reader an idea of the layout of
//          local memory in her compiler
#include <stdio.h>
#include <iostream.h>

int main(int nArgc, char* pszArgs[])
{
    int    m1;
    int    n;
    long   l;
    float  f;
    double d;
    int    m2;

    // set output to hex mode
    cout.setf(ios::hex);

    // output the address of each variable
    // in order to get an idea of the size
    // of each variable
    cout << "--- = 0x" << (long)&m1 << "\n";
    cout << "&n  = 0x" << (long)&n  << "\n";
    cout << "&l  = 0x" << (long)&l  << "\n";
    cout << "&f  = 0x" << (long)&f  << "\n";
    cout << "&d  = 0x" << (long)&d  << "\n";
    cout << "--- = 0x" << (long)&m2 << "\n";

    return 0;
}
```

The output from this program is shown in Listing 13-1. From this, you can see that the variable n was stored at location 0x65fdf0.

Note

Don't worry if the values you see when running this program are different. The relationship between the locations is what matters.

From the comparison of locations we can also infer that the size of n is 4 bytes (0x65fdf4 – 0x65fdf0), the size of the long 1 is also 4 (0x65fdf0 – 0x65fdec), and so forth.

This demonstration only makes sense if you assume that variables are laid out immediately next to each other, which is the case in GNU C++. This is only the case in Visual C++ if a certain project setting is specified correctly.

Listing 13-1
Results of executing the Layout program

```
--- = 0x65fdf4
&n  = 0x65fdf0
&l  = 0x65fdec
&f  = 0x65fde8
&d  = 0x65fde0
--- = 0x65fddc
Press any key to continue
```

There is nothing in the definition of C++ that dictates that the layout of variables is anything like that shown in Listing 13-1. As far as we are concerned, it is purely an accident that GNU C++ and Visual C++ chose the same variable layout.

Introduction to Pointer Variables

Let's begin with a new definition and a couple of new operators. A *pointer variable* is a variable that contains an address, usually the address of another variable. Add to this definition the new operators shown in Table 13-2.

Table 13-2
Pointer Operators

Operator	Meaning
& (unary)	the address of
* (unary)	(in an expression) the thing pointed at by (in a declaration) pointer to

The use of these new features is best described by example:

```
void fn()
{
   int nInt;
   int* pnInt;

   pnInt = &nInt;    // pnInt now points to nInt
   *pnInt = 10;      // stores 10 into int location
                     // pointed at by pnInt
}
```

The function fn() begins with the declaration of nInt. The next statement declares the variable pnInt to be a variable of type "pointer to an int."

 Pointer variables are declared similar to normal variables except for the addition of the unary * character. This "splat" character can appear anywhere between the base type name, in this case int, and the variable name; however, it is becoming increasingly common to add the splat to the end of the variable type.

 Just as the names of integer variables start with an n, pointer variables begin with a p. Thus, pnX is a pointer to an integer variable X. Again, this is just a convention to help keep things straight — C++ doesn't care what names you use.

In an expression, the unary operator & means "the address of." Thus, we would read the first assignment as "store the address of nInt in pnInt."

To make this more concrete, let's assume that the memory for function fn() starts at location 0x100. In addition, let's assume that nInt is at address 0x102 and that pnInt is at 0x106. The lay out here is simpler than the actual results from the Layout program, but the concepts are identical.

The first assignment is shown in Figure 13-1. Here you can see that the value of &nInt (0x102) is stored in pnInt.

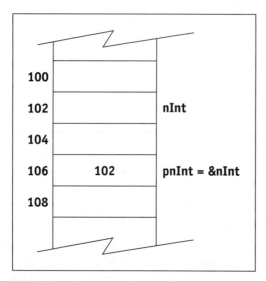

Figure 13-1
Storing the address of nInt in pnInt.

The second assignment in the small program snippet says "store 10 in the location pointed at by pnInt." Figure 13-2 demonstrates this. The value 10 is stored in the address contained in pnInt, which is 0x102 (the address of nInt).

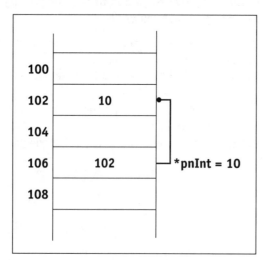

Figure 13-2
Storing 10 in the address pointed at by pnInt.

Types of Pointers

Remember that every expression has a type as well as a value. The type of the &nInt expression is a pointer to an integer, which is written as int*. A comparison of this expression type to the declaration of pnInt shows that the types match exactly:

```
pnInt = &nInt;   // both sides of the assignment are of type int*
```

Similarly, because pnInt is of type int*, the type of *pnInt is int.

```
*pnInt = 10;     // both sides of the assignment are of type int
```

Expressed in plain English, the type of the thing pointed to by pnInt is int.

Despite the fact that a pointer variable has different types, such as int* and double*, the pointer is an intrinsic type. Irrespective of what it might point to, a pointer on a Pentium class machine takes 4 bytes.

Matching types is extremely important. Consider what might happen if the following were allowed:

```
int   n1;
int* pnInt;
pnInt = &n1;
*pnInt = 100.0;
```

The second assignment attempts to store the 8-byte double value 100.0 in the 4-byte space allocated for n1. The result is that variables nearby are wiped out. This is demonstrated graphically in the following LayoutError program shown in Listing 13-2. The output from this program appears at the end of the listing.

Listing 13-2
LayoutError program with output shown

```
// LayoutError - demonstrate the results of
// messing up a pointer usage
#include <stdio.h>
#include <iostream.h>

int main(int nArgc, char* pszArgs[])
```

Continued

Listing 13-2 *Continued*

```
{
    int    upper = 0;
    int    n     = 0;
    int    lower = 0;

    // output the values of the three variables before...
    cout << "upper = " << upper << "\n";
    cout << "n     = " << n     << "\n";
    cout << "lower = " << lower << "\n";

    // now store a double in the space
    // allocated for an int
    cout << "\nPerforming assignment of double\n";
    double* pD = (double*)&n;
    *pD = 13.0;

    // display the results
    cout << "upper = " << upper << "\n";
    cout << "n     = " << n     << "\n";
    cout << "lower = " << lower << "\n";

    return 0;
}
```

Output:

```
upper = 0
n     = 0
lower = 0

Performing assignment of double
upper = 1076494336
n     = 0
lower = 0
Press any key to continue
```

The first three lines in main() declare three integers in the normal fashion. The assumption here is that these three variables are laid out next to each other.

The next three executable lines output the value of the three variables. Not surprisingly, all three variables display as 0. The assignment *pD = 13.0; stores the double value 13.0 into the integer variable n. The three output statements display the values of all three variables after the assignment.

After assigning the double value 13.0 to the integer variable n, n itself is not modified; however, the nearby variable upper is filled with a garbage value.

The following casts a pointer from one type to another:

```
double* pD = (double*)&n;
```

Here &n **is of type** int* **whereas the variable** pD **is of type** double*. **The cast** (double*) **changes the type of the value** &n **to match that of** pD **in the same way that:**

```
double d = (double)n;
```

casts the int **value contained in** n **into a double.**

Passing Pointers to Functions

One of the uses of pointer variables is in passing arguments to functions. To understand why this is important, you need to understand how arguments are passed to a function.

Pass by value

You may have noticed that it is not normally possible to change the value of a variable passed to a function from within the function. Consider this code segment:

```
void fn(int nArg)
{
    nArg = 10;
    // value of nArg at this point is 10
}

void parent(void)
{
    int n1 = 0;
    fn(n1);
    // value of n1 at this point is 0
}
```

The parent() function initializes the integer variable n1 to zero. The value of n1 is then passed to fn(). On entering the function, nArg is equal to 10, the value passed. fn() changes the value of nArg before returning to parent(). Perhaps surprisingly, on return to parent(), the value of n1 is still 0.

The reason is that C++ doesn't pass a variable to a function. Instead, C++ passes the value contained in the variable at the time of the call. That is, the expression is evaluated, even if it is just a variable name, and the result is passed. Passing the value of a variable to a function is known as *pass by value.*

It is easy for a speaker to get lazy and say something similar to "pass the variable x to the function fn()**." This really means, "pass the value of the expression x."**

Passing pointer values

Like any other intrinsic type, a pointer may be passed as an argument to a function:

```
void fn(int* pnArg)
{
    *pnArg= 10;
}

void parent(void)
{
    int n = 0;
    fn(&i);          // this passes the address of i
                     // now the value of n is 10
}
```

In this case, the address of n is passed to the function fn() rather than the value of n. The significance of this difference is apparent when you consider the assignment in fn().

Let's return to our earlier example values. Suppose n is located at address 0x102. Rather than the value 10, the call fn(&n) passes the "value" 0x106. Within fn(), the assignment *pnArg = 10 stores the value 10 in the int variable located at location 0x102, thereby overwriting the value 0. On return to parent(), the value of n is 10 because n is just another name for 0x102.

Passing by reference

C++ provides a shorthand method for passing the variable that doesn't involve the hassle of dealing with pointers yourself. In the following example, the variable n is passed by reference. In *pass by reference* the parent function passes a reference to the variable rather than the value. Reference is another word for address.

```
void fn(int& nArg)
{
    nArg = 10;
}

void parent(void)
{
    int n = 0;
    fn(n)
                        // here the value of n is 10
}
```

In this case, a reference to n is passed to fn() rather than the value. The fn() function stores the value 10 into int location referenced by nArg.

Notice that "reference" is not an actual type. Thus, the function's full name is fn(int) **and not** fn(int&).

**10 Min.
To Go**

Heap Memory

Just as it is possible to pass a pointer to a function, it is also possible for a function to return a pointer. A function that returns the address of a double would be declared as follows:

```
double* fn(void);
```

However, one must be very careful when returning a pointer. To understand the dangers, you must know something about variable scope.

Scope

C++ variables have a property in addition to their value and type known as scope. *Scope* is the range over which a variable is defined. Consider this code snippet:

```cpp
// the following variable is accessible to
// all functions and defined as long as the
// program is running(global scope)
int nGlobal;

// the following variable nChild is accessible
// only to the function and is defined only
// as long as C++ is executing child() or a
// function which child() calls (function scope)
void child(void)
{
    int nChild;
}

// the following variable nParent has function
// scope
void parent(void)
{
    int nParent = 0;
    fn();

    int nLater = 0;
    nParent = nLater;
}

int main(int nArgs, char* pArgs[])
{
    parent();
}
```

Execution begins with main(). The function main() immediately invokes parent(). The first thing that the processor sees in parent() is the declaration of nParent. At that point, nParent goes into scope — that is, nParent is defined and available for the remainder of the function parent().

The second statement in parent() is the call to child(). Once again, the function child() declares a local variable, this time nChild. The variable nChild is within the scope of child(). Technically, nParent is not within the scope of child()because child() doesn't have access to nParent; however, the variable nParent continues to exist.

When child() exits, the variable nChild goes out of scope. Not only is nChild no longer accessible but it no longer even exists. (The memory occupied by nChild is returned to the general pool to be used for other things.)

As parent() continues executing, the variable nLater goes into scope at the declaration. At the point that parent() returns to main(), both nParent and nLater go out of scope.

The programmer may declare a variable outside of any function. A *global variable* is a variable declared outside of any function. Such a variable remains in scope for the duration of the program.

Because nGlobal is declared globally in this example, it is available to all three functions and remains available for the life of the program.

The scope problem

The following code segment compiles without error but does not work:

```
double* child(void)
{
    double dLocalVariable;
    return &dLocalVariable;
}

void parent(void)
{
    double* pdLocal;
    pdLocal = child();
    *pdLocal = 1.0;
}
```

The problem is that dLocalVariable is defined only within the scope of the function fn(). Thus, by the time that the memory address of dLocalVariable is returned from child() it refers to a variable that no longer exists. The memory that dLocalVariable formerly occupied is probably being used for something else.

This is a very common error because it can creep up in a number of different ways. Unfortunately, this error does not cause the program to instantly stop. In fact, the program may work perfectly well most of the time — as long as the memory formerly occupied by dLocalVariable is not reused immediately, the program continues to work. Such intermittent problems are the most difficult to solve.

The heap solution

The scope problem occurs because C++ returns the locally defined memory before the programmer is ready. What is needed is a block of memory controlled by the programmer. The programmer can allocate the memory and put it back when the programmer wants and not because C++ thinks it a good idea. Such a block of memory is called the heap.

The *heap* is a segment of memory that is explicitly controlled by the program.

Heap memory is allocated using the new command followed by the type of object to allocate. For example, the following allocates a double variable off the heap.

```
double* child(void)
{
    double* pdLocalVariable = new double;
    return pdLocalVariable;
}
```

Even though the variable pdLocalVariable goes out of scope when the function child() returns, the memory to which pdLocalVariable refers does not.

A memory location returned by new does not go out of scope until it is explicitly returned to the heap using the delete command:

```
void parent(void)
{
    // child() returns the address of a block
    // of heap memory
    double* pdMyDouble = child();

    // store a value there
    *pdMyDouble = 1.1;
```

```
// ...

// now return the memory to the heap
delete pdMyDouble;
pdMyDouble = 0;

// ...
}
```

Done!

Here the pointer returned by child() is used to store a double value. After the function is finished with the memory location, it is returned to the heap. Setting the pointer to 0 after the delete is not necessary, but it is a good idea. That way, if the programmer mistakenly attempts to store something in *pdMyDouble after the delete, the program will crash immediately.

A program that crashes immediately on encountering an error is much easier to fix than one that is intermittent in its behavior.

Pointers to Functions

In addition to pointers to intrinsic types, it is possible to declare pointers to functions. For example, the following declares a pointer to a function that takes an integer argument and returns a double:

```
double (*pFN)(int);
```

There are a number of uses for a variable such as this; the twists and turns of pointers to functions, however, are beyond the scope of this book.

Part III—Saturday Afternoon
Session 13

REVIEW

Pointer variables are a powerful, if dangerous, mechanism for accessing objects by their memory address. This is probably the single most important language feature and it is probably the feature most responsible for the dominance of C and later C++ over other computer languages.

- Pointer variables are declared by adding a '*', known as the asterisk or splat character, to the variable type. The splat character may appear anywhere between the variable name and the root type; however, it makes more sense to append the splat to the end of the variable type.

- The address of operator & returns the address of an object while the splat operator * returns the object pointed at by an address or a pointer type variable.

- Variable types such as int* are their own variable types and are not equivalent to int. The address of operator & converts a type such as int into a pointer type such as int*. The splat operator * converts a pointer type such as int* into a base type such as int. One pointer type can be converted to another, but at considerable risk.

Subsequent lessons review some of the additional ways that pointers can be used to extend the C++ programmer's bag of tricks.

QUIZ YOURSELF

1. If a variable x contains the value 10 and is stored at location 0x100 what is the value of x? What is the value of &x? (See "Introduction to Pointer Variables.")

2. If x is an int, what is the type of &x? (See "Types of Pointers.")

3. Why would you pass a pointer to a function? (See "Passing Pointer Values.")

4. What is heap memory and how do you gain access to it? (See "Heap Memory.")

A Few More Pointers

Session Checklist

✔ Introducing mathematical operations on character pointers

✔ Examining the relationship between pointers and arrays

✔ Applying this relationship to increase program performance

✔ Extending pointer operations to different pointer types

✔ Explaining the arguments to main() in our C++ program template

**30 Min.
To Go**

The pointer types introduced in Session 13 allow for some interesting operations. Storing the address of a variable only to turn around and use that address more or less like the variable itself, is an interesting party trick, but it has limited use except for the capability to permanently modify variables passed to a function.

What makes pointers more interesting is the capability to perform mathematical operations. Of course, because multiplying two addresses is illogical, it is not allowed. However, the capability to compare two addresses or to add an integer offset opens interesting possibilities that are examined here.

Pointers and Arrays

Some of the same operators applicable to integers are applicable to pointer types. This section examines the implications of this both to pointers and to the array types studied so far.

Operations on pointers

Table 14-1 lists the three fundamental operations that are defined on pointers.

Table 14-1
Three Operations Defined on Pointer Types

Operation	Result	Meaning
pointer + offset	pointer	calculate the address of the object integer entries from pointer
pointer - offset	pointer	the opposite of addition
pointer2 - pointer1	offset	calculate the number of entries between pointer2 and pointer1

(Although not listed in Table 14-1, derivative operators, such as pointer += offset and pointer++, are also defined as variations of addition.)

The simplistic memory model used in Session 13 to explain the concept of pointers is useful here to explain how these operations work. Consider an array of 32 1-byte characters called cArray. If the first byte of this array is stored at address 0x110, then the array would extend over the range 0x110 through 0x12f. While cArray[0] is located at address 0x110, cArray[1] is at 0x111, cArray[2] at 0x112, and so forth.

Now assume a pointer ptr located at address 0x102. After executing the expression:

```
ptr = &cArray[0];
```

the pointer ptr contains the address 0x110. This is demonstrated in Figure 14-1.

Addition of an integer offset to a pointer is defined so that the relationships shown in Table 14-2 are true. Figure 14-2 also demonstrates why adding an offset n to ptr calculates the address of the nth element in cArray.

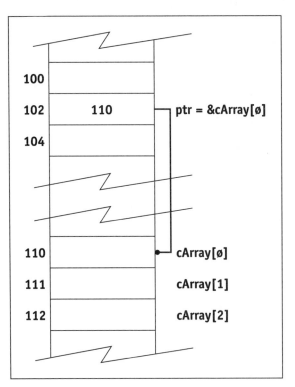

Figure 14-1
After the assignment ptr = &cArray[0] the pointer ptr points to the
beginning of the array cArray.

Table 14-2
Pointer Offsets and Arrays

Offset	Result	Corresponds to . . .
+ 0	0x110	cArray[0]
+ 1	0x111	cArray[1]
+ 2	0x112	cArray[2]
. . .	. . .	. . .
+ n	0x110+ n	cArray[n]

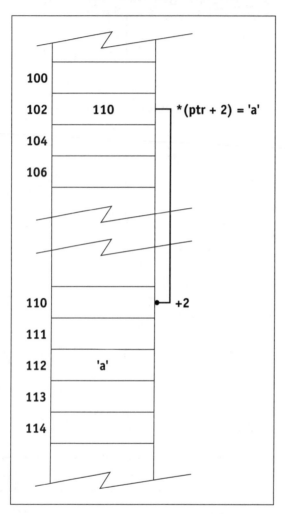

Figure 14-2
The expression ptr + i results in the address of cArray[i].

Thus, given that

```
char* ptr = &cArray[0];
```

then

```
*(ptr + n) ← corresponds with → cArray[n]
```

Because * has higher precedence than addition, *ptr + n adds n **to the character which** ptr **points to. The parentheses are needed to force the addition to occur before the indirection. The expression** *(ptr + n) **retrieves the character pointed at by the pointer** ptr **plus the offset** n.

In fact, the correspondence between the two forms of expression is so strong that C++ considers array[n] nothing more than a simplified version of *(ptr + n) where ptr points to the first element in array.

```
array[n] -- C++ interprets as → *(&array[0] + n)
```

To complete the association, C++ takes a second short cut. Given

```
char cArray[20];
```

then

```
cArray == &cArray[0]
```

That is, the name of an array without any subscript present is the address of the array itself. Thus, we can further simplify the association to

```
array[n] → C++ interprets as → *(array + n)
```

This is a powerful statement. For example, the displayArray() function from Session 11, which is used to display the contents of an array of integers, could be written:

```
// displayArray - display the members of an
//                array of length nSize
void displayArray(int nArray[], int nSize)
{
    cout << "The value of the array is:\n";

    // point at the first element of nArray
    int* pArray = nArray;
    while(nSize--)
    {
        cout.width(3);

        // output the integer pointed at by pArray...
        cout << i << ": " << *pArray << "\n";
```

```
    // ...and move the pointer over to the next
    // member of nArray
    pArray++;
  }
  cout << "\n";
}
```

The new `displayArray()` begins by creating a pointer to an integer `pArray` that points at the first element of `nArray`.

According to our naming convention, the p indicates pointer.

The function then loops through each element of the array (using `nSize` as the number of entries in the array). On each loop, `displayArray()` outputs the current integer, that is, the integer pointed at by `pArray` before incrementing the pointer to the next entry in `pArray`.

This use of pointers to access arrays is nowhere more common than in the accessing of character arrays.

Character arrays

**20 Min.
To Go**

Session 11 also explained how C++ uses a character array with a null character at the end to serve as a quasistring variable type. C++ programmers often use character pointers to manipulate such strings. The following code examples compare this technique to the earlier technique of indexing in the array.

Pointer vs. array-based string manipulation

The `concatString()` function was declared in the Concatenate example in Session 11 as:

```
void concatString(char szTarget[], char szSource[]);
```

The prototype declaration describes the type of arguments that the function accepts, as well as the return type. This declaration appears the same as a function definition with no function body.

To find the null at the end of the szTarget array, the concatString() function iterated through szTarget string using the following while loop:

```
void concatString(char szTarget[], char szSource[])
{
    // find the end of the first string
    int nTargetIndex = 0;
    while(szTarget[nTargetIndex])
    {
        nTargetIndex++;
    }

    // ...
```

Using the relationship between pointers and arrays, concatString() could have been prototyped as follows:

```
void concatString(char* pszTarget, char* pszSource);
```

The sz refers to a string of characters that ends in a 0 (null).

The pointer version of concatString() contained in the program ConcatenatePtr is written:

```
void concatString(char* pszTarget, char* pszSource)
{
    // find the end of the first string
    while(*pszTarget)
    {
        pszTarget++;
    }

    // ...
```

The while loop in the array version of concatString() looped until szTarget[nTargetIndex] was equal to 0. This version iterates through the array by incrementing nTargetIndex on each pass through the loop until the character pointed at by pszTarget is null.

The expression ptr++ **is a shortcut for** ptr = ptr + 1.

Upon exiting the while loop, pszTarget points to the null character at the end of the szTarget string.

 It is no longer correct to say "the array pointed at by pszTarget" because pszTarget no longer points to the beginning of the array.

The complete concatString() example

The following is the complete ConcatenatePtr program:

```
1.   // ConcatenatePtr - concatenate two strings
2.   //                  with a " - " in the middle
3.   //                  using pointer arithmetic
4.   //                  rather than array subscripts
5.   #include <stdio.h>
6.   #include <iostream.h>
7.
8.   void concatString(char* pszTarget, char* pszSource);
9.
10.  int main(int nArg, char* pszArgs[])
11.  {
12.      // read first string...
13.      char szString1[256];
14.      cout << "Enter string #1:";
15.      cin.getline(szString1, 128);
16.
17.      // ...now the second string...
18.      char szString2[128];
19.      cout << "Enter string #2:";
20.      cin.getline(szString2, 128);
21.
22.      // ...concatenate a " - " onto the first...
23.      concatString(szString1, " - ");
24.
25.      // ...now add the second string...
26.      concatString(szString1, szString2);
27.
28.      // ...and display the result
29.      cout << "\n" << szString1 << "\n";
```

```
30.
31.       return 0;
32.   }
33.
34.   // concatString - concatenate *pszSource onto the
35.   //                 end of *pszTarget
36.   void concatString(char* pszTarget, char* pszSource)
37.   {
38.       // find the end of the first string
39.       while(*pszTarget)
40.       {
41.           pszTarget++;
42.       }
43.
44.       // tack the second to the end of the first
45.       // (copy the null at the end of the source array
46.       // as well - this terminates the concatenated
47.       // array)
48.       while(*pszTarget++ = *pszSource++)
49.       {
50.       }
51.   }
```

The main() portion of the program does not differ from its array-based cousin. The concatString() function is significantly different, however.

As noted, the equivalent declaration of concatString() is now based on char* type pointers. In addition, the initial while() loop within concatString() searches for the terminating null at the end of the pszTarget array.

The extremely compact loop that follows copies the pszSource array to the end of the pszTarget array. The while() clause does all the work, executing as follows:

1. Fetch the character pointed at by pszSource.

2. Increment pszSource to the next character.

3. Save the character in the character position pointed at by pszTarget.

4. Increment pszTarget to the next character.

5. Execute the body of the loop if the character is not null.

After executing the empty body of the `while()` loop, control passes back up to the `while()` clause itself. This loop is repeated until the character copied to `*pszTarget` is the null character.

Why bother with array pointers?

The sometimes-cryptic nature of pointer-based manipulation of character strings might lead the reader to wonder why. That is, what advantage does the `char*` pointer version of `concatString()` have over the easier-to-read index version?

The pointer version of `concatenate()` **is much more common in C++ programs than the array version from Session 11.**

The answer is partially historic and partially human nature. As complicated as it might appear to the human reader, a statement such as line 48 can be converted to an amazingly small number of machine-level instructions. Older computer processors were not very fast by today's standards. When C, the progenitor of C++, was created some 30 years ago, saving a few computer instructions was a big deal. This gave C a big advantage over other languages of the day, notably Fortran, which did not offer pointer arithmetic.

In addition, programmers like to generate clever program statements to combat what can be a repetitively boring job. Once C++ programmers learn how to write compact and cryptic but efficient statements, there is no getting them back to searching arrays with indices.

Do not generate complex C++ expressions in order to create a more efficient program. There is no obvious relationship between the number of C++ statements and the number of machine instructions generated. For example, the following two expressions might generate the same amount of machine code:

```
*pszArray1++ = '\0';
```

```
*pszArray2 = '\0';
pszArray2 = pszArray2 + 1;
```

In the old days, when compilers were simpler, the first version would definitely have generated fewer instructions.

Operations on different pointer types

The two examples of pointer manipulation shown so far, concatString(char*, char*) and displayArray(int*), have a fundamental difference.

It is not too hard to convince yourself that szTarget + n points to szTarget [n] when you consider that each char in szTarget occupies a single byte. After all, if szTarget were stored at 0x100, then the sixth element is located at 0x105 (0x100 + 5 equals 0x105).

Because C++ arrays begin counting at 0, szTarget[5] **is the sixth element in the array.**

It is not obvious that pointer addition works for nArray because each element in nArray is an int that occupies 4 bytes. If the first element in nArray is located at 0x100, then the sixth element is located at 0x114 (0x100 + (5 * 4) = 0x114).

Fortunately for us, in C++ array + n points at array[n] no matter how large a single element of array might be.

A good analogy is a city block of houses. If all of the street addresses on each street were numbered consecutively with no gaps, then house number 1605 would be the sixth house of the 1600 block. In order not to confuse the mail carrier too much, this relationship is true no matter how big the houses might be.

Differences between pointers and arrays

Despite the equivalent types, there are some differences between an array and a pointer. For one, the array allocates space for the data whereas the pointer does not:

```
void arrayVsPointer()
{
    // allocate storage for 128 characters
    char cArray[128];

    // allocate space for a pointer
    char* pArray;
}
```

Here cArray occupies 128 bytes, the amount of storage required to store 128 characters. pArray occupies only 4 bytes, the amount of storage required by a pointer.

The following function does not work:

```
void arrayVsPointer()
{
    // access elements with an array
    char cArray[128];
    cArray[10] = '0';
    *(cArray + 10) = '0';

    // access an 'element' of an array
    // which does not exist
    char* pArray;
    pArray[10] = '0';
    *(pArray + 10) = '0';
}
```

The expressions cArray[10] and *(cArray + 10) are equivalent and legal. The two expressions involving pArray don't make sense. While they are both legal to C++, the uninitialized pArray contains some random value. Thus, this second pair of statements attempts to store a 0 character somewhere randomly in memory.

 This type of mistake is generally caught by the CPU resulting in the dreaded segment violation error that you see from time to time issuing from your favorite applications.

A second difference is that cArray is a constant whereas pArray is not. Thus, the following for loop used to initialize the array cArray does not work:

```
void arrayVsPointer()
{
char cArray[10];
for (int i = 0; i < 10; i++)
{
    *cArray = '\0';    // this makes sense...
    cArray++;          // ...this does not
}
}
```

The expression cArray++ makes no more sense than does 10++. The correct version is:

```
void arrayVsPointer()
{
char cArray[10];
char* pArray = cArray;
for (int i = 0; i < 10; i++)
{
    *pArray = '\0';    // this works great
    pArray++;
}
}
```

Arguments to the Program

Arrays of pointers are another type of array of particular interest. This section examines how to use these arrays to simplify your program.

Arrays of pointers

Just as arrays may contain other data types, an array may contain pointers. The following declares an array of pointers to ints.

```
int* pnInts[10];
```

Given the above declaration, pnInt[0] is a pointer to an int value. Thus, the following is true:

```
void fn()
{
    int n1;
    int* pnInts[3];
    pnInts[0] = &n1;
    *pnInts[0] = 1;
}
```

or

```
void fn()
```

```
{
    int n1, n2, n3;
    int* pnInts[3] = {&n1, &n2, &n3};
    for (int i = 0; i < 3; i++)
    {
        *pnInts[i] = 0;
    }
}
```

or even

```
void fn()
{
    int* pnInts[3] = {(new int),
                      (new int),
                      (new int)};
    for (int i = 0; i < 3; i++)
    {
        *pnInts[i] = 0;
    }
}
```

The latter declares three int objects off the heap.

The most common use for arrays of pointers is to create arrays of character strings. The following two examples show why arrays of character strings are useful.

Arrays of character strings

Suppose a function that returns the name of the month corresponding to an integer argument passed it is needed. For example, if the program is passed the value 1, it responds by returning a pointer to the string "January".

The function could be written as follows:

```
// int2month() - return the name of the month
char* int2month(int nMonth)
{
    char* pszReturnValue;

    switch(nMonth)
    {
```

**10 Min.
To Go**

```
        case 1: pszReturnValue = "January";
                break;
        case 2: pszReturnValue = "February";
                break;
        case 3: pszReturnValue = "March";
                break;
        // ...and so forth...
        default: pszReturnValue = "invalid";
    }
}
```

When passed a 1 for the month, control would pass to the first case statement and the function would dutifully return a pointer to the string "January"; when passed a 2, "February"; and so on.

The switch() **control command is similar to a sequence of** if **statements.**

A more elegant solution uses the integer value for the month as an index to an array of pointers to the names of the months. In use, this appears as follows:

```
// int2month() - return the name of the month
char* int2month(int nMonth)
{
    // first check for a value out of range
    if (nMonth < 1 || nMonth > 12)
    {
    return << "invalid";
    return;
    }

    // nMonth is valid - return the name of the month
    char* pszMonths[] = {"invalid",
                         "January",
                         "February",
                         "March",
                         "April",
                         "May",
                         "June",
```

```
                                   "July",
                                   "August",
                                   "September",
                                   "October",
                                   "November",
                                   "December"};
        return pszMonths[nMonth];
    }
```

Here `int2month()` first checks to make sure that `nMonth` is a number between 1 and 12, inclusive (the `default` clause of the `switch` statement handled that for us in the previous example). If `nMonth` is valid, the function uses it as an offset into an array containing the names of the months.

The arguments to main()

You have seen another application of arrays of pointers to strings: the arguments to `main()`.

The arguments to a program are the strings that appear with the program name when you launch it. For example, suppose I entered the following command at the MS-DOS prompt:

```
MyProgram file.txt /w
```

MS-DOS executes the program contained in the file `MyProgram.exe` passing it the arguments `file.txt` and `/w`.

The use of the term *arguments* is a little confusing. The arguments to a program and the arguments to a C++ function follow a different syntax but the meaning is the same.

Consider the following simple program:

```
// PrintArgs - write the arguments to the program
//             to the standard output
#include <stdio.h>
#include <iostream.h>

int main(int nArg, char* pszArgs[])
{
    // print a warning banner
```

```
cout << "The arguments to " << pszArgs[0] << "\n";

// now write out the remaining arguments
for (int i = 1; i < nArg; i++)
{
    cout << i << ":" << pszArgs[1] << "\n";
}

// that's it
cout << "That's it\n";
return 0;
}
```

As always, the function main() accepts two arguments. The first argument is an int that I have called nArgs. This variable is the number of arguments passed to the program. The second argument is an array of pointers of type char* that I have called pszArgs. Each of these char* elements points to an argument passed to the program.

Consider the program PrintArgs. If I invoke the program

```
PrintArgs arg1 arg2 arg3 /w
```

from the command line of an MS-DOS window, nArgs would be 5 (one for each argument). The first argument is the name of the program itself. Thus, pszArgs[0] points to PrintArgs. The remaining elements in pszArgs point to the program arguments. The element pszArgs[1] points to arg1, pszArgs[2] to arg2, and so on. Because MS-DOS does not place any significance on /w, this string is also passed as an argument to be processed by the program.

The same is not true of the redirection symbols "<", ">" and "|". These are significant to MS-DOS and are not passed to the program.

There are several ways to pass arguments to a function under test. The easiest way is to simply execute the program from the MS-DOS prompt. Both the Visual C++ and rhide debuggers provide a mechanism for passing arguments during debug.

In Visual C++, select the Debug tab in the Project Settings dialog box. Input your arguments in the Program Arguments edit window as shown in Figure 14-3. The next time you start the program, Visual C++ passes these arguments.

Done!

In rhide, select Arguments... under the Run menu. Enter any arguments in the edit window that appears. This is demonstrated in Figure 14-4.

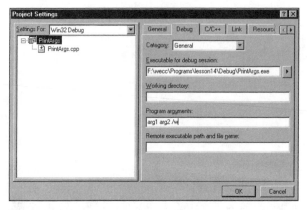

Figure 14-3
Visual C++ uses the Project Settings to pass arguments to the program under debug.

Figure 14-4
In rhide, the program arguments are found in the Run menu.

REVIEW

All languages base array indexing upon simple math operations on pointers; however, by allowing the programmer to have direct access to these types of operations, C++ gives the programmer tremendous semantic freedom. The C++ programmer can examine and use the relationship between the manipulation of arrays and pointers to her own advantage.

In this session you saw that

- Indexing in an array involves simple mathematical operations performed on pointers. C++ is practically unique in enabling the programmer to perform these operations himself or herself.

- Pointer operations on character arrays offered the greatest possibility for performance improvement in the early C and C++ compilers. Whether this is still true is debatable; however, the use of character pointers is a part of everyday life now.

- C++ adjusts pointer arithmetic to account for the size of the different types of objects pointed at. Thus, while incrementing a character pointer might increase the value of the pointer by 1, incrementing a double pointer would increase the value by 8. Incrementing the pointer of class object might increase the address by hundreds of bytes.

- Arrays of pointers can add significant efficiencies to a program for functions which convert an integer value to some other constant type, such as a character string or a bit field.

- Arguments to a program are passed to the `main()` function as an array of pointers to character strings.

QUIZ YOURSELF

1. If the first element of an array of characters `c[]` is located at address 0x100, what is the address of `c[2]`? (See "Operations on Pointers.")

2. What is the index equivalent to the pointer expression `*(c + 2)`? (See "Pointer vs. Array-Based String Manipulation.")

3. What is the purpose of the two arguments to `main()`? (See "The Arguments to main().")

Pointers to Objects

Session Checklist

✔ Declaring and using pointers to class objects

✔ Passing objects using pointers

✔ Allocating objects off of the heap

✔ Creating and manipulating linked lists

✔ Comparing linked list of objects to arrays of objects

**30 Min.
To Go**

S ession 12 demonstrated how combining the array and the class structures
into arrays of objects solved a number of problems. Similarly, the introduction of pointers to objects solves some problems not easily handled by arrays
of class objects.

Pointers to Objects

A pointer to a programmer defined structure type works essentially the same as a
pointer to an intrinsic type:

```
int* pInt;
class MyClass
```

```
{
   public:
        int  n1;
        char c2;
};
MyClass  mc;
MyClass* pMS = &mc;
```

The type of pMS **is "pointer to MyClass," which is also written** MyClass*.

Members of such an object may be accessed as follows:

```
(*pMS).n1 = 1;
(*pMS).c2 = '\0';
```

Literally, the first expression says, "assign 1 to the member n1 of the MS object pointed at by pMS."

The parentheses are required because "." has higher precedence than "*". The expression *mc.pN1 **means "the integer pointed at by the** pN1 **member of the object** mc.

Just as C++ defines a shortcut for use with arrays, C++ defines a more convenient operator for accessing members of an object. The -> operator is defined as follows:

```
(*pMS).n1 is equivalent to pMS->n1
```

The arrow operator is used almost exclusively because it is easier to read; however, the two forms are completely equivalent.

Passing objects

A pointer to a class object can be passed to a function in the same way as simple pointer type.

```
// PassObjectPtr - demonstrate functions that
//                 accept an object pointer
#include <stdio.h>
```

```cpp
#include <iostream.h>

// MyClass - a meaningless test class
class MyClass
{
    public:
        int n1;
        int n2;
};

// myFunc - pass by value version
void myFunc(MyClass mc)
{
    cout << "In myFunc(MyClass)\n";
    mc.n1 = 1;
    mc.n2 = 2;
}

// myFunc - pass by reference
void myFunc(MyClass* pMS)
{
    cout << "In myFunc(MyClass*)\n";
    pMS->n1 = 1;
    pMS->n2 = 2;
}

int main(int nArg, char* pszArgs[])
{
    // define a dummy object
    MyClass mc = {0, 0};
    cout << "Initial value = \n";
    cout << "n1 = " << mc.n1 << "\n";

    // pass by value
    myFunc(mc);
    cout << "Result = \n";
    cout << "n1 = " << mc.n1 << "\n";

    // pass by reference
    myFunc(&mc);
```

```
    cout << "Result = \n";
    cout << "n1 = " << mc.n1 << "\n";
    return 0;
}
```

The main program creates an object of class MyClass. The object is first passed
to the function myFunc(MyClass) and then its address to the function myFunc
(MyClass*). Both functions change the value of the object — only the changes
made from within myFunc(MyClass*) "stick."

In the call to myFunc(MyClass), C++ makes a copy of the object. Changes to mc
in this function are not copied back to main(). The call to myFunc(MyClass*)
passes an address to the original object in main(). The object retains any changes
when control returns to main().

This copy versus original comparison is exactly analogous to a function such as
fn(int) versus fn(int*).

**Besides retaining changes, passing a 4-byte pointer, rather than
creating a copy of the entire object, may be significantly faster.**

References

You can use the reference feature to let C++ perform some of the pointer
manipulation:

```
// myFunc - mc remains changed in calling function
void myFunc(MyClass& mc)
{
    mc.n1 = 1;
    mc.n2 = 2;
}

int main(int nArgs, char* pszArgs[])
{
    MyClass mc;
    myFunc(mc);
    // ...
```

You've already seen this feature. The ClassData **example in Session 12 used a reference to the class object in the call to** getData(NameDataSet&) **in order that the data read could be returned to the caller.**

Return to the heap

One must be careful not to return a reference to an object defined locally to the function:

```
MyClass* myFunc()
{
    MyClass  mc;
    MyClass* pMC = &mc;
    return pMC;
}
```

Upon return from myFunc(), the mc object goes out of scope. The pointer returned by myFunc() is not valid in the calling function. (See Session 13 for details.)

Allocating the object off of the heap solves the problem:

```
MyClass* myFunc()
{
    MyClass* pMC = new MyClass;
    return pMC;
}
```

The heap is used to allocate objects in a number of different situations.

**20 Min.
To Go**

The Array Data Structure

As a container of objects the array has a number of advantages including the capability to access a particular entry quickly and efficiently:

```
MyClass mc[100];           // allocate room for 100 entries
mc[n];                     // access the n'th ms entry
```

Weighed against that are a number of disadvantages:

Arrays are of fixed length. You can calculate the number of array entries to allocate at run time, but once created the size of the array can not be changed:

```
void fn(int nSize)
{
    // allocate an array to hold n number of
    // MyClass objects
    MyClass* pMC = new MyClass[n];

    // size of the array is now fixed and cannot
    // be changed

    // ...
}
```

In addition, each entry in the array must be of exactly the same type. It is not possible to mix objects of class MyClass and YourClass in the same array.

Finally, it is difficult to add an object to the middle of an array. To add or remove an object, the program must copy each of the adjoining elements up or down in order to make or remove a gap.

There are alternatives to the array that do not suffer from these limitations. The most well-known of these is the linked list.

Linked Lists

The linked list uses the same principle as the "holding hands to cross the street" exercise when you were a child. Each object contains a link to the next object in the chain. The "teacher," otherwise known as the head pointer, points to the first element in the list.

A linkable class is declared as follows:

```
class LinkableClass
{
    public:
        LinkableClass* pNext;

        // other members of the class
};
```

Here pNext points to the next entry in the list. This is shown in Figure 15-1.

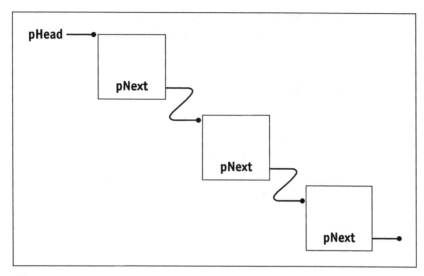

Figure 15-1
A linked list consists of a number of objects, each of which points to the next element in the list.

The head pointer is simply a pointer of type LinkableClass*:

```
LinkableClass* pHead = (LinkableClass*)0;
```

Always initialize any pointer to 0. Zero, generally known as null when used in the context of pointers, is universally known as the "nonpointer." In any case, referring to address 0 will always cause the program to halt immediately.

The cast from the int 0 to LinkableClass* is not necessary. C++ understands 0 to be of all types, sort of the "universal pointer." However, I find it a good practice.

Adding to the head of a linked list

To see how linked lists work in practice consider the following simple function which adds the argument passed it to the beginning of the list:

```
void addHead(LinkableClass* pLC)
{
    pLC->pNext = pHead;
    pHead = pLC;
}
```

The process is shown graphically in Figure 15-2. After the first line, the *pLC object points to the first object in the list (the same one pointed at by pHead), shown here as step A. After the second statement, the head pointer points to the object passed, *pLC shown in step B.

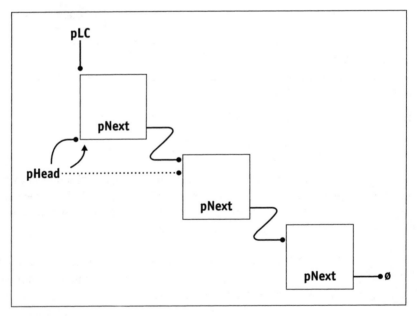

Figure 15-2
Adding an object to the head of a linked list is a two-step process.

Other operations on a linked list

Adding an object to the head of a list is the simplest of the operations on a linked list. Adding an element to the end of the list is a bit trickier:

```
void addTail(LinkableClass* pLC)
{
    // start with a pointer to the beginning
    // of the linked list
    LinkableClass* pCurrent = pHead;

    // iterate through the list until we find
    // the last object in the list - this will
    // be the one with the null next pointer
    while(pCurrent->pNext != (LinkableClass*)0)
    {
        // move pCurrent over to the next entry
        pCurrent = pCurrent->pNext;
    }

    // now make that object point to LC
    pCurrent->pNext = pLC;

    // make sure that LC's next pointer is null
    // thereby marking it as the last element in
    // the list
    pLC->pNext = (LinkableClass*)0;
}
```

The addTail() function begins by iterating through the loop looking for the entry who's pNext pointer is null — this is the last entry in the list. With that in hand, addTail() links the *pLC object to the end.

(Actually, as written addTail() has a bug. A special test must be added for pHead itself being null, indicating that the list was previously empty.)

A remove() function is similar. This function removes the specified object from the list and returns a 1 if successful or a 0 if not.

```
int remove(LinkableClass* pLC)
{
    LinkableClass* pCurrent = pHead;
```

```
// if the list is empty, then obviously
// we couldn't find *pLC in the list
if (pCurrent == (LinkableClass*)0)
{
    return 0;
}

// iterate through the loop looking for the
// specified entry rather than the end of
// the list
while(pCurrent->pNext)
{
    // if the next entry is the *pLC object...
    if (pLC == pCurrent->pNext)
    {
        // ...then point the current entry at
        // the next entry instead
        pCurrent->pNext = pLC->pNext;

        // not abolutely necessary, but remove
        // the next object from *pLC so as not
        // to get confused
        pLC->pNext = (LinkableClass*)0;
        return 1;
    }
}
return 0;
}
```

The remove() function first checks to make sure that the list is not empty — if it is, remove() returns a fail indicator because obviously the *pLC object is not present if the list is empty. If the list is not empty, remove() iterates through each member until it finds the object that points to *pLC. If it finds that object, remove() moves the pCurrent->pNext pointer around *pLC. This process is shown graphically in Figure 15-3.

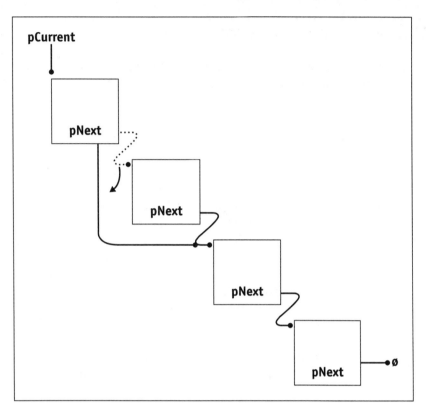

Figure 15-3
"Wire around" an entry to remove it from a linked list.

Properties of linked lists

Linked lists are everything that arrays are not. Linked lists can expand and contract at will as entries are added and removed. Inserting an object in the middle of a linked list is quick and simple — existing members do not need to be copied about. Similarly, sorting elements in a linked list is much quicker than the same process on the elements of an array.

On the negative side of the ledger, finding a member in a linked list is not nearly as quick as referencing an element in an array. Array elements are directly accessible via the index — no similar feature is available for the linked list. Programs must search sometimes the entire list to find any given entry.

A Linked NameData Program

The LinkedListData program shown here is a linked-list version of the array-based ClassData program from Session 12.

```cpp
// LinkedListData - store name data in
//                   a linked list of objects
#include <stdio.h>
#include <iostream.h>
#include <string.h>

// NameDataSet - stores name and social security
//                   information
class NameDataSet
{
    public:
        char szFirstName[128];
        char szLastName [128];
        int  nSocialSecurity;

        // the link to the next entry in the list
        NameDataSet* pNext;
};

// the pointer to the first entry
// in the list
NameDataSet* pHead = 0;

// addTail - add a new member to the linked list
void addTail(NameDataSet* pNDS)
{
    // make sure that our list pointer is NULL
    // since we are now the last element in the list
    pNDS->pNext = 0;

    // if the list is empty,
    // then just point the head pointer to the
    // current entry and quit
    if (pHead == 0)
    {
```

```
        pHead = pNDS;
        return;
    }


    // otherwise find the last element in the list
    NameDataSet* pCurrent = pHead;
    while(pCurrent->pNext)
    {
        pCurrent = pCurrent->pNext;
    }


    // now add the current entry onto the end of that
    pCurrent->pNext = pNDS;
}

// getData - read a name and social security
//           number; return null if no more to
//           read
NameDataSet* getData()
{
    // get a new entry to fill
    NameDataSet* pNDS = new NameDataSet;

    // read the first name
    cout << "\nEnter first name:";
    cin  >> pNDS->szFirstName;

    // if the name entered is 'exit'...
    if ((strcmp(pNDS->szFirstName, "exit") == 0)
        ||
        (strcmp(pNDS->szFirstName, "EXIT") == 0))
    {
        // ...delete the still empty object...
        delete pNDS;

        // ...return a null to terminate input
        return 0;
    }

    // read the remaining members
```

```
    cout << "Enter last name:";
    cin  >> pNDS->szLastName;

    cout << "Enter social security number:";
    cin  >> pNDS->nSocialSecurity;

    // zero the pointer to the next entry
    pNDS->pNext = 0;

    // return the address of the object created
    return pNDS;
}

// displayData - output the index'th data set
void displayData(NameDataSet* pNDS)
{
    cout << pNDS->szFirstName
         << " "
         << pNDS->szLastName
         << "/"
         << pNDS->nSocialSecurity
         << "\n";
}

int main(int nArg, char* pszArgs[])
{
    cout << "Read name/social security information\n"
         << "Enter 'exit' for first name to exit\n";

    // create (another) NameDataSet object
    NameDataSet* pNDS;
    while (pNDS = getData())
    {
        // add it onto the end of the list of
        // NameDataSet objects
        addTail(pNDS);
    }

    // to display the objects, iterate through the
    // list (stop when the next address is NULL)
```

```
        cout << "Entries:\n";
        pNDS = pHead;
        while(pNDS)
        {
            // display current entry
            displayData(pNDS);

            // get the next entry
            pNDS = pNDS->pNext;
        }
        return 0;
    }
```

Although somewhat lengthy, the `LinkedListData` program is relatively simple. The `main()` function begins by calling `getData()` to fetch another `NameDataSet` entry from the user. If the user enters exit, then `getData()` returns a null. `main()` calls `addTail()` to add the entry returned from `getData()` to the end of the linked list.

After there are no more `NameDataSet` objects forthcoming from the user, `main()` iterates through the list, displaying each using the `displayData()` function.

The `getData()` function first allocates an empty `NameDataSet` object from the heap. `getData()` continues by reading the first name of the entry to add. If the user enters a first name of exit or EXIT, the function deletes the object and returns a null to the caller. `getData()` continues by reading the last name and social security number. Finally, `getData()` zeroes out the `pNext` pointer before returning.

Never leave link pointers uninitialized. Use the old programmer's wives tale: "Zero them out when in doubt." (All wives of old programmers say that.)

The `addTail()` function appearing here is similar to the `addTail()` function demonstrated earlier in the chapter. Unlike that earlier version, this `addTail()` checks whether the list is empty before starting. If `pHead` is null, then `addTail()` points it at the current entry and terminates.

The `displayData()` function is a pointer-based version of the earlier `displayData()` functions.

Other Containers

Done!

A *container* is a structure designed to contain objects. Arrays and linked lists are specific instances of containers. The heap is also a form of container; it contains a separate block of memory that is available to your program.

You may have heard of other types of containers including the FIFO (first-in-first-out) and the LIFO (last-in-first-out), also known as the stack. These provide two functions, one to add and the other to remove objects. FIFO removes the oldest object, while LIFO removes the most recent object.

REVIEW

Creating pointers to class objects makes it possible to modify the value of class objects from within a function. Passing a reference to a class object is also considerably more efficient than passing a class object by reference. However, adding a pointer data member to a class introduces the possibility of linking objects from one object to another into a linked list. The linked list data structure offers certain advantages over arrays while giving up other efficiencies.

- Pointers to class objects work in essentially the same way as pointers to other data types. This includes the capability to pass objects by reference to functions.

- A pointer to a local object has no meeting once control passes from the function. Objects allocated off the heap do not have scope limitations and, therefore, can be passed from function to function. However, it is incumbent upon the programmer to remember to return objects back to the heap or face fatal and difficult-to-trace memory leaks.

- Objects can be strung together in linked lists if the class includes a pointer to an object of its own type. It is easy to remove and add objects to linked lists. Although not demonstrated here, sorting the objects in a linked list is also easier than sorting an array. Object pointers are also useful in the creation of other types of containers not demonstrated here.

QUIZ YOURSELF

1. Given the following:

```
class MyClass
{
    int n;
}
MyClass* pM;
```

   how would you reference the data member m from the pointer pM?
   (See "Pointers to Objects.")

2. What is a container? (See "Other Containers.")

3. What is a linked list? (See "Linked Lists.")

4. What is a head pointer? (See "Linked Lists.")

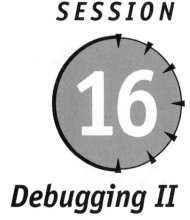
Debugging II

Session Checklist

✔ Stepping through a program

✔ Setting breakpoints

✔ Viewing and modifying variables

✔ Debugging a program using the debugger

**30 Min.
To Go**

S ession 10 presented a technique for debugging programs based on writing key data to cout standard output. We used this so-called write-statement technique to debug the admittedly very simple ErrorProgram example.

For small programs the write statement technique works reasonably well. Problems with this approach don't really become obvious until the size of the program grows beyond the simple programs you've seen so far.

In larger programs, the programmer often doesn't generally know where to begin adding output statements. The constant cycle of add write statements, execute the program, add write statements, and on and on becomes tedious. Further, in order to change an output statement, the programmer must rebuild the entire program. For a large program, this rebuild time can itself be significant.

A second, more sophisticated technique is based on a separate utility known as a debugger. This approach avoids many of the disadvantages of the write-statement

approach. This session introduces you to the use of the debugger by fixing
a small program.

Much of this part of the book is dedicated to studying the programming capabilities made possible by pointer variables. However, pointer capabilities come at a price: pointer errors are easy to make and extremely hard to find. The write-statement approach is not up to the task of finding and removing pointer problems. Only a good debugger can ferret out such errors.

Which Debugger?

Unlike the C++ language, which is standardized across manufacturers, each
debugger has its own command set. Fortunately, most debuggers offer the same
basic commands. The commands we need are available in both the Microsoft Visual
C++ and the GNU C++ rhide environments. Both environments offer the basic command set via drop-down menus. In addition, both debuggers offer quick access
to common debugger commands via the function keys. Table 16-1 lists these
commands in both environments.

For the remainder of this session, I refer to the debug commands by name.
Use Table 16-1 to find the corresponding keystroke to use.

Table 16-1
Debugger Commands for Microsoft Visual C++ and GNU rhide

Command	Visual C++	GNU C++ (rhide)
Build	Shift+F8	F9
Step in	F11	F7
Step over	F10	F8
View variable	see text	Ctl+F4
Set breakpoint	F9	Ctl+F8
Add watch	see text	Ctl+F7
Go	F5	Ctl+F9
View User Screen	Click on Program Window	Alt+F5
Program reset	Shift+F5	Ctl+F2

To avoid confusion over the slight differences that exist between the two debuggers, I describe the debug process I used with rhide first. I then debug the program using more or less the same steps with the Visual C++ debugger.

The Test Program

I wrote the following "buggy" program. Writing a buggy program is particularly easy for me because my programs rarely work the first time.

This file is contained on the accompanying CD-ROM in the file Concatenate (Error).cpp.

```cpp
// Concatenate - concatenate two strings
//                with a " - " in the middle
//                (this version crashes)
#include <stdio.h>
#include <iostream.h>

void concatString(char szTarget[], char szSource[]);

int main(int nArg, char* pszArgs[])
{
    cout << "This program concatenates two strings\n";
    cout << "(This version crashes.)\n\n";

    // read first string...
    char szString1[256];
    cout << "Enter string #1:";
    cin.getline(szString1, 128);

    // ...now the second string...
    char szString2[128];
    cout << "Enter string #2:";
    cin.getline(szString2, 128);

    // ...concatenate a " - " onto the first...
    concatString(szString1, " - ");
```

```
    // ...now add the second string...
    concatString(szString1, szString2);

    // ...and display the result
    cout << "\n" << szString1 << "\n";

    return 0;
}


// concatString - concatenate the string szSource
//                 to the end of szTarget
void concatString(char szTarget[], char szSource[])
{
    int nTargetIndex;
    int nSourceIndex;

    // find the end of the first string
    while(szTarget[++nTargetIndex])
    {
    }

    // tack the second to the end of the first
    while(szSource[nSourceIndex])
    {
        szTarget[nTargetIndex] =
            szSource[nSourceIndex];
        nTargetIndex++;
        nSourceIndex++;
    }
}
```

The program builds without problem. I next execute the program. When it asks
for string #1, I enter this is a string. For string #2, I enter THIS IS A STRING. Rather
than generate the proper output, however, the program terminates with an exit
code of 0xff. I click OK. In an attempt to offer some solace, the debugger opens
the Message Window underneath the edit window shown in Figure 16-1.

The first line of the message window indicates that rhide thinks that the error
occurred on or about line 46 of the module Concatenate(error1). In addition,
the function that crashed was called from line 29 of the same module. This would
seem to indicate that the initial while loop within concatString() is faulty.

Figure 16-1
The rhide debugger gives some hint as to the source of the error when a program crashes.

Because I don't see any problem with the statement, I decide to bring the rhide debugger to my aide.

Actually, I see the problem based on the information that rhide has already provided, but work with me here.

Single-Stepping Through a Program

**20 Min.
To Go**

I press Step Over to begin debugging the program. rhide opens an MS-DOS window as if it were about to execute the program; however, before the program can execute, the debugger closes the program window and displays the program edit window with the first executable line of the program highlighted.

An *executable statement* is a statement other than a declaration or a comment. An executable statement is one that generates machine code when compiled.

The debugger has actually executed the program up through the first line of the main() function and then snatched control of the program. The debugger is waiting for you to decide what to do next.

By repetitively pressing Step Over I can execute through the program until it crashes. This should tell me a lot about what went wrong.

Executing a program one line at a time is commonly known as *single-stepping* the program.

When I try to Step Over the `cin.getline()` command, the debugger does not take control back from MS-DOS window as it normally would. Instead, the program appears to be frozen at the prompt to enter the first string.

On reflection, I realize that the debugger does not take control back from the program until the C++ statement finishes executing — the statement containing the call to `getline()` cannot finish until I enter a string of text from the keyboard.

I enter a line of text and press Enter. The rhide debugger stops the program at the next statement, the `cout << "Enter string #2"`. Again I single–step, entering the second line of text in response to the second call to `getline()`.

If the debugger seems to halt without returning when single-stepping through a program, your program is waiting for something to happen. Most likely, the program is waiting for input, either from you or from external device.

Eventually I single-step down to the call to `concatString()`, as shown in Figure 16-2. When I try to Step Over the call, however, the program crashes as before.

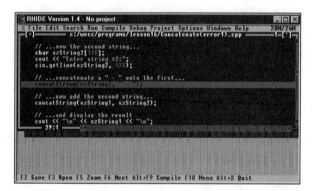

Figure 16-2
Something in the concatString() function causes the program to crash.

This doesn't tell me a lot more than I knew before. What I need is to be able to execute into the function rather than simply "stepping over" it.

Single-Stepping into a Function

I decide to start over. First, I press Program Reset in order to start the debugger at the beginning of the program.

Always remember to press Program Reset before starting over. It doesn't hurt to press the key too often. You might get into the habit of entering Program Reset before starting in the debugger every time.

Again, I single-step through the program using the Step Over key until I reach the call to concatString(). This time rather than step over the call, I use the Step In command to move into the function. Immediately the pointer moves to the first executable line in concatString() as shown in Figure 16-3.

There is no difference between the Step Over and Step In commands when not executing a function call.

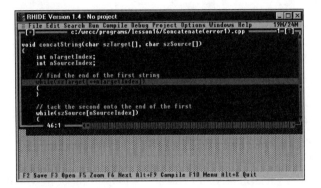

Figure 16-3
The Step In command moves control to the first executable line in concatString().

If you accidentally Step In to a function that you did not mean to, the debugger may ask you for the source code to some file that you've never heard of before. This asked-for file is the library module that contains the function you just stepped into. Press Cancel to view a listing of machine instructions, which are not very useful to even the most hardened techies. To return to sanity, open the edit window, set a break point as described in the next section to the statement after the call, and press Go.

With high hopes, I press the Step Over key to execute the first statement in the function. The rhide debugger responds by reporting a Segmentation violation as shown in Figure 16-4.

Figure 16-4
Single-stepping the first line of the concatString() function generates a Segmentation violation.

 A segmentation violation generally indicates that the program has accessed an invalid section of memory either because a pointer has gone awry or because an array is being addressed way beyond its bounds. To keep things interesting, let's pretend that I don't know that.

Now I know for sure that something about the while loop is not correct and that executing it even the first time crashes the program. To find out what it is, I need to stop the program right before it executes the offending line.

Using Breakpoints

Again, I press Program Reset to move the debugger back to the beginning of the program. I could single-step back through the program to the while loop as I did before. Instead, I decide to employ a shortcut. I place the cursor on the while statement and enter the Set breakpoint command. The editor highlights the statement in red as shown in Figure 16-5.

Figure 16-5
The breakpoint command

A *breakpoint* tells the debugger to halt on that statement if control ever passes this way. A breakpoint enables the program to execute normally up to the point that we want to take control. Breakpoints are useful either when we know where to stop or when we want the program to execute normally until it's time to stop.

With the breakpoint set, I press Go. The program appears to execute normally up to the point of the `while` call. At that point, the program obediently jumps back to the debugger.

Viewing and Modifying Variables

10 Min. To Go

There isn't much point in executing the `while` statement again — I know that it will crash. I need more information about what the program is doing to determine why it crashed. For example, I would like to see the value of `nTargetIndex` immediately prior to the execution of the `while` loop.

First, I double-click the variable name nTargetIndex. Next, I press View Variable. A window appears with the name nTargetIndex in the upper field. I click Eval in order to find the current value of the variable. The results, which are shown in Figure 16-6, are obviously nonsensical.

Looking back at the C++ code, I realize that I neglected to initialize either the `nTargetIndex` or `nSourceIndex` variables. To test this theory, I enter a 0 in the New Value window and click Change. I repeat the process for `nSourceIndex`. I then close the window and click Step Over to continue executing.

Figure 16-6
The Evaluate and Modify window enables the programmer to evaluate and optionally change the value of in-scope variables.

With the index variables initialized, I single-step into the `while` loop. The program does not crash. Each Step Over or Step In command executes one iteration of the `while` loop. Because the cursor ends up right where it started, there appears to be no change; however, after one loop `nTargetIndex` has incremented to 1.

Because I don't want to go through the work of reevaluating `nTargetIndex` on each iteration, I double-click on `nTargetIndex` and enter the Add Watch command. A window appears with the variable `nTargetIndex` and the value 1 to the right. I press Step In a few more times. `nTargetIndex` increments on each iteration through the loop. After several iterations, control eventually passes outside of the loop.

I set a breakpoint on the closing brace of the `concatString` function and press Go. The program stops immediately prior to returning from the function.

To check the string generated, I double-click on `szTarget` string and press View Variable. The results shown in Figure 16-7 are not what I expected.

The 0x6cceeO is the address of the string in memory. This information can be useful when tracking pointers. For example, this information would be extremely helpful in debugging a linked-list application.

It would appear as if the target string has not been updated, yet I know that the second `while` loop was executed. On the off chance that the second string is in fact there, I attempt to look past the initial string. `szTarget + 17` should be the address of the first character after the `null` at the end of "this is a string," the value I entered. In fact, the " - " appears there, followed by a "T" which appears to be incorrect. This is shown in Figure 16-8.

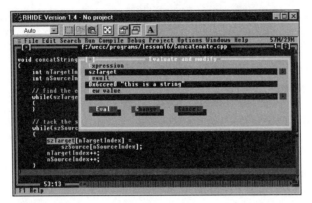

Figure 16-7
The target string does not appear to be modified upon returning from the concatString() function.

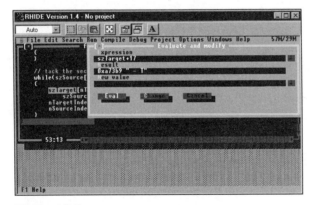

Figure 16-8
The target string appears appended to the source string in the wrong place.

After careful consideration, it is obvious that szSource was appended to szTarget after the terminating null. In addition, it is clear that the resulting target string was not terminated at all (hence the extra "T" at the end).

Modifying a string after the terminating null or forgetting to terminate a string with a null are by far the two most common string-related errors.

Because I now know two errors, I press Program Reset and fix the concatString() function to append the second string in the correct place and to append a terminating null to the resulting string. The updated concatString() function appears as follows:

```
void concatString(char szTarget[], char szSource[])
{
    int nTargetIndex = 0;
    int nSourceIndex = 0;

    // find the end of the first string
    while(szTarget[nTargetIndex])
    {
        nTargetIndex++;
    }

    // tack the second onto the end of the first
    while(szSource[nSourceIndex])
    {
        szTarget[nTargetIndex] =
            szSource[nSourceIndex];
        nTargetIndex++;
        nSourceIndex++;
    }

    // terminate the string properly
    szTarget[nTargetIndex] = '\0';
}
```

Because I suspect that I may still have a problem, I set a watch on szTarget and nTargetIndex while executing the second loop. Sure enough, the source string appears to be copied to the end of the target string as shown in Figure 16-9. (The second call to concatString() is shown in Figure 16-9 because it is the more obvious to understand.)

You really need to execute this one yourself. It's the only way you can get a feel for how neat it is to watch one string grow while the other string shrinks on each iteration through the loop.

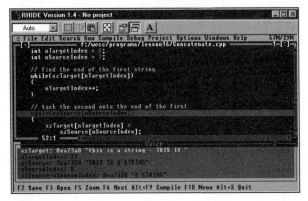

Figure 16-9
The appropriate watch variables demonstrate how the source string is appended to the end of the target string.

Reexamining the string immediately prior to adding the terminating `null`, I notice that the `szTarget` string is correct except for the extra characters at the end as shown in Figure 16-10.

Figure 16-10
Prior to adding the terminating null, the string resulting from concatenating the target and source strings displays extra characters.

As soon as I press Step Over, the program adds the terminating `null` and the noise characters disappear from the watch window.

Using the Visual C++ Debugger

The steps used to debug the Concatenate program using the Visual C++ debugger are similar to those used under rhide. A major difference, however, is that the Visual C++ debugger opens the program under execution in a separate MS-DOS window rather than as part of the debugger itself. When you press Go, a new tab appears along the Windows Task Bar bearing the name of the program, in this case Concatenate. The programmer can view the user window by selecting the program window.

A second difference is the way that the Visual C++ debugger handles the viewing of local variables. When execution is halted at a breakpoint, the programmer may simply place the cursor on a variable. If the variable is in scope, the debugger displays its value in a popup window as shown in Figure 16-11.

```
Concatenate(error1).cpp                                    _ □ X
         // ...concatenate a " - " onto the first...
         concatString(szString1, " - ");

         // ...now add the second string...
         concatString(szString1, szString2);

         // ...and display the result
         cout << "\n" << szString1 << "\n";

         return 0;
    }

    void concatString(char szTarget[], char szSource[])
    {
         int nTargetIndex;
         int nSourceIndex;
                       | nSourceIndex = -858993460 |
         // find the end of the first string
    ⟲    while(szTarget[++nTargetIndex])
         {
         }

         // tack the second onto the end of the first
         while(szSource[nSourceIndex])
         {
             szTarget[nTargetIndex] =
                 szSource[nSourceIndex];
             nTargetIndex++;
```

Figure 16-11
Visual C++ displays the value of a variable by placing the cursor on it.

In addition, the Visual C++ debugger offers a convenient view of all "local" variables (these are variables declared locally to the function). Select View, then Debug Windows, and finally Variables. From within the Variables Window, select the Locals tab. Alternatively, you may enter Alt+4. This window even highlights the variable which has changed since the last break point. Figure 16-12 shows this window while single-stepping through the copy of the source to the destination string.

Done!

The "I" characters at the end of szTarget **reflect the fact that the string has yet to be terminated.**

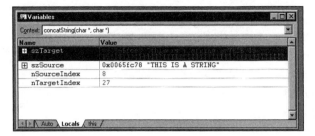

Figure 16-12
*The Variables window in the Visual C++ debugger tracks values of variables
as you single-step through the code.*

REVIEW

Let's compare the debugger approach to finding problems as shown here with the
write approach demonstrated in Session 10. The debugger approach is not as easy
to learn. I'm sure that many of the commands entered here seem foreign. Once
you feel comfortable with the debugger, however, you can use it to learn a great
deal about your program. The capability to move slowly through a program while
viewing and modifying different variables is a powerful feature.

**I prefer to use the debugger the first time I execute a newly
written program. Stepping through a program provides a good
understanding of what's really going on.**

I was forced to restart the program several times using the debugger approach;
however, I only edited and rebuilt the program once, even though I found more
than one problem. This is a distinct advantage when debugging a large program
that may take several minutes to rebuild.

**I have been on projects where it took the computer the entire
night to rebuild the system. While this was an extreme case,
5 to 30 minutes per rebuild is not out of the ordinary in real-
world applications.**

Finally, the debugger gives you access to information that you couldn't easily
see using the write approach. For example, viewing the contents of a pointer is
straightforward using the debugger. While possible, it is clumsy to repeatedly
write out address information.

QUIZ YOURSELF

1. What is the difference between Step Over and Step In?
   (See "Single-Stepping into a Function.")

2. What is a breakpoint? (See "Using Breakpoints.")

3. What is a watch? (See "Viewing and Modifying Variables.")

PART

III

Saturday
Afternoon

1. Define a student class to hold a student's last name, grade (as in first grade, second grade, and so forth), and grade-point average (GPA).

2. Write a function to read one student object and output the information.

3. Read in three grades and average them in the GPA before writing the object back out.

   Hints:

   a. Use some number-to-grade mapping. For example, 1 for first grade, 2 for second grade, and so forth.

   b. GPA is a floating-point number.

4. If the following variables are "packed" in memory with no wasted space, how many bytes of memory does each variable consume in a program created from Visual C++ or GNU C++:

   a. `int n1; long l1; double d1;`

   b. `int nArray[20];`

   c. `int* pnPt1; double* pdPt2;`

5. Consider the following function:

```
void fn(int n1)
{
    int* pnVar1 = new int;
    *pnVar1 = n1;
}
```

    a. Does it compile?

    b. What's wrong with it?

    c. Why might this function cause problems?

    d. What makes this type of problem difficult to find?

6. Describe the memory layout of `double dArray[3]`. Assume that the array begins at location 0x100.

7. Using the array described in problem 6, describe the effect of the following:

```
double dArray[3];
double* pdPtr = &dArray[1];
*pdPtr = 1.0; // assignment #1
int*    pnPtr = (int*)&dArray[2];
*pnPtr = 2;   // assignment #2
```

8. Write a function `LinkableClass* removeHead()` that removes the first entry from a list of `LinkableClass` objects and returns it to the caller.

Hints:

    a. Don't forget that the list may already be empty.

    b. Return a null if the list is empty.

    c. If you're having trouble worrying about empty lists, start out by just assuming that the list is not empty and go from there. After your function is finished, try to go back and add the special case of an empty list.

9. Write a function `LinkableClass* returnPrevious(LinkableClass* pTarget)` that returns the predecessor to `pTarget` in a linked list, that is, returns the entry in the linked list that points to `pTarget`. Return a `null` if the list is empty or if `pTarget` is not found.

Hint: You can't just assume that `pTarget` is in the list. Remember to check for the end of the list as well.

10. Write a function `LinkableClass* returnTail()` that returns the address of the last entry using `returnPrevious()` defined in problem 9.

Hint: Remember that the next pointer of the last entry is `null`.

Extra credit: Write a function `LinkableClass* removeTail()` that removes the last entry and returns it to the caller.

Hints:

a. Try to use the returnPrevious() function. It should be capable of doing most of the work.

b. If the previous entry to the last entry is null, then the list has only one entry in it.

11. Update the Concatenate program with the following faulty pointer version of concatString using either the rhide or Visual C++ debugger:

```
void concatString(char* pszTarget, char* pszSource)
{
    // tack the second onto the end of the first
    while(*pszTarget)
    {
        *pszTarget++ = *pszSource++;
    }

    // terminate the string properly
    *pszTarget = '\0';
}
```

PART

IV

Saturday Evening

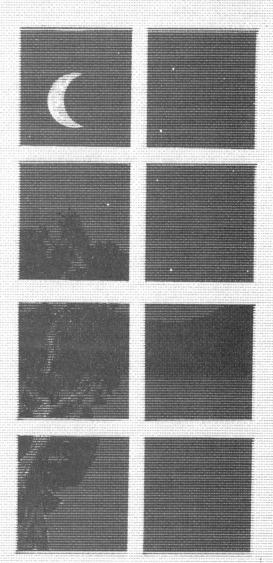

Object Programming

Session Checklist

✔ Identifying objects in the real world

✔ Classifying objects into classes

✔ Comparing the object-oriented approach to the functional
approach to programming

✔ Making nachos

**30 Min.
To Go**

Examples of object programming can be found in everyday life. In fact, objects
abound. Right in front of me is a chair, a table, a computer and a half-eaten
bagel. Object programming applies these concepts to the world of programming.

Abstraction and Microwave Ovens

Sometimes when my son and I watch football, I whip up a terribly unhealthy batch
of nachos. I dump some chips on a plate, throw on some beans, cheese, and lots of
jalapeños, and nuke the whole mess in the microwave oven for five minutes.

To use the microwave, I open the door, throw the stuff in, and punch a few buttons on the front. After a few minutes, the nachos are done.

This doesn't sound very profound, but think for a minute about all the things I don't do to use my microwave:

- I don't look inside the case of my microwave; I don't look at the listings of the code that goes into the central processor; and I don't study the wiring diagram.

- I don't rewire or change anything inside the microwave to get it to work. The microwave has an interface that lets me do everything I need to do — the front panel with all the buttons and the little timer display.

- I don't reprogram the software used to drive the little processor inside my microwave, even if I cooked a different dish the last time I used it.

- Even if I were a microwave designer and knew all about the inner workings of a microwave, including its software, I wouldn't think about that stuff when I use it.

These are not profound observations. We can think about only so much at one time. To reduce the number of things we must deal with, we work at a certain level of detail.

In object-oriented (OO) terms, the level of detail at which we are working is called the *level of abstraction*. When I'm working on nachos, I view my microwave oven as a box. As long as I use the microwave only through its interface (the keypad), there should be nothing that I can do that will cause the microwave to

1. Enter an inconsistent state and crash;

2. Worse, turn my nachos into a blackened, flaming mass; or

3. Worst of all, catch on fire and burn down the house.

Functional nachos

Suppose I were to ask my son to write an algorithm for how Dad makes nachos. After he understood what I wanted, he would probably write "open a can of beans, grate some cheese, cut the jalapeños," and so on. When it came to the part about microwaving the concoction, he would write something similar to "cook in the microwave for five minutes."

That description is straightforward and complete. But it's not how a functional programmer would code a program to make nachos. Functional programmers live in a world devoid of objects such as microwave ovens and other appliances. They tend to worry about flowcharts with their myriad functional paths. In a functional solution to the nachos problem, the flow of control would pass through my finger to the front panel and then to the internals of the microwave. Soon, the flow would be wriggling through complex logic paths about how long to turn on the microwave energy and whether to sound the "come and get it" tone.

In a world like this, it's difficult to think in terms of levels of abstraction. There are no objects, no abstractions behind which to hide inherent complexity.

Object-oriented nachos

**20 Min.
To Go**

In an object-oriented approach to making nachos, we would first identify the types of objects in the problem: chips, beans, cheese, and an oven. Then we would begin the task of modeling these objects in software, without regard to the details of how they will be used in the final program.

While we are writing object-level code, we are said to be working (and thinking) at the level of abstraction of the basic objects. We need to think about making a useful oven, but we don't have to think about the logical process of making nachos yet. After all, the microwave designers didn't think about the specific problem of my making a snack. Rather, they set about the problem of designing and building a useful microwave.

After we have successfully coded and tested the objects we need, we can ratchet up to the next level of abstraction. We can start thinking at the nacho-making level, rather than at the microwave-making level. At this point, we can pretty much translate my son's instructions directly into C++ code.

Actually we could keep going up the chain. The next level up might be to get up, go to work, return home, eat, rest, and sleep with nacho consumption falling somewhere in the eat-rest phases.

Classification and Microwave Ovens

Critical to the concept of abstraction is that of classification. If I were to ask my son, "What's a microwave?" he would probably say, "It's an oven that. . . ." If I then asked, "What's an oven?" he might reply, "It's a kitchen appliance that. . . ." I could keep asking this question until we eventually ended up at "It's a thing," which is another way of saying, "It's an object."

My son understands that our particular microwave is an example of the type of things called microwave ovens. In addition, he sees microwave ovens as just a special type of oven, which is, in turn, a special type of kitchen appliance.

The technical way of saying this is that my microwave is an *instance* of the class *microwave*. The class *microwave* is a *subclass* of the class *oven* and the class *oven* is a *superclass* of the class *microwave*.

Humans classify. Everything about our world is ordered in taxonomies. We do this to reduce the number of things that we have to remember. Consider, for example, the first time that you saw the new Ford-based Jaguar (or the new Neon for the rest of us). The advertisement called the Jaguar "revolutionary, a new type of car." But you and I know that that just isn't so. I like the looks of the Jaguar — I like them a lot — but it is just a car. As such, it shares all of (or at least most of) the properties of other cars. It has a steering wheel, seats, a motor, brakes, and so on. I bet I could even drive one without help.

I don't have to clutter my limited storage with all the things that a Jaguar has in common with other cars. All I have to remember is that "a Jaguar is a car that . . ." and tack on those few things that are unique to a Jaguar. Cars are a subclass of wheeled vehicles, of which there are other members, such as trucks and pickups. Maybe wheeled vehicles are a subclass of vehicles, which include boats and planes. And on and on and on.

Why Build Objects This Way?

It might seem easier to design and build a microwave oven specifically for our one problem, rather than to build a separate, more generic oven object. Suppose, for example, that I wanted to build a microwave to cook nachos and nachos only. There would be no need to put a front panel on it, other than a START button. You always cook nachos the same amount of time. We could dispense with all that DEFROST and TEMP COOK nonsense. It could be tiny. It would only need to hold one flat little plate. Three cubic feet of space would be wasted on nachos.

For that matter, let's just dispense with the concept of "microwave oven" altogether. All we really need is the guts of the oven. Then, in the recipe, we put the instructions to make it work: "Put nachos in the box. Connect the red wire to the black wire. Notice a slight hum." Stuff like that.

Nevertheless, the functional approach does have some problems:

- **Too complex.** We don't want the details of oven building mixed in with the details of nacho building. If we can't define the objects and pull them out of the morass of details to deal with separately, we must deal with all the complexities of the problem at the same time.

- **Not flexible.** If we need to replace the microwave oven with some other type of oven, we should be able to do so as long as the interface to the new oven is the same as the old one. Without a simple and clearly delineated interface, it becomes impossible to cleanly remove an object type and replace it with another.

- **Not reusable.** Ovens are used to make many different dishes. We don't want to create a new oven each time we encounter a new recipe. Having solved a problem once, it would be nice to reuse the solution in future programs.

It does cost more to write a generic object. It would be cheaper to build a microwave made specifically for nachos. We could dispense with expensive timers, buttons, and the like, that are not needed to make nachos. After we have used a generic object in more than one application, however, the costs of a slightly more expensive class more than outweigh the repeated costs of building cheaper, less flexible classes for every new application.

Self-Contained Classes

**10 Min.
To Go**

Let's reflect on what we have learned. In an object-oriented approach to programming

- The programmer identifies the classes necessary to solve the problem. I knew right off that I was going to need an oven to make decent nachos.

- The programmer creates self-contained classes that fit the requirements of the problem, and doesn't worry about the details of the overall application.

- The programmer writes the application using the classes just created without thinking about how they work internally.

An integral part of this programming model is that each class is responsible for itself. A class should be in a defined state at all times. It should not be possible to crash the program by calling a class with illegal data or with an illegal sequence of correct data.

Paradigm **is another word for programming model.**

Many of the features of C++ that are shown in subsequent chapters deal with giving the class the capability to protect itself from errant programs just waiting to trip it up.

REVIEW

In this Session, you saw the fundamental concepts of object-oriented programming.

- Object-oriented programs consist of a loosely coupled set of classes.
- Each class represents a real-world concept.
- Object-oriented classes are written to be somewhat independent of the programs that use them.
- Object-oriented classes are responsible for their own well-being.

QUIZ YOURSELF

1. What does the term *level of abstraction* mean? (See "Abstractions and Microwave Ovens.")

2. What is meant by the term *classification*? (See "Classification and Microwave Ovens.")

3. What are three problems with the functional approach to programming that object programming attempts to solve? (See "Why Build Objects This Way?")

4. How do you make nachos? (See "Abstractions and Microwave Ovens.")

Active Classes

Session Checklist

✔ Turning classes into active agents through the addition of member functions

✔ Naming member functions

✔ Defining member functions both inside and outside of the class

✔ Calling a member function

✔ Accumulating class definitions in `#include` files

✔ Accessing `this`

**30 Min.
To Go**

Real-world objects are independent agents (aside from their dependence on things such as electricity, air, and so forth). A class should be as self-sufficient as possible as well. It is impossible for a struct to be independent of its surroundings. The functions that manipulate these classes must be external to the class itself. Active classes have the capability to bundle these manipulator functions into the class itself.

Class Review

A class enables you to group related data elements in a single entity. For example, we might define a class Student as follows:

```
class Student
{
  public:
    int    nNSemesterHours;  // hours earned toward
                             // graduation
    float gpa;
};
```

Every instance of Student contains its own two data elements:

```
void fn(void)
{
    Student s1;
    Student s2;
    s1.nNSemesterHours = 1;  // this is not the same as...
    s2.nNSemesterHours = 2;  // ...this one
}
```

The two nNSemesterHours differ because they belong to two different students (s1 and s2).

A class with nothing but data members is also known as a *structure* and is defined using the keyword struct. The struct keyword's origins are in C. A struct is identical to a class except that the public keyword is not necessary.

It is possible to define pointers to class objects and to allocate these objects off of the heap as the following example illustrates:

```
void fn()
{
    Student* pS1 = new Student;
    pS1->nNSemesterHours = 1;
}
```

It is also possible to pass class objects to a function as follows:

```
void studentFunc(Student s);
void studentFunc(Student* pS);
```

```
void fn()
{
    Student s1 = {12, 4.0};
    Student* pS = new Student;

    fn(s1);              // call studentFunc(Student)
    fn(ps);              // call studentFunc(Student*)
}
```

Limitations of Struct

Classes with only data members have significant limitations.

Programs exist in the real world. That is, any nontrivial program is designed to provide some real-world function. Usually, but not always, this function is some analog of what could have been done manually. For example, a program might be used to calculate the grade point average (GPA) of a student. This function could be done by hand with pencil and paper, but it's a lot easier and faster to do it electronically.

The closer that a program can be made to mimic life, the easier it is for the programmer to understand. Thus, if there is a type of thing called a "student," then it would be nice to have a Student class that had all the relevant properties of a student. An instance of class Student would be analogous to an individual student.

A small class Student that describes the properties necessary to keep track of a student's GPA is found at the beginning of this lesson. The problem with this class is that it addresses only passive properties of the student. That is, a student has a number-of-classes-taken property and a GPA property. (The student also has a name, social security number, and so on, but it's OK to leave these properties off if they are not germane to the problem we're trying to solve.) Students start classes, drop classes, and complete classes. These are active properties of the class.

A functional fix

Of course, it is possible to add active properties to a class by defining a set of functions to accompany the class:

```
// define a class to contain the passive properties of
// a student
class Student
{
```

```
  public:
    int   nNSemesterHours;  // hours earned toward graduation
    float gpa;
};

// a Course class
class Course
{
  public:
    char* pszName;
    int   nCourseNumber;
    int   nNumHours;
};

// define a set of functions to describe the active
// properties of a student
void startCourse(Student* pS,
                 Course* pC);
void dropCourse(Student* pS, int nCourseNumber);
void completeCourse(Student* pS, int nCourseNumber);
```

This solution does work — in fact, this is the solution adopted by nonobject-oriented languages such as C. However, there is a problem with this solution.

The way this excerpt is written Student has only passive properties. There is a nebulous "thing" out there that has active agents, such as startCourse(), that operates on Student objects (and Course objects, for that matter). Furthermore, this nebulous thing has no data properties of its own. This description, though workable, does not correspond to reality.

We would like to take the active properties out of this undefined thing and attribute them to the Student class itself so that each instance of Student is outfitted with a complete set of properties.

 Adding active properties to the class rather than leaving them unassigned may seem minor now, but it will grow in importance as we make our way through the remainder of the book.

Defining an Active Class

The active properties of a student may be added to the Student class as follows:

```
class Student
{
  public:
    // the passive properties of a class
    int   nNSemesterHours;  // hours earned toward graduation
    float gpa;

    // the active properties of a class
    float startCourse(Course*);
    void  dropCourse(int nCourseNumber);
    void  completeCourse(int nCourseNumber);
};
```

The function startCourse(Course*) is a property of the class as are nNSemesterHours and gpa.

A function that is a member of a class is called a *member function*. For historical reasons that have little to do with C++, a member function is also referred to as a *method*. Probably because the term *method* is the more confusing of the two, it is the term of preference.

There isn't a name for functions or data that are not members of a class. I refer to them as nonmembers. All the functions that have been shown so far are nonmember functions because they didn't belong to a class.

C++ doesn't care about the order of members within a class. The data members may come before or after the member functions or they appear mixed together. My personal preference is to put the data members first with the member functions bringing up the rear.

Naming member functions

The full name of the function startCourse(Course*) is Student::startCourse (Course*). The class name in front indicates that the function is a member of the class Student. (The class name is added to the extended name of the function just as arguments are added to an overloaded function name.) We could have other functions called startCourse() that are members of other classes, such as Teacher::startCourse(). A function startCourse() without any class name in front is a conventional nonmember function.

Actually, the full name of the nonmember function addCourse() is ::addCourse(). **The** :: **without any class name in front indicates expressly that it is not a member of any class.**

Data members are not any different than member functions with respect to extended names. Outside a structure, it is not sufficient to refer to nSemester Hours by itself. The data member nSemesterHours makes sense only in the context of the class Student. The extended name for nSemesterHours is Student::nSemesterHours.

The :: is called the *scope resolution operator* because it indicates the class to which a member belongs. The :: operator can be used with a nonmember function as well as with a null structure name. The nonmember function startCourse() should actually be referred to as ::startCourse().

The operator is optional except when two functions of the same name exist. For example:

```
float startCourse(Course*);

class Student
{
  public:
    int    nSemesterHours;  // hours earned toward graduation
    float gpa;

    // add a completed course to the record
    float startCourse(Course* pCourse)
    {
      // ...whatever stuff...

      startCourse(pCourse);// call global function(?)
```

```
        // ...more stuff...
    }
};
```

We want the member function Student::startCourse() to call the non-member function ::startCourse(). Without the :: operator, however, a call to startCourse() from Student refers to Student::startCourse(). This results in the function calling itself. Adding the :: operator to the front directs the call to the global version, as desired:

```
class Student
{
  public:
    int   nSemesterHours;  // hours earned toward graduation
    float gpa;

    // add a completed course to the record
    float startCourse(Course* pCourse)
    {
        ::startCourse(pCourse);// call global function
    }
};
```

Thus, the fully extended name of a nonmember function includes not only the arguments, as we saw in Session 9, but also the class name to which the function belongs.

Defining a Member Function in the Class

A member function can be defined either in the class or separately. Consider the following in-class definition of a method addCourse(int, float):

```
class Student
{
  public:
    int   nSemesterHours;  // hours earned toward graduation
    float gpa;

    // add a completed course to the record
    float addCourse(int hours, float grade)
    {
```

```
    float weightedGPA;

    weightedGPA = nSemesterHours * gpa;

    // now add in the new course
    nSemesterHours += hours;
    weightedGPA += grade * hours;
    gpa = weightedGPA / nSemesterHours;
    return gpa;
}
};
```

The code for addCourse(int, float) doesn't appear different than that of any other function except that it appears embedded within the class.

Member functions defined in the class default to inline (see sidebar). Mostly, this is because a member function defined in the class is usually very small, and small functions are prime candidates for inlining.

Inline Functions

Normally a function definition causes the C++ compiler to generate machine code in one particular place in the executable program. Each time the function is called, C++ inserts a type of jump to the location where that function is stored. When the function completes, control passes back to the point where it was when it was originally called.

C++ defines a special type of function called an *inline* function. When an inline function is invoked, C++ compiles the machine code into the spot of the call. Each call to the inline function gets its own copy of machine code.

Inline functions execute more quickly because the computer does not need to jump to some other location and set up before starting to execute. Keep in mind, however, that inline functions take up more space. If an inline function is called 10 times, the machine code is duplicated in 10 different locations.

Because the difference in execution speed is small between an inline and a conventional, sometimes referred to an outline function, only small functions are candidates for inlining. In addition, certain other constructs force an inline function outline.

Writing Member Functions Outside of the Class

For larger functions, putting the code directly in the class definition can lead to some very large, unwieldy class definitions. To prevent this, C++ lets us define member functions outside of the class.

When written outside the class definition, our addCourse() method looks like this:

```
class Student
{
  public:
    int   nSemesterHours;  // hours earned toward graduation
    float gpa;

    // add a completed course to the record
    float addCourse(int hours, float grade);
};
float Student::addCourse(int hours, float grade)
{
    float weightedGPA;

    weightedGPA = nSemesterHours * gpa;

    // now add in the new course
    nSemesterHours += hours;
    weightedGPA += grade * hours;
    gpa = weightedGPA / nSemesterHours;
    return gpa;
}
```

Here we see that the class definition contains nothing more than a prototype *declaration* for the function addCourse(). The actual function *definition* appears separately.

A *declaration* defines the type of a thing. A *definition* defines the contents of a thing.

The analogy with a prototype declaration is exact. The declaration in the structure is a prototype declaration and, like all prototype declarations, is required.

When the function was among its Student buddies in the class, it wasn't necessary to include the class name with the function name — the class name was assumed. When the function is by itself, the fully extended name is required. It's just like at my home. My wife calls me only by my first name (provided I'm not in the doghouse). Among the family, the last name is assumed. Outside the family (and my circle of acquaintances), others call me by my full name.

Include files

It is common to place class definitions and function prototypes in a file carrying the extension .h separate from the .cpp file that contains the actual function definitions. The .h file is subsequently "included" in the .cpp source file as follows.

The student.h include file is best defined as follows:

```
class Student
{
  public:
    int   nSemesterHours;  // hours earned toward graduation
    float gpa;

    // add a completed course to the record
    float addCourse(int hours, float grade);
};
```

The student.cpp file would appear as follows:

```
#include "student.h";
float Student::addCourse(int hours, float grade)
{
    float weightedGPA;

    weightedGPA = nSemesterHours * gpa;

    // now add in the new course
    nSemesterHours += hours;
    weightedGPA += grade * hours;
    gpa = weightedGPA / nSemesterHours;
    return gpa;
}
```

The #include directive says "replace this directive with the contents of the student.h file."

The #include directive doesn't have the format of a C++ statement because it is interpreted by a separate interpreter that executes before the C++ compiler.

Including class definitions and function prototypes in an include file enables multiple C++ source modules to include the same definitions without the need to repeat them. This reduces effort and, more important, it reduces the chances that multiple source files will get out of synch.

10 Min. To Go

Calling a Member Function

Before we look at how to call a member function, let's review how to reference a data member:

```
#include "student.h"
Student s;
void fn(void)
{  // access one of the data members of s
   s.nSemesterHours = 10;
   s.gpa          = 3.0;
}
```

We must specify an object along with the member name when referencing an object member. In other words, the following makes no sense:

```
#include "student.h"
void fn(void)
{
   Student s;

   // access one of the data members of s
   // neither of these is legal
   nSemesterHours = 10;    // member of what object
                           // of what class?
   Student::nSemesterHours = 10; // okay, I know the class
                           // but I still don't know which
                           // object
```

```
   s.nSemesterHours = 10; // this is OK
}
```

Member functions are invoked with an object just as data members are:

```
void fn()
{
   Student s;

   // reference the data members of the class
   s.nSemesterHours = 10;
   s.gpa            = 3.0;

   // now access the member function
   s.addCourse(3, 4.0);
}
```

Calling a member function without an object makes no more sense than refer-encing a data member without an object. The syntax for calling a member function looks like a cross between the syntax for accessing a data member and for calling a conventional function.

Calling a member function with a pointer

The same parallel for the objects themselves can be drawn for pointers to objects. The following references a data member of an object with a pointer:

```
#include ""student.h"

void someFn(Student *pS)
{
   // access the data members of the class
   pS->nSemesterHours = 10;
   pS->gpa            = 3.0;

   // now access the member function
   // (that is, call the function)
   pS->addCourse(3, 4.0);
}

int main()
{
```

```
    Student s;

    someFn(&s);
    return 0;
}
```

Calling a member function with a reference to an object appears identical to using the object itself. Remember that when passing or returning a reference as an argument to a function, C++ passes only the address of the object. In using a reference, however, C++ dereferences the address automatically, as the following example shows:

```
#include "student.h"

// same as before, but this time using references
void someFn(Student &refS)
{
    refS.nSemesterHours = 10;
    refS.gpa            = 3.0;
    refS.addCourse(3, 4.0);   // call the member function
}

Student s;
int main()
{
    someFn(s);
    return 0;
}
```

Accessing other members from a member function

It is clear why you can't access a member of a class without an object. You need to know, for example, which gpa from which Student object? Take a second look at the definition of the member function Student::addCourse().This function is accessing class members without reference to an object in direct contradiction to my previous statement.

You still can't reference a member of a class without an object; however, from within a member function the object is taken to be the object on which the call was made. It's easier to see this with an example:

```
#include "student.h"
float Student::addCourse(int hours, float grade)
```

```
{
    float weightedGPA;
    weightedGPA = nSemesterHours * gpa;

    // now add in the new course
    nSemesterHours += hours;
    weightedGPA += hours * grade;
    gpa = weightedGPA / nSemesterHours;
    return gpa;
}

int main(int nArgs, char* pArgs[])
{
    Student s;
    Student t;

    s.addCourse(3, 4.0);  // here's an A+
    t.addCourse(3, 2.5);  // give this guy a C
    return 0;
}
```

When addCourse() is invoked with the object s, all of the otherwise unqualified member references in addCourse() refer to s. Thus, nSemesterHours becomes s.nSemesterHours, gpa becomes s.gpa. In the call t.addCourse() on the next line, these same references refer to t.nSemesterHours and t.gpa instead.

The object with which the member function is invoked is the "current" object, and all unqualified references to class members refer to this object. Put another way, unqualified references to class members made from a member function are always against the current object.

How does the member function know what the current object is? It's not magic — the address of the object is passed to the member function as an implicit and hidden first argument. In other words, the following conversion occurs:

```
s.addCourse(3, 2.5);
```

is like

```
Student::addCourse(&s, 3, 2.5);
```

(You can't actually use this interpretive syntax; this is just a way of understanding what C++ is doing.)

Inside the function, this implicit pointer to the current object has a name, in case you need to refer to it. The hidden object pointer is called this, as in "Which object? *this* object." The type of this is always a pointer to an object of the appropriate class. Thus within the Student class, this is of type Student*.

Anytime that a member function refers to another member of the same class without providing an object explicitly, C++ assumes this. You also can refer to this explicitly. We could have written Student::addCourse() as follows:

```
#include "student.h"
float Student::addCourse(int hours, float grade)
{
    float weightedGPA;

    // refer to 'this' explicitly
    weightedGPA = this->nSemesterHours * this->gpa;

    // same calculation with 'this' understood
    weightedGPA = this->nSemesterHours * gpa;

    // now add in the new course
    this->nSemesterHours += hours;
    weightedGPA += hours * grade;
    this->gpa = weightedGPA / this->nSemesterHours;
    return this->gpa;
}
```

Whether we explicitly include this or leave it implicit, as we did before, the effect is the same.

Overloading Member Functions

Member functions can be overloaded in the same way that conventional functions are overloaded. Remember, however, that the class name is part of the extended name. Thus, the following functions are all legal:

```
class Student
{
  public:
    // grade - return the current grade point average
    float grade();
```

```
    // grade - set the grade and return previous value
    float grade(float newGPA);

    // ...data members and stuff...
};

class Slope
{
  public:
    // grade - return the percentage grade of the slope
    float grade();

    // ...stuff goes here too...
};

// grade - return the letter equivalent of a numerical grade
char grade(float value);

int main(int nArgs, char* pArgs[])
{
    Student s;
    Slope o;

    // invoke the different variations on grade()
    s.grade(3.5);           // Student::grade(float)
    float v = s.grade();    // Student::grade()
    char c = grade(v);      // ::grade(float)
    float m = o.grade();    // Slope::grade()
    return 0;
}
```

Each call made from main() is noted in the comments with the extended name of the function called.

When calling overloaded functions, both the arguments of the function and the type of the object (if any) with which the function is invoked are used to disambiguate the call.

The term *disambiguate* is object-oriented talk for "decide at compile time which overloaded function to call." One can also say that the calls are being *resolved*.

Done!

In the example code segment, the first two calls to the member functions `Student::grade(float)` and `Student::grade()` are differentiated by their argument lists. The third call has no object, so it unambiguously denotes the nonmember function `grade(float)`. Because the final call is made with an object of type `Slope`, it must refer to the member function `Slope::grade()`.

REVIEW

The closer you can model the problem to be solved with C++ classes, the easier it is to solve the problem. Those classes containing only data members can only model the passive properties of objects. Adding member functions makes the class much more like a real-world object in that it can now respond to the "outside world," that is the remainder of the program. In addition, the class can be made responsible for its own health, in the same sense that real-world objects protect themselves.

- Members of a class can be functions as well as data. Such member functions give the class an active aspect. The full name of a member function includes the name of the class.

- Member functions may be defined either inside or outside the class. Member functions written outside of the class are more difficult to associate with the class, but avoid cluttering up the class definition.

- From within a member function, the current object is referred to by the keyword `this`.

QUIZ YOURSELF

---

1. What's wrong with defining functions external to the class that directly manipulates class data members? (See "A Functional Fix.")

2. A function that is a member of a class is known as a what? There are two answers to this question. (See "Defining an Active Class.")

3. Describe the significance of the order of the functions within a class. (See "Defining an Active Class.")

4. If a class X has a member `Y(int)`, what is the "full" name of the function? (See "Writing Member Functions Outside of the Class.")

5. Why is an include file called by that name? (See "Include Files.")

Maintaining Class Integrity

Session Checklist

✔ Writing and using a constructor

✔ Constructing data members

✔ Writing and using a destructor

✔ Controlling access to data members

**30 Min.
To Go**

An object cannot be made responsible for it's own well-being if it has no control over how it is created and how it is accessed. This Session examines the facilities C++ provides for maintaining object integrity.

Creating and Destroying Objects

C++ can initialize an object as part of the declaration. For example:

```
class Student
{
  public:
    int    semesterHours;
```

```
      float gpa;
};

void fn()
{
   Student s = {0, 0};
   //...function continues...
}
```

Here fn() has total control of the Student object.

We could outfit the class with an initialization function that the application calls as soon as the object is created. This gives the class control over how its data members are initialized. This solution appears as follows:

```
class Student
{
  public:
    // data members
    int    semesterHours;
    float gpa;

    // member functions
    // init - initialize an object to a valid state
    void init()
    {
       semesterHours = 0;
       gpa = 0.0;
    }
};

void fn()
{
   // create a valid Student object
   Student s;      //create the object...
   s.init();       //...then initialize it in valid state

   //...function continues...
}
```

The problem with this "init" solution is that the class must rely on the application to call the init() function. This is still not the solution we seek. What we really want is a mechanism that automatically initializes an object when it is created.

The constructor

C++ enables a class to assume responsibility for initializing its objects via a special function called the constructor.

A *constructor* is a member function that is called automatically when an object is created. Similarly, a *destructor* is called when an object expires.

C++ embeds a call to the constructor whenever an object is created. The constructor carries the same name as the class. That way, the compiler knows which member function is the constructor.

The designers of C++ could have made up a different rule, such as: "The constructor must be called init()**."The Java language uses just such a rule. A different rule wouldn't make any difference, as long as the compiler could recognize the constructor from among the other member functions.**

With a constructor, the class Student appears as follows:

```cpp
class Student
{
  public:
    // data members
    int     semesterHours;
    float gpa;

    // member functions
    Student()
    {
        semesterHours = 0;
        gpa = 0.0;
    }
};
```

```
void fn()
{
    Student s;        //create an object and initialize it

    //...function continues...
}
```

At the point of the declaration of s, the compiler inserts a call to the constructor Student::Student().

This simple constructor was written as an inline member function. Constructors can be written also as outline functions. For example:

```
class Student
{
  public:
    // data members
    int    semesterHours;
    float gpa;

    // member functions
    Student();
};

Student::Student()
{
    semesterHours = 0;
    gpa = 0.0;
}
int main(int nArgc, char* pszArgs)
{
    Student s;        //create the object and initialize it
    return 0;
}
```

I added a small main() function here so that you can execute this program. You really should single-step this simple program in your debugger before going any further.

As you single-step through this example, control eventually comes to rest at the Student s; declaration. Press Step In one more time and control magically jumps to Student::Student(). Continue single-stepping through the constructor. When the function has finished, control returns to the statement after the declaration.

Multiple objects can be declared on a single line. Rerun the single-step process with fn() declared as follows:

```
int main(int nArgc, char* pszArgs)
{
    Student s[5];    //create an array of objects
}
```

The constructor is invoked five times, once for each element in the array.

 If you can't get the debugger to work (or you just don't want to bother), add an output statement to the constructor so that you can see output to the screen whenever the constructor is invoked. The effect is not as dramatic, but it is convincing.

**20 Min.
To Go**

Limitations on the constructor

The constructor can only be invoked automatically. It cannot be called like a normal member function. That is, you cannot use something similar to the following to reinitialize a Student object:

```
void fn()
{
    Student s;         //create and initialize the object

    //...other stuff...

    s.Student();       //reinitilize it; this doesn't work
}
```

The constructor has no return type, not even void. The constructors you see here also have void arguments.

 The constructor with no arguments is known as the default or void constructor.

The constructor can call other functions. Thus, if you want to be able to reinitialize an object at will, write the following:

```
class Student
{
```

```
public:
  // data members
  int     semesterHours;
  float gpa;

  // member functions
  // constructor - initialize the object automatically
                  when it is created
  Student()
  {
      init();
  }

  // init - initialize the object
  void init()
  {
      semesterHours = 0;
      gpa = 0.0;
  }
};

void fn()
{
    Student s;        //create and initialize the object

  //...other stuff...
    s.init();         //reinitilize it
}
```

Here the constructor calls a universally available init() function, which performs the actual initialization.

Constructing data members

The data members of a class are created at the same time as the object itself. The object data members are actually constructed in the order in which they appear and immediately before the rest of the class. Consider the ConstructMembers program in Listing 19-1. Write statements were added to the constructors of the individual class so that you can see the order in which the objects are created.

Listing 19-1
The ConstructMembers Program

```
// ConstructMembers - create an object with data members
//                     that are also objects of a class
#include <stdio.h>
#include <iostream.h>
class Student
{
  public:
    Student()
    {
      cout << "Constructing student\n";
    }
};

class Teacher
{
  public:
    Teacher()
    {
      cout << "Constructing teacher\n";
    }
};

class TutorPair
{
  public:
    Student student;
    Teacher teacher;
    int     noMeetings;

    TutorPair()
    {
      cout << "Constructing tutor pair\n";
      noMeetings = 0;
    }
};
```

Continued

Listing 19-1 *Continued*

```
int main(int nArgc, char* pArgs[])
{
    cout << "Creating a tutor pair\n";

    TutorPair tp;

    cout << "Back in main\n";
    return 0;
}
```

Executing this program generates this output:

```
Creating a tutor pair
Constructing student
Constructing teacher
Constructing tutor pair
Back in main
```

Creating the object tp in main invokes the constructor for TutorPair automatically. Before control passes to the body of the TutorPair constructor, however, the constructors for the two member objects — student and teacher — are invoked.

The constructor for Student is called first because it is declared first. Then the constructor for Teacher is called. After these objects are constructed, control returns to the open brace and the constructor for TutorPair is allowed to initialize the remainder of the object.

It would not do for TutorPair **to be responsible for initializing** student **and** teacher**. Each class is responsible for initializing its own objects.**

The destructor

Just as objects are created, so are they destroyed. If a class can have a constructor to set things up, it should also have a special member function that's called to destruct, or take apart, the object.

The *destructor* is a special member function that is called when an object is destroyed or, to use C++ parlance, is destructed.

A class may allocate resources in the constructor; these resources need to be deallocated before the object ceases to exist. For example, if the constructor opens a file, the file needs to be closed. Or, if the constructor allocates memory from the heap, this memory must be freed before the object goes away. The destructor allows the class to do these clean-up tasks automatically without relying on the application to call the proper member functions.

The destructor member has the same name as the class, but a tilde (~) precedes it. Like a constructor, the destructor has no return type. For example, the class Student with a destructor added appears as follows:

```
class Student
{
  public:
    // data members
    // the roll up figures
    int   semesterHours;
    float gpa;

    // an array to hold each individual grade
    int*  pnGrades;

    // member functions
    // constructor - called when object created;
    //               initializes data members including
    //               allocating an array off of the heap
    Student()
    {
        semesterHours = 0;
        gpa = 0.0;

        // allocate room for 50 grades
        pnGrades = new int[50];
    }

    // destructor - called when object destroyed to put the
    //              heap memory back
    ~Student()
    {
        //return memory to the heap
        delete pnGrades;
```

```
        pnGrades = 0;
    }
};
```

If more than one object is being destructed, then the destructors are invoked in the reverse order from the order in which the constructors were called. This is also true when destructing objects that have class objects as data members. Listing 19-2 shows the output from the program shown in Listing 19-1 with the addition of destructors to all three classes.

Listing 19-2
Output of ConstructMembers After Destructors Are Added

```
Creating a tutor pair
Constructing student
Constructing teacher
Constructing tutor pair
Back in main
Destructing tutor pair
Destructing teacher
Destructing student
```

The entire program is contained on the accompanying CD-ROM.

The constructor for TutorPair is invoked at the declaration of tp. The Student and Teacher data objects are created in the order that they are contained in TutorPair before the body of TutorPair() is given control. Upon reaching the close brace of main(), tp goes out of scope. C++ calls ~TutorPair to destruct tp. After the destructor has finished disassembling the TutorPair object, ~Student and ~Teacher destruct the data member objects.

Access Control

**10 Min.
To Go**

Initializing an object into a known state is only half the battle. The other half is to make sure that external functions cannot "reach into" an object and diddle with its data members.

Allowing external functions access to the data members of a class is akin to allowing me access to the internals of my microwave. If I reach into the microwave and change the wiring, I can hardly blame the designer if the oven catches fire.

The protected keyword

C++ also enables a class to declare members to be off limits to nonmember functions. C++ uses the keyword `protected` to flag a set of class members as not being accessible from functions external to the class.

A class member is *protected* if it can only be accessed from other members of the class.

The opposite of *protected* is *public*. A *public* member can be accessed from both member and nonmember functions.

For example, in the following version of `Student`, only the functions `grade(double, int)` and `grade()` are accessible to external functions.

```
// ProtectedMembers - demonstrate the use of
//                    protected members
#include <stdio.h>
#include <iostream.h>

// Student
class Student
{
  protected:
    double dCombinedScore;
    int    nSemesterHours;

  public:
    Student()
    {
        dCombinedScore = 0;
        nSemesterHours = 0;
```

```cpp
    }

    // grade - add in the effect of another course grade
    double grade(double dNewGrade, int nHours)
    {
        // if the arguments represent legal values...
        if (dNewGrade >= 0 && dNewGrade <= 4.0)
        {
            if (nHours >0 && nHours <= 5)
            {
                // ...update the GPA information
                dCombinedScore += dNewGrade * nHours;
                nSemesterHours += nHours;
            }
        }
        return grade();
    }

    // grade - return the current GPA
    double grade()
    {
        return dCombinedScore / nSemesterHours;
    }

    // semesterHours - return the number of semester
    //                 hours the student has attended
    //                 school
    int semesterHours()
    {
        return nSemesterHours;
    }
};

int main(int nArgc, char* pszArgs[])
{
    // create a student object from the heap
    Student* pS = new Student;

    // add in a few grades
    pS->grade(2.5, 3);
```

```
        pS->grade(4.0, 3);
        pS->grade(3, 3);

        // now retrieve the current GPA
        cout << "Resulting GPA is " << pS->grade() << "\n";

        return 0;
    }
```

This version of Student maintains two data members. dCombinedScore reflects the sum of the weighted grades, while nSemesterHours reflects the total number of semester hours completed. The function grade(double, int) updates both the sum of the weighted grades and the number of semester hours. Its namesake function, grade(), returns the current GPA, which it calculates as the ratio of the weighted grades and the total number of semester hours.

grade(double, int) **adds the effect of a new course to the overall GPA whereas** grade(void**) returns the current GPA. This dichotomy of one function updating a value while the other simply returns it is very common.**

A grade() function which returns the value of some data member is called an access function because it provides access to the data member.

While certainly not foolproof, the grade(double, int) function demonstrates a little of how a class can protect itself. The function runs a few rudimentary checks to make sure that the data being passed it is reasonable. The Student class knows that valid grades stretch from 0 to 4. Further, the class knows that the number of semester hours for one course lies between 0 and 5 (the upper range is my own invention).

The basic checks made by the grade() method, when added to the fact that the data members are not accessible by outside functions, guarantees a certain amount of data integrity.

There is another access control level called *private*. **The distinction between** *private* **and** *protected* **will become clearer when we discuss inheritance in Session 21.**

The member function semesterHours() does nothing more than return the value of nSemesterHours.

A function that does nothing more than give external functions access to the value of a data member is called an *access function*. An access function enables nonmember functions to read the value of a data member without the capability to change it.

A function that can access the protected members of a class is called a *trusted function*. All member functions are trusted. Nonmember functions can also be designated as trusted using the `friendly` keyword. A function that is friendly to a class is trusted. All of the member functions of a friendly class are friendly. The proper use of `friendly` is beyond the scope of this book.

Static data members

No matter how many members we had protected, our `LinkList` class in Session 15 would still have been vulnerable to outside functions through the global head pointer. What we really want is to draw that pointer back into the protection of the class where we could make it protected. However, we cannot use a normal data member because these are created separately for each instance of `LinkList` — there can be only one head pointer for the entire linked list. C++ provides a solution in the format of static data member.

A *static data member* is one that is not instanced separately for each object. All objects of a given class share the same static data member.

The syntax for declaring a static data member is a bit tortured:

```
class LinkedList
{
  protected:
    // declare pHead to be a member of the class
    // but common to all objects
    static LinkedList* pHead;

    // the standard pNext pointer is instanced separately
    // for each object
    LinkedList* pNext;

    // addHead - add a data member to the beginning
    //           of the list
    void addHead()
    {
```

```
            // make the current entry point to the
            // current beginning of the list
            pNext = pHead;

            // make the current head pointer point to
            // the current object (this)
            pHead = this;
        }

    // ...whatever else...
};

// now allocate a memory location to house the static
// data memory; be sure to initialize the static here
// because the object constructor will not handle it
LinkedList* LinkedList::pHead = 0;
```

The static declaration in the class makes pHead a member of the class but does not allocate memory for it. That must be done outside of the class as shown.

The same function addHead() accesses pHead just as it would access any other data member. First, it points the current object's next pointer to the beginning of the list — the entry pointed at by pHead. Second, it changes the head pointer to point to the current entry.

Remember that the address of the "current entry" is referenced by the keyword this.

Done!

As simple as addHead() is, examine it very carefully: all objects of class LinkedList **refer to the same** pHead **member, whereas each object has its own** pNext **pointer.**

It is also possible to declare a member function static; this book, however, does not cover such functions.

REVIEW

The constructor is a special member function that C++ calls automatically when an object is created, whether it's because a local variable goes into scope or when an object is allocated off of the heap. It is the responsibility of the constructor to initialize the data members to a legal state. The data members of a class are constructed automatically before the class constructor is called. By comparison, C++ calls a special function known as the destructor when the object is to be destroyed.

- The class constructor gives the class control over how the object is to be created. This keeps the class object from starting life in an illegal state. Constructors are declared the same as other member functions except that they carry the same name as the class and have no return type (not even void).

- The class destructor gives the class a chance to return any resources allocated by the constructor. The most common such resource is memory.

- Declaring a member protected makes it inaccessible to untrusted member functions. Member functions are automatically considered trusted.

QUIZ YOURSELF

1. What is a constructor? (See "The Constructor.")

2. What is wrong with calling a function init() to initialize an object when it is created? (See "The Constructor.")

3. What is the full name of a constructor for the class Teacher? What is its return type? (See "The Constructor.")

4. What is the order of construction for object data members? (See "Constructing Data Members.")

5. What is the full name of the destructor for the class Teacher? (See "The Destructor.")

6. What is the significance of the keyword static when it is used in connection with data members? (See "Static Data Members.")

Class Constructors II

Session Checklist

✔ Creating constructors that have arguments

✔ Passing arguments to the constructors of data members

✔ Determining the order of construction of data members

✔ Examining the special properties of the copy constructor

30 Min.
To Go

A very simple constructor worked well for the simple Student class in Session 19. However, the Student class would not become very complex before the limitations of such a constructor became clear. Consider, for example, that a student has a name and a social security number-based ID. The constructor in Session 19 had no arguments, so it had no choice but to initialize the object as "empty." The constructor is supposed to create a valid object — a no-named student with a null ID probably does not represent a valid student.

Constructors with Arguments

C++ enables the programmer to define a constructor with arguments as shown in Listing 20-1.

Listing 20-1
Defining a Constuctor with Arguments

```cpp
// NamedStudent - this program demonstrates how adding
//                arguments to the constructor makes
//                for a more realistic class
#include <stdio.h>
#include <iostream.h>
#include <string.h>

// Student
class Student
{
  public:
    Student(char *pszName, int nID)
    {
        // Store a copy of the person's name in the object:
        // allocate from the heap the same
        // size string as that passed
        int nLength = strlen(pszName) + 1;
        this->pszName = new char[nLength];

        // now copy the name passed into the
        // newly allocated buffer
        strcpy(this->pszName, pszName);

        // finally save off the student id
        this->nID = nID;
    }

    ~Student()
    {
        delete pszName;
        pszName = 0;
    }

  protected:
    char* pszName;
    int   nID;
```

```
};

void fn()
{
    // create a local student
    Student  s1("Stephen Davis", 12345);

    // now create a student off of the heap
    Student* pS2 = new Student("Kinsey Davis", 67890);

    // be sure to return any objects allocated from
    // the heap
    delete pS2;
}
```

The Student(char*, int) constructor begins by allocating a block of heap memory to hold a copy of the string passed it. The function strlen() returns the number of bytes in a character string; however, because strlen() does not count the null, we have to add 1 to that count to calculate the amount of heap memory that is needed. The Student constructor copies the string passed it to this block of memory. Finally, the constructor assigns the student ID in the class.

The function fn() creates two Student objects, one local to the function and a second off of the heap. In both cases, fn() passes the name and ID number of the Student object being created.

In this NamedStudent **example, the arguments to the** Student **constructor carry the same name as the data members that they initialize. This is not a requirement of C++, just a convention that I prefer. However, a locally defined variable has precedence over a data member of the same name. Thus, an unqualified reference within** Student() **to** pszName **refers to the argument; however,** this->pszName **always refers to the data member irrespective of any locally declared variables. While some find this practice confusing, I think it highlights the connection between the argument and the data member. In any case, you should be acquainted with this common practice.**

Constructors can be overloaded in the same way that functions with arguments can be overloaded.

Remember that to overload a function means to have two functions with the same name, which are differentiated by their different types of arguments.

C++ chooses the proper constructor based on the arguments in the declaration. For example, the class Student can simultaneously have the three constructors shown in the following snippet:

```cpp
#include <iostream.h>
#include <string.h>
class Student
{
  public:
    // the available constructors
    Student();
    Student(char* pszName);
    Student(char* pszName, int nID);
    ~Student();

  protected:
    char* pszName;
    int   nID;
};

//the following invokes each constructor in turn
int main(int nArgs, char* pszArgs[])
{
    Student noName;
    Student freshMan("Smel E. Fish");
    Student xfer("Upp R. Classman", 1234);
    return 0;
}
```

Because the object noName appears with no arguments, it is constructed using the constructor Student::Student(). This constructor is called the *default*, or *void, constructor*. (I prefer the latter name, but the former is more common so I use it in this book.)

It is often the case that the only difference between one constructor and another is the addition of a default value for the missing argument. Suppose, for example, that a student created without a student ID is given the ID of 0. To help avoid extra work, C++ enables the programmer to designate a default argument. I could have combined the latter two constructors as follows:

```
Student(char* pszName, int nID = 0);

Student s1("Lynn Anderson", 1234);
student s2("Stella Prater");
```

Both s1 and s2 are constructed using the same Student(char*, int) constructor. In Stella's case, a default value of 0 is supplied to the constructor.

Default values for arguments can be supplied to any function; however, they find the greatest use in reducing the number of constructors.

Constructing Class Members

C++ constructs data member objects at the same time that it constructs the object itself. There is no obvious way to pass arguments when constructing member objects.

In the examples shown in Session 19, there was no need to pass arguments to the data member constructors — that version of Student relied on the application to call an init() function to initialize the object to some reasonable value.

Consider Listing 20-2 in which the class Student includes an object of class StudentId. I outfitted both with WRITE statements in the constructor in order to see what's going on.

Listing 20-2
Student Constructor with a member object of class StudentID

```
// DefaultStudentId - create a student object using the
//                    the next available student ID
#include <stdio.h>
#include <iostream.h>
#include <string.h>
```

Continued

Listing 20-2 *Continued*

```cpp
// StudentId
int nNextStudentId = 0;
class StudentId
{
  public:
    StudentId()
    {
        nId = ++nNextStudentId;
        cout << "Assigning student id " << value << "\n";
    }

    ~StudentId()
    {
        cout << "Destructing student id " << value << "\n";
  protected:
    int nId;
};

// Student
class Student
{
  public:
    // constructor - create a student with the name
    //               supplied (use default of "no name")
    Student(char *pszName  = "no name")
    {
        cout << "Constructing student " << pszName << "\n";

        // copy the string passed to the local member
        this->pszName = new char[strlen(pszName) + 1];
        strcpy(this->pszName, pszName);
    }

    ~Student()
    {
        cout << "Destructing student " << pszName << "\n";
        delete pszName;
        pszName = 0;
```

```
     }

  protected:
    char* pszName;
    StudentId id;
};

int main(int nArgs, char* pszArg[])
{
   Student s("Randy");
   return 0;
}
```

A student ID is assigned to each student as the `Student` object is constructed. In this example, IDs are handed out sequentially using the global variable `nextStudentId` to store the next ID to be assigned.

The output from executing this simple program follows:

```
Assigning student id 1
Constructing student Randy
Destructing student Randy
Destructing student id 1
```

Notice that the message from the `StudentId` constructor appears before the output from the `Student` constructor and the message from the `StudentId` destructor appears after the output from the `Student` destructor.

With all these constructors performing output, you might think that constructors must output something. Most constructors don't output a darned thing. Book constructors do because readers usually don't take the good advice provided by authors and single-step the programs.

If the programmer does not provide a constructor, the default constructor provided by C++ automatically invokes the default constructors for any data members. The same is true come harvesting time. The destructor for the class automatically invokes the destructor for any data members that have destructors. The C++ provided destructor does the same.

Okay, this is all great for the default constructor. But what if we wanted to invoke a constructor other than the default? Where do we put the object? To demonstrate, let's assume that instead of calculating the student ID, it is provided to the Student constructor, which passes the ID to the constructor for class StudentId.

First, let's look at what doesn't work. Consider the program shown in Listing 20-3.

Listing 20-3
An incorrect way to construct a data member object

```
// FalseStudentId - the following attempts to create
//                  the student id data member using
//                  a non-default constructor.

#include <stdio.h>
#include <iostream.h>
#include <string.h>

class StudentId
{
  public:
    StudentId(int nId = 0)
    {
        this->nId = nId;
        cout << "Assigning student id " << nId << "\n";
    }

    ~StudentId()
    {
        cout << "Destructing student id " << nId << "\n";
    }
  protected:
    int nId;
};

class Student
{
  public:
    // constructor - create an object with a specified
    //               name and student id
    Student(char* pszName  = "no name", int ssId = 0)
    {
```

```
        cout << "Constructing student " << pszName << "\n";
        this->pszName = new char[strlen(pszName) + 1];
        strcpy(this->pszName, pszName);

        //don't try this at home kids. It doesn't work
        StudentId id(ssId);      //construct a student id
    }

    ~Student()
    {
        cout << "Destructing student " << this->pszName << "\n";
        delete this->pszName;
        pszName = 0;
    }
  protected:
    char* pszName;
    StudentId id;
};

int main()
{
    Student s("Randy", 1234);
    cout << "This message from main\n";
    return 0;
}
```

The constructor for StudentId was changed to accept a value externally (the default value is necessary to get the example to compile, for reasons that become clear shortly). Within the constructor for Student, the programmer (that's me) has (cleverly) attempted to construct a StudentId object named id.

The output from this program shows a problem:

```
Assigning student id 0
Constructing student Randy
Assigning student id 1234
Destructing student id 1234
This message from main
Destructing student Randy
Destructing student id 0
```

First, the constructor appears to be invoked twice, the first time with zero before the Student constructor begins and a second time with the expected 1234 from within the Student constructor. Apparently, a second StudentId object has been created within the constructor for Student different from the StudentId data member

The explanation for this rather bizarre behavior is that the data member id already exists by the time the body of the constructor is entered. Rather than constructing an existing data member id, the declaration provided in the constructor creates a local object of the same name. This local object is destructed upon returning from the constructor.

Somehow we need a different mechanism to indicate "construct the existing member; don't create a new one." C++ defines the new construct as follows:

```
class Student
{
  public:
    Student(char* pszName  = "no name", int ssId = 0)
        : id(ssId) // construct the data member id to the
                   // specified value
    {
      cout << "Constructing student " << pszName << "\n";
      this->pszName = new char[strlen(pszName) + 1];
      strcpy(this->pszName, pszName);
    }
    // ...
};
```

Take particular notice of the first line of the constructor. We haven't seen this before. The : means that what follows are calls to the constructors of data members of the current class. To the C++ compiler, this line reads: "Construct the member id using the argument ssId of the Student constructor. Whatever data members are not called out in this fashion are constructed using the default constructor."

The entire program appears on the accompanying CD-ROM with the name StudentId.

This new program generates the expected result:

```
Assigning student id 1234
Constructing student Randy
This message from main
Destructing student Randy
Destructing student id 1234
```

The object s is created in main() with a student name of "Randy" and a student id of 1234. This object is automatically destructed upon reaching the end of main().

The : syntax must also be used to assign values to const or reference type members. Consider the following silly class:

```
class SillyClass
{
  public:
    SillyClass(int& i) : nTen(10), refI(i)
    {
    }
  protected:
    const int nTen;
    int& refI;
};
```

By the time that the program begins executing the code contained in the body of the constructor, the data members nTen and refI are already created. These data member types must be initialized before control enters the constructor body.

Any data member can be declared using the preceding syntax.

Order of Construction

When there are multiple objects, all with constructors, the programmer usually doesn't care about the order in which things are built. If one or more of the constructors have side effects, however, the order can make a difference.

A *side effect* is some change in state caused by a function but not part of the arguments or the returned object. For example, if a function assigns a value to a global variable, that would be a side effect.

The rules for the order of construction are:

- Locals and static objects are constructed in the order in which their declarations are invoked.
- Static objects are constructed only once.
- All global objects are constructed before main().
- Global objects are constructed in no particular order.
- Members are constructed in the order in which they are declared in the class.

Let's consider each rule in turn.

Local objects are constructed in order

Local objects are constructed in the order in which the program encounters their declaration. Normally, this is the same as the order in which the objects appear in the function, unless your function jumps around particular declarations. (By the way, jumping around declarations is a bad thing to do. It confuses the reader and the compiler.)

Static objects are constructed only once

Static objects are similar to other local variables, except they are constructed only once. This is to be expected because they retain their value from one invocation of the function to the next. However, unlike C, which is free to initialize statics when the program begins, C++ must wait until the first time control passes through the static's declaration to perform the construction. Consider the following trivial program:

```
class DoNothing
{
  public:
    DoNothing(int initial)
    {
    }
};
```

```
void fn(int i)
{
    static DoNothing staticDN(1);
    DoNothing localDN(2);
}
```

The variable `staticDN` is constructed the first time that `fn()` is called. The second time that `fn()` is invoked, the program only constructs `localDN`.

All global objects are constructed before main()

All global variables go into scope as soon as the program starts. Thus, all global objects are constructed before control is passed to `main()`.

Global objects are constructed in no particular order

Figuring out the order of construction of local objects is easy. An order is implied by the flow of control. With globals, there is no such flow to give order. All globals go into scope simultaneously, remember? Okay, you argue, why can't the compiler just start at the top of the file and work its way down the list of global objects? That would work fine for a single file (and I presume that's what most compilers do).

Unfortunately, most programs in the real world consist of several files that are compiled separately and then built together. Because the compiler has no control over the order in which these files are linked, it cannot affect the order in which global objects are constructed from file to file.

Most of the time this is ho-hum stuff. Occasionally, though, it can generate bugs that are extremely difficult to track down. (It happens just often enough to make it worth mentioning in a book.)

Consider this example:

```
class Student
{
  public:
    Student (unsigned id) : studentId(id)
    {
    }
    const unsigned studentId;
};

class Tutor
```

```
{
  public:
    // constructor - assign the tutor to a student
    //                 by recording the student's id
    Tutor(Student &s)
    {
        tutoredId = s.studentId;
    }
  protected:
    unsigned tutoredId;
};

// create a student globally
Student randy(1234);

//assign that student a tutor
Tutor    jenny(randy);
```

Here the constructor for Student assigns a student ID. The constructor for
Tutor records the ID of the student to help. The program declares a student
randy and then assigns that student a tutor jenny.

The problem is that we are making the implicit assumption that randy gets
constructed before jenny. Suppose that it was the other way around. Then jenny
would get constructed with a block of memory that had not yet been turned into
a Student object and, therefore, had garbage for a student ID.

**This example is not too difficult to figure out and more than a
little contrived. Nevertheless, problems deriving from global
objects being constructed in no particular order can appear in
subtle ways. To avoid this problem, don't allow the constructor
for one global object to refer to the contents of another global
object.**

Members are constructed in the order in which they are declared

Members of a class are constructed according to the order in which they are
declared within the class. This is not quite as obvious as it might sound. Consider
this example:

```
class Student
{
```

```
public:
  Student (unsigned id, unsigned age) : sAge(age), sId(id)
  {
  }
  const unsigned sId;
  const unsigned sAge;
};
```

In this example, sId is constructed before sAge even though it appears second in the constructor's initialization list. The only time you could probably detect any difference in the construction order is if both of these were members of classes that had constructors and these constructors had some mutual side effect.

Destructors are invoked in the reverse order of the constructors

Finally, no matter in what order the constructors kick off, you can be assured that the destructors are invoked in the reverse order. (It's nice to know that there's at least one rule in C++ that has no if's, and's, or but's.)

**10 Min.
To Go**

The Copy Constructor

A copy constructor is a constructor that has the name X::X(X&), where X is any class name. That is, it is the constructor of class X which takes as its argument a reference to an object of class X. Now, I know that this sounds really useless, but think for a moment about what happens when you call a function similar to the following:

```
void fn1(Student fs)
{
   //...
}
int fn2()
{
   Student ms;
   fn1(ms);
   return 0;
}
```

As you know, a copy of the object ms — and not the object itself — is passed to the function fn1(). C++ could just make an exact copy of the object and pass that to fn1().

This is not acceptable in C++. First, as I have pointed out, it takes a constructor to create an object, even a copy of an existing object. Second, what if we don't want a simple copy of the object? (Let's ignore the "why?" of this for a little while.) We need to be able to specify how the copy should be constructed.

The CopyStudent program shown in Listing 20-4 demonstrates the point.

Listing 20-4
Copy Constructor in Action

```cpp
// CopyStudent - demonstrate a copy constructor by
//                passing an object by value
#include <stdio.h>
#include <iostream.h>
#include <string.h>

class Student
{
  public:
    // create an initialization function
    void init(char* pszName, int nId, char* pszPreamble = "\0")
    {
        int nLength = strlen(pszName)
                    + strlen(pszPreamble)
                    + 1;
        this->pszName = new char[nLength];
        strcpy(this->pszName, pszPreamble);
        strcat(this->pszName, pszName);
        this->nId = nId;
    }

    //conventional constructor
    Student(char* pszName  = "no name", int nId = 0)
    {
        cout << "Constructing new student " << pszName << "\n";
        init(pszName, nId);
    }
```

```
   //copy constructor
   Student(Student &s)
   {
      cout << "Constructing Copy of "
           << s.pszName
           << "\n";
      init(s.pszName, s.nId, "Copy of ");
   }

   ~Student()
   {
      cout << "Destructing " << pszName << "\n";
      delete pszName;
   }
 protected:
   char* pszName;
   int   nId;
};

//fn - receives its argument by value
void fn(Student s)
{
   cout << "In function fn()\n";
}

int main(int nArgs, char* pszArgs[])
{
   // create a student object
   Student randy("Randy", 1234);

   // now pass it by value to fn()
   cout << "Calling fn()\n";
   fn(randy);
   cout << "Returned from fn()\n";

   // done
   return 0;
}
```

The output from executing this program is:

```
Constructing new student Randy
Calling fn()
Constructing Copy of Randy
In function fn()
Destructing Copy of Randy
Returned from fn()
Destructing Randy
```

Starting with `main()`, we can see how this program works. The normal constructor generates the first message. `main()` generates the "Calling . . ." message. C++ calls the copy constructor to make a copy of `randy` to pass to `fn()`, which generates the next line of output. The copy is destructed at the return from `fn()`. The original object, `randy`, is destructed at the end of `main()`.

(This copy constructor does a little bit more than just make a copy of the object; it tacks the phrase `Copy of` to the front of the name. That was for your benefit. Normally, copy constructors should restrict themselves to just making copies. But, if the truth be known, they can do anything they want.)

Shallow copies versus deep copies

C++ considers the copy constructor to be so important that if you don't provide one with your class, C++ creates one for you. The default copy constructor that C++ provides performs a member-by-member copy.

Performing a member-by-member copy seems the obvious thing to do in a copy constructor. Other than adding the capability to tack silly things such as `Copy of` to the front of students' names, when would we ever want to do anything but a member-by-member copy?

Consider what happens if the constructor allocates an asset such as memory off the heap. If the copy constructor simply makes a copy of that asset without allocating its own, we end up with a troublesome situation: two objects thinking they have exclusive access to the same asset. This becomes nastier when the destructor is invoked for both objects and they both try to put the same asset back. To make this more concrete, consider our `Student` class again:

```
class Student
{
  public:
    Person(char *pszName)
    {
```

```
        pszName = new char[strlen(pszName) + 1];
        strcpy(pName, pN);
    }
    ~Person()
    {
        delete pszName;
    }
  protected:
    char* pszName;
};
```

Here, the constructor allocates memory off the heap to store the person's name — the destructor dutifully puts this heap memory back as it should. Were this object to be passed to a function by value, C++ would make a copy of the Student object, including the pointer pszName. The program now has two Student objects both pointing to the same block of memory containing the student's name. When the first object is destructed, the block is returned to memory. Destructing the second object results in the same memory being returned to the stack twice — a fatal act for a program to perform.

Heap memory is not the only asset that requires a deep copy constructor, but it is the most common. Open files, ports, and allocated hardware (such as printers) also require deep copies. These are the same types of assets that destructors must return. Thus, a good rule of thumb is that if your class requires a destructor to deallocate assets, it also requires a copy constructor.

A "fall back" copy constructor

There are times when you don't want copies of your object being created. This could be because you cannot or don't want to write the code to perform a deep copy. This is also the case when the object is very large and making a copy, whether shallow or deep, could take a considerable amount of time.

A simple fall back position to avoid the problem of shallow copies being created without your knowledge is to create a protected copy constructor.

If you do not create a copy constructor, C++ creates one for you.

In the following example, C++ cannot make a copy of the BankAccount class, thereby ensuring that the program does not mistakenly make a deposit to or withdrawal from a copy of the account and not the account itself.

```
class BankAccount
{
    protected:
     int nBalance;
     BankAccount(BankAccount& ba)
     {
     }

    public:
     // ...remainder of class...
};
```

Done!

REVIEW

The constructor is designed to create an object in an initial, valid state; however, many objects do not have a valid default state. For example, it is not possible to create a valid Student object without a name and a student ID. A constructor with arguments enables the parent program to pass initial values for the newly created object. These arguments may also be passed along to any constructors for data members of the class. The order of construction of these members is well defined in the C++ standard (one of the few things that is well defined).

- Arguments to constructors enable the initial state of the object to be determined by the parent program; however, in the event that these initial arguments are illegal, the class must have a "fall back" state.

- Care must be taken with constructors that have side effects, such as changing the value of global variables, because one or more constructors can clash when constructing an object with data members which are objects in their own right.

- A special constructor, the copy constructor, has a prototype of X::X(X&) where X is the name of some class. This class is used to create a copy of an existing object. Copy constructors are extremely important if the object contains a resource that is returned to the resource pool in the destructor.

Although the principles of object-based programming have been explored, we still aren't where we want to be. We've built a microwave oven, we've built a box around the working parts, and we've defined a user interface; but we haven't drawn a relationship between microwave ovens and other types of ovens. This is the essence of object-oriented programming, which is discussed in Part 5.

Quiz yourself

1. Why would a class such as Student have a constructor in the form Student(char* pszName, int nId)? (See "Constructors with Arguments.")

2. How can you tell what order global objects are constructed? (See "Global Objects Are Constructed in No Particular Order.")

3. Why would a class need a copy constructor? (See "The Copy Constructor.")

4. What is the difference between a shallow copy and a deep copy? (See "Shallow Copies versus Deep Copies.")

Exercises

Problems

Write a copy constructor and a destructor for the following LinkedList class:

```
#include <stdio.h>
#include <iostream.h>
#include <string.h>

class LinkedList
{
  protected:
    LinkedList* pNext;
    static LinkedList* pHead;

    char* pszName;

  public:
    // constructor - copy the name provided
    LinkedList(char* pszName)
```

```
    {
        int nLength = strlen(pszName) + 1;
        this->pszName = new char[nLength];
        strcpy(this->pszName, pszName);
        pNext = 0;
    }

    // assume that these two member functions exist
    void addToList();
    void removeFromeList();

    // destructor -
    ~LinkedList()
    {
        // ...what goes here?
    }
    LinkedList(LinkedList& l)
    {
        // ...and here?
    }
};
```

Hint

1. Consider what happens if the object is still in the linked list when it is destructed.

2. Remember that the memory allocated off the heap should be returned before the pointer is lost.

My solution

This is my version of the destructor and copy constructor:

```
// destructor - remove the object and
//              remove the entry
~LinkedList()
{
    // if the current object is in a list...
    if (pNext)
```

```
        {
            // ...then remove it
            removeFromList();
        }

        // if the object has a block of memory...
        if (pszName)
        {
            // ...return it to the heap
            delete pszName;
        }
        pszName = 0;
    }

    // copy constructor - called to create a copy of
    //                     an existing object
    LinkedList(LinkedList& l)
    {
        // allocate a block of the same size
        // off of the heap
        int nLength = strlen(l.pszName) + 1;
        this->pszName = new char[nLength];

        // now copy the name into this new block
        strcpy(this->pszName, l.pszName);

        // zero out the length as long as the object
        // is not in a linked list
        pNext = 0;
    }
```

If the object is a member of a linked list, then the destructor must remove it before the object is reused and the pNext pointer is lost. In addition, if the object "owns" a block of heap memory, it must also be returned. Similarly, the copy constructor performs a deep copy by allocating a new block of memory off the heap to hold the object name. The copy constructor does not add the object to the existing linked list (although it could).

P A R T

IV

Saturday Evening

1. Think about the contents of your clothes closet. Build an informal taxonomy of what you find there.

2. Consider shoes. Describe the "interface" to shoes.

3. Name two different types of shoes. What is the effect of applying one in place of the other?

4. Write a constructor for a class defined as follows:

```
class Link
{
    static Link* pHead;
    Link* pNextLink;
};
```

5. Write a copy constructor and a destructor for the following LinkedList class:

```
#include <stdio.h>
#include <iostream.h>
#include <string.h>

class LinkedList
{
  protected:
    LinkedList* pNext;
    static LinkedList* pHead;
```

```
    char* pszName;

public:
    // constructor - copy the name provided
    LinkedList(char* pszName)
    {
        int nLength = strlen(pszName) + 1;
        this->pszName = new char[nLength];
        strcpy(this->pszName, pszName);
        pNext = 0;
    }

    // assume that these two member functions exist
    void addToList();
    void removeFromeList();

    // destructor -
    ~LinkedList()
    {
        // ...what goes here?
    }
    LinkedList(LinkedList& l)
    {
        // ...and here?
    }
};
```

Hints:

a. Consider what happens if the object is still in the linked list when it is destructed.

b. Remember that the memory allocated off of the heap should be returned before the pointer is lost.

☑ **Friday**

☑ **Saturday**

☑ **Sunday**

PART

V

Sunday Morning

Session Checklist

✔ Defining inheritance

✔ Inheriting a base class

✔ Constructing the base class

✔ Exploring the IS_A versus the HAS_A relationship

**30 Min.
To Go**

In this Session, we discuss inheritance. *Inheritance* is the capability of one class of things to assume capabilities or properties from another class. For example, I am a human. I inherit from the class *Human* certain properties, such as my ability to converse intelligently (more or less) and my dependence on air, water, and food. These properties are not unique to humans. The class *Human* inherits the dependencies on air, water, and nourishment from the class *Mammal*, of which it is a member.

Advantages of Inheritance

The capability to pass down properties is a powerful one. It allows us to describe things in an economical way. For example, when my son asks "What's a duck?" I can say, "It's a bird that goes quack." Despite what you might think, that answer conveys a considerable amount of information to him. He knows what a bird is, and now he knows all those same things about a duck plus the duck's additional quacking ability.

There are several reasons why inheritance was introduced into C++. Of course, the major reason is the capability to express the inheritance relationship. (I'll return to that in a moment.) A minor reason is to reduce the amount of typing. Suppose we have a class `Student`, and we are asked to add a new class called `GraduateStudent`. Inheritance can drastically reduce the number of things we have to put in the class. All we really need in the class `GraduateStudent` are things that describe the differences between students and graduate students.

A more important, related issue is that major buzzword of the '90s, reuse. Software scientists have realized for some time that it doesn't make much sense to start from scratch with each new project, rebuilding the same software components.

Compare the situation in software to other industries. How many car manufacturers start from ore to build a car? And even if they did, how many would start completely over from ore with the next model? Practitioners in other industries have found it makes more sense to start from screws, bolts, nuts, and even larger off-the-shelf components such as motors and compressors.

Unfortunately, except for very small functions, like those found in the Standard C library, it's rare to find much reuse of software components. One problem is that it's virtually impossible to find a component from an earlier program that does exactly what you want. Generally, these components require "tweaking."

There's a rule of thumb that says, "If you open it, you've broken it." In other words, if you have to modify a function or class to adapt it to a new application, you will have to retest everything, not just the parts you add. Changes can introduce bugs anywhere in existing code. ("The one who last touched it is the one who gets to fix it.")

Inheritance allows existing classes to be adapted to new applications without the need for modification. The existing class is inherited into a new subclass that contains any necessary additions and modifications.

This carries with it a third benefit. Suppose we inherit from some existing class. Later we find that the base class has a bug that must be corrected. If we have modified the class to reuse it, we must manually check for, correct, and retest the bug in each application separately. If we have inherited the class without changes, we can probably adopt the fixed base class without further ado.

Class Factoring

To make sense out of our surroundings, humans build extensive taxonomies. *Fido* is a special case of *dog* which is a special case of *canine* which is a special case of *mammal* and so it goes. This shapes our understanding of the world.

To use another example, a student is a (special type of) person. Having said this, I already know a lot of things about students. I know they have social security numbers, they watch too much TV, they drive a car too fast, and they don't exercise enough. I know all these things because these are properties of all people.

In C++, we call this *inheritance*. We say that the class Student *inherits* from the class Person. We say also that Person is a *base class* of Student and Student is a *subclass* of Person. Finally, we say that a Student *IS_A* Person (I use all caps as my way of expressing this unique relationship). C++ shares this terminology with other object-oriented languages.

Notice that although Student IS_A Person, the reverse is not true. A Person is not a Student. (A statement like this always refers to the general case. It could be that a particular Person is, in fact, a Student.) A lot of people who are members of class Person are not members of class Student. This is because the class Student has properties it does not share with class Person. For example, Student has a grade point average, but Person does not.

The inheritance property is transitive however. For example, if I define a new class GraduateStudent as a subclass of Student, GraduateStudent must also be Person. It has to be that way: if a GraduateStudent IS_A Student and a Student IS_A Person, then a GraduateStudent IS_A Person.

20 Min. To Go

Implementing Inheritance in C++

To demonstrate how to express inheritance in C++, let's return to the GraduateStudent example and fill it out with a few example members:

```
// GSInherit - demonstrate how the graduate
//             student class can inherit
//             the properties of a Student
#include <stdio.h>
#include <iostream.h>
#include <string.h>

// Advisor - let's provide an empty class
//           for now
```

```
class Advisor
{
};

// Student - this class includes all types of
//           students
class Student
{
  public:
    Student()
    {
        // start out a clean slate
        pszName = 0;
        dGPA = nSemesterHours = 0;
    }
    ~Student()
    {
        // if there is a name...
        if (pszName != 0)
        {
            // ...then return the buffer
            delete pszName;
            pszName = 0;
        }
    }

    // addCourse - add in the effects of completing
    //             a course by factoring the
    //             dGrade into the GPA
    void addCourse(int nHours, double dGrade)
    {
        // first find the current weighted GPA
        int ndGradeHours = (int)(nSemesterHours * dGPA + dGrade);

        // now factor in the number of hours
        // just completed
        nSemesterHours += nHours;

        // from that calculate the new GPA
        dGPA = ndGradeHours / nSemesterHours;
    }
```

```cpp
    // the following access functions allow
    // the application access to important
    // properties
    int    hours( )
    {
        return nSemesterHours;
    }
    double gpa( )
    {
        return dGPA;
    }

  protected:
    char*  pszName;
    int    nSemesterHours;
    double dGPA;

    // copy constructor - I don't want any
    //                    copies being created
    Student(Student& s)
    {
    }
};

// GraduateStudent - this class is limited to
//                   students who already have a
//                   BA or BS
class GraduateStudent : public Student
{
  public:
    GraduateStudent()
    {
        dQualifierGrade = 2.0;
    }

    double qualifier( )
    {
        return dQualifierGrade;
    }
```

```
    protected:
        // all graduate students have an advisor
        Advisor advisor;

        // the qualifier grade is the
        // grade below which the gradstudent
        // fails the course
        double dQualifierGrade;
};

int main(int nArgc, char* pszArgs[])
{
    // first create a student
    Student llu;

    // now let's create a graduate student
    GraduateStudent gs;

    // the following is perfectly OK
    llu.addCourse(3, 2.5);
    gs.addCourse(3, 3.0);

    // the following is not
    gs.qualifier();        // this is legal
    llu.qualifier();       // but this isn't
    return 0;
}
```

The class Student has been declared in the conventional fashion. The declaration for GraduateStudent, however, is different from previous declarations. The name of the class followed by the colon followed by public Student declares class GraduateStudent to be a subclass of Student.

The appearance of the keyword public **implies that there is probably protected inheritance as well. It's true, but I want to hold off discussing this type of inheritance for a moment.**

The function main() declares two objects, llu and gs. The object llu is a conventional Student object, but the object gs is something new. As a member of a subclass of Student, gs can do anything that llu can do. It has the data

members pszName, dSemesterHours, and dAverage and the member function
addCourse( ). After all, gs quite literally IS_A Student — it's just a little bit
more than a Student. (You'll get tired of me reciting this "IS_A" stuff before
the book is over.) In fact, GraduateStudent has the qualifier() property
which Student does not have.

The next two lines add a course to the two students 11u and gs. Remember that
gs is also a Student.

The last two lines in main( ) are incorrect. It is OK to retrieve the qualifier
grade of the graduate student gs. It is not OK, however, to try to retrieve the
qualifier property of the 11u object. The 11u object is only a Student and
does not share the properties unique to GraduateStudent.

Now consider the following scenario:

```
// fn - performs some operation on a Student
void fn(Student &s)
{
    //whatever fn it wants to do
}

int main(int nArgc, char* pszArgs[])
{
    // create a graduate student...
    GraduateStudent gs;

    // ...now pass it off as a simple student
    fn(gs);
    return 0;
}
```

Notice that the function fn( ) expects to receive as its argument an object of
class Student. The call from main( ) passes it an object of class GraduateStudent.
However, this is fine because once again (all together now) "a GraduateStudent
IS_A Student."

Basically, the same condition arises when invoking a member function of Student
with a GraduateStudent object. For example:

```
int main(int nArgc, char* pszArgs[])
{
   GraduateStudent gs;
   gs.addCourse(3, 2.5); //calls Student::addCourse( )
   return 0;
}
```

Constructing a Subclass

Even though a subclass has access to the protected members of the base class and could initialize them in its own constructor, we would like the base class to construct itself. In fact, this is what happens. Before control passes beyond the open brace of the constructor for GraduateStudent, control passes to the default constructor of Student (because no other constructor was indicated). If Student were based on another class, such as Person, the constructor for that class would be invoked before the Student constructor got control. Like a skyscraper, the object gets constructed starting at the basement class and working its way up the class structure one story at a time.

Just as with member objects, we sometimes need to be able to pass arguments to the base class constructor. We handle this in almost the same way as with member objects, as the following example shows:

```
// Student - this class includes all types of
//           students
class Student
{
  public:
    // constructor - use default argument to
    // create a default constructor as well as
    // the specified constructor type
    Student(char* pszName = 0)
    {
        // start out a clean slate
        this->pszName = 0;
        dGPA = nSemesterHours = 0;

        // if there is a name provided...
        if (pszName != 0)
        {
            this->pszName =
                    new char[strlen(pszName) + 1];
            strcpy(this->pszName, pszName);
        }
    }
    ~Student()
    {
```

```cpp
        // if there is a name...
        if (pszName != 0)
        {
            // ...then return the buffer
            delete pszName;
            pszName = 0;
        }
    }
    // ...remainder of class definition...
};

// GraduateStudent - this class is limited to
//                   students who already have a
//                   BA or BS
class GraduateStudent : public Student
{
  public:
    // constructor - create a Graduate Student
    //               with an advisor, a name and
    //               a qualifier grade
    GraduateStudent(
            Advisor &adv,
            char*    pszName = 0,
            double   dQualifierGrade = 0.0)
                : Student(pName),
                  advisor(adv)
    {
        // executed only after the other constructors
        // have executed
        dQualifierGrade = 0;
    }
  protected:
    // all graduate students have an advisor
    Advisor advisor;

    // the qualifier grade is the
    // grade below which the gradstudent
    // fails the course
    double dQualifierGrade;
};
```

```
void fn(Advisor &advisor)
continued
{
    // sign up our new marriage counselor
    GraduateStudent gs("Marion Haste",
                       advisor,
                       2.0);
    //...whatever this function does...
}
```

Here a GraduateStudent object is created with an advisor, the name "Marion Haste" and a qualifier grade of 2.0. The the constructor for GraduateStudent invokes the Student constructor, passing it the student name. The base class is constructed before any member objects; thus, the constructor for Student is called before the constructor for Advisor. After the base class has been constructed, the Advisor object advisor is constructed using the copy constructor. Only then does the constructor for GraduateStudent get a shot at it.

The fact that the base class is constructed first has nothing to do with the order of the constructor statements after the colon. The base class would have been constructed before the data member object even if the statement had been written advisor(adv), Student(pszName). **However, it is a good idea to write these clauses in the order in which they are executed just as not to confuse anyone.**

**10 Min.
To Go**

Following our rule that destructors are invoked in the reverse order of the constructors, the destructor for GraduateStudent is given control first. After it's given its last full measure of devotion, control passes to the destructor for Advisor and then to the destructor for Student. If Student were based on a class Person, the destructor for Person would get control after Student.

The destructor for the base class Student **is executed even though there is no explicit** ~GraduateStudent **constructor.**

This is logical. The blob of memory which will eventually become a GraduateStudent object is first converted to a Student object. Then it is the job of the GraduateStudent constructor to complete its transformation into a GraduateStudent. The destructor simply reverses the process.

Note a few things in this example. First, default arguments have been provided to the GraduateStudent constructor in order to pass along this ability to the Student base class. Second, arguments can only be defaulted from right to left. The following would not have been legal:

```
GraduateStudent(char* pszName = 0, Advisor& adv)...
```

The non-defaulted arguments must come first.

Notice that the class GraduateStudent contains an Advisor object within the class. It does not contain a pointer to an Advisor object. The latter would have been written:

```
class GraduateStudent : public Student
{
  public:
    GraduateStudent(
            Advisor& adv,
            char*    pszName = 0)
                : Student(pName),
    {
        pAdvisor = new Advisor(adv);
    }
  protected:
    Advisor* pAdvisor;
};
```

Here the base class Student is constructed first (as always). The pointer is initialized within the body of the GraduateStudent constructor.

The HAS_A Relationship

Notice that the class GraduateStudent includes the members of class Student and Advisor, but in a different way. By defining a data member of class Advisor, we know that a Student has all the data members of an Advisor within it, yet we say that a GraduateStudent HAS_A Advisor. What's the difference between this and inheritance?

Let's use a car as an example. We could logically define a car as being a subclass of *vehicle*, and so it inherits the properties of other vehicles. At the same time, a car has a motor. If you buy a car, you can logically assume that you are buying a motor as well.

Now if some friends asked you to show up at a rally on Saturday with your vehicle of choice and you came in your car, there would be no complaint because a car IS_A vehicle. But if you appeared on foot carrying a motor, they would have reason to be upset because a motor is not a vehicle. It is missing certain critical properties that vehicles share. It's even missing properties that cars share.

From a programming standpoint, it's just as straightforward. Consider the following:

```
class Vehicle
{
};
class Motor
{
};
class Car : public Vehicle
{
  public:
    Motor motor;
};
void VehicleFn(Vehicle &v);
void motorFn(Motor &m);
int main(int nArgc, char* pszArgs[])
{
    Car c;
    VehicleFn(c);    //this is allowed
    motorFn(c);      //this is not allowed
    motorFn(c.motor);//this is, however
    return 0;
}
```

The call `VehicleFn(c)` is allowed because c IS_A `Vehicle`. The call `motorFn(c)` is not because c is not a `Motor`, even though it contains a `Motor`. If what was intended was to pass the motor portion of c to the function, this must be expressed explicitly, as in the call `motorFn(c.motor)`.

Of course, the call `motorFn(c.motor)` **is only allowed if** `c.motor` **is public.**

Done!

One further distinction: the class `Car` has access to the protected members of `Vehicle`, but not to the protected members of `Motor`.

REVIEW

Understanding inheritance is critical to understanding the whole point behind object-oriented programming. It's also required in order to understand the next chapter. If you feel you've got it down, move on to Chapter 19. If not, you may want to reread this chapter.

QUIZ YOURSELF

1. What is the relationship between a graduate student and a student? Is it an IS_A or a HAS_A relationship? (See "The HAS_A Relationship.")

2. Name three benefits from including inheritance to the C++ language? (See "Advantages of Inheritance.")

3. Which of the following terms does not fit: *inherits*, *subclass*, *data member* and *IS_A*? (See "Class Factoring.")

Polymorphism

Session Checklist

✔ Overriding member functions in a subclass

✔ Applying polymorphism (alias late binding)

✔ Comparing polymorphism to early binding

✔ Taking special considerations with polymorphism

**30 Min.
To Go**

Inheritance gives us the capability to describe one class in terms of another. Just as importantly, it highlights the relationship between classes. Once again, a microwave oven is a type of oven. However, there's still a piece of the puzzle missing.

You have probably noticed this already, but a microwave oven and a conventional oven look nothing alike. These two types of ovens don't work exactly alike either. Nevertheless, when I say "cook" I don't want to worry about the details of how each oven performs the operation. This session describes how C++ handles this problem.

Overriding Member Functions

It has always been possible to overload a member function in one class with a member function in the same class as long as the arguments are different. It is also possible to overload a member in one class with a member function in another class even if the arguments are the same.

Inheritance introduces another possibility: a member function in a subclass can overload a member function in the base class.

Overloading a member function in a subclass is called overriding. This relationship warrants a different name because of the possibilities it introduces.

Consider, for example, the simple EarlyBinding program shown in Listing 22-1.

Listing 22-1
EarlyBinding Demonstration Program

```cpp
// EarlyBinding - calls to overridden member functions
//                are resolved based on the object type

#include <stdio.h>
#include <iostream.h>

class Student
{
  public:
    double calcTuition()
    {
        return 0;
    }
};
class GraduateStudent : public Student
{
  public:
    double calcTuition()
    {
```

```
            return 1;
        }
};

int main(int nArgc, char* pszArgs[])
{
    // the following expression calls
    // Student::calcTuition();
    Student s;
    cout << "The value of s.calcTuition is "
         << s.calcTuition()
         << "\n";

    // this one calls GraduateStudent::calcTuition();
    GraduateStudent gs;
    cout << "The value of gs.calcTuition is "
         << gs.calcTuition()
         << "\n";
    return 0;
}
```

Output

```
The value of s.calcTuition is 0
The value of gs.calcTuition is 1
```

As with any case of overriding, when the programmer refers to `calcTuition()`, C++ has to decide which `calcTuition()` is intended. Normally, the class is sufficient to resolve the call, and this example is no different. The call `s.calcTuition()` refers to `Student::calcTuition()` because s is declared locally as a `Student`, whereas `gs.calcTuition()` refers to `GraduateStudent::calcTuition()`.

The output from the program `EarlyBinding` shows that calls to overridden member functions are resolved according to the type of the object.

Resolving calls to overridden member functions based on the type of the object is called *compile-time* binding. This is also called *early binding.*

Enter Polymorphism

Overriding functions based on the class of the object is all very nice, but what if the class of the object making the call can't be determined unambiguously at compile time? To demonstrate how this can occur, let's change the preceding program in a seemingly trivial way. The result is the program AmbiguousBinding shown in Listing 22-2.

Listing 22-2
AmbiguousBinding Program

```
// AmbiguousBinding - the situation gets confusing
//                    when the compile-time type and
//                    run-time type don't match
#include <stdio.h>
#include <iostream.h>

class Student
{
  public:
    double calcTuition()
    {
        return 0;
    }
};
class GraduateStudent : public Student
{
  public:
    double calcTuition()
    {
        return 1;
    }
};

double fn(Student& fs)
{
    // to which calcTuition() does this call refer?
    // which value is returned?
    return fs.calcTuition();
```

```
}

int main(int nArgc, char* pszArgs[])
{
    // the following expression calls
    // Student::calcTuition();
    Student s;
    cout << "The value of s.calcTuition when "
         << "called through fn() is "
         << fn(s)
         << "\n";

    // this one calls GraduateStudent::calcTuition();
    GraduateStudent gs;
    cout << "The value of gs.calcTuition when "
         << "called through fn() is "
         << fn(gs)
         << "\n";
    return 0;
}
```

The only difference between Listing 22-2 and Listing 22-1 is that the calls to calcTuition() are made through an intermediate function, fn(). The function fn(Student& fs) is declared as receiving a Student, but depending on how fn() is called, fs can be a Student or a GraduateStudent. (Remember? A GraduateStudent IS_A Student.) But these two types of objects calculate their tuition differently.

Neither main() nor fn() really care anything about how tuition is calculated. We would like fs.calcTuition() to call Student::calcTuition() when fs is a Student, but call GraduateStudent::calcTuition() when fs is a GraduateStudent. But this decision can only be made at run time when the actual type of the object passed is determinable.

In the case of the AmbiguousBinding program, we say that the compile-time type of fs, which is always Student, differs from the run-time type, which may be GraduateStudent or Student.

The capability to decide which of several overridden member functions to call based on the run-time type is called *polymorphism,* or *late binding. Polymorphism* comes from *poly* (meaning multiple) and *morph* (meaning form).

**20 Min.
To Go**

Polymorphism and Object-Oriented Programming

Polymorphism is key to the power of object-oriented programming. It's so important that languages that don't support polymorphism cannot advertise themselves as object-oriented languages. Languages that support classes but not polymorphism are called *object-based languages.* Ada is an example of such a language.

Without polymorphism, inheritance has little meaning.

Remember how I made nachos in the oven? In this sense, I was acting as the late binder. The recipe read: "Heat the nachos in the oven." It didn't read: "If the type of oven is a microwave, do this; if the type of oven is conventional, do that; if the type of oven is convection, do this other thing." The recipe (the code) relied on me (the late binder) to decide what the action (member function) heat means when applied to the oven (the particular instance of class Oven) or any of its variations (subclasses), such as a microwave oven (Microwave). This is the way people think, and designing a language along these lines enables the software model to more accurately describe what people are thinking.

There also are the mundane issues of maintenance and reusability. Suppose that I had written this great program that used the class Student. After months of design, coding, and testing, I release this application.

Time passes and my boss asks me to add to this program the capability to handle graduate students who are similar but not identical to normal students. Deep within the program, someFunction() calls the calcTuition() member function as follows:

```
void someFunction(Student &s)
{
    //...whatever it might do...
    s.calcTuition();
    //...continues on...
}
```

If C++ did not support late binding, I would need to edit someFunction() to something similar to the following to add class GraduateStudent:

```
#define STUDENT 1
#define GRADUATESTUDENT 2
void someFunction(Student &s)
{
    //...whatever it might do...
    //add some member type that indicates
```

```
        //the actual type of the object
        switch (s.type)
        {
            STUDENT:
                s.Student::calcTuition();
                break;
            GRADUATESTUDENT:
                s.GraduateStudent::calcTuition();
                break;
        }
        //...continues on...
    }
```

By using the full name of the function, the expression
s.GraduateStudent::calcTuition() **forces the call to the**
GraduateStudent **version even though** s **is declared to be a**
Student.

I would add the member type to the class, which I would then set to STUDENT
in the constructor for Student and to GRADUATESTUDENT in the constructor for
GraduateStudent. The value of type would refer to the run-time type of s. I
would then add the test in the preceding code snippet to call the proper member
function depending on the value of this member.

That doesn't seem so bad, except for three things. First, this is only one function. Suppose calcTuition() is called from a lot of places and suppose that
calcTuition() is not the only difference between the two classes. The chances
are not good that I will find all the places that need to be changed.

Second, I must edit (read "break") code that was debugged, checked in, and
working, introducing opportunities for error. Edits can be time-consuming and
boring, which increases the possibility of error. Any one of my edits may be wrong
or may not fit in with the existing code. Who knows?

Finally, after I've finished editing, redebugging, and retesting everything, I now
have two versions to track (unless I can drop support for the original version). This
means two sources to edit when bugs are found and some type of accounting system to keep them straight.

What happens when my boss wants yet another class added? (My boss is like
that.) Not only do I get to repeat the process, but I'll also have three copies to track.

With polymorphism, there's a good chance that all I need to do is add the new
subclass and recompile. I may need to modify the base class itself, but at least it's
all in one place. Modifications to the application should be minimal to none.

This is yet another reason to leave data members protected and access them through public member functions. Data members cannot be polymorphically overridden by a subclass, whereas a member function can.

How Does Polymorphism Work?

Given all that I've said so far, it may be surprising that the default for C++ is early binding. The output from the AmbiguousBinding program is shown below.

```
The value of s.calcTuition when called through fn() is 0
The value of gs.calcTuition when called through fn() is 0
```

The reason is simple. Polymorphism adds a small amount of overhead both in terms of data storage and code needed to perform the call. The founders of C++ were concerned that any additional overhead they introduced would be used as a reason not to adopt C++ as the systems language of choice, so they made the more efficient early binding the default.

To indicate polymorphism, the programmer must flag the member function with the C++ keyword virtual, as shown in program LateBinding contained in Listing 22-3.

Listing 22-3
LateBinding Program

```
// LateBinding - in late binding the decision as to
//               which of two overridden functions
//               to call is made at run-time
#include <stdio.h>
#include <iostream.h>

class Student
{
  public:
    virtual double calcTuition()
    {
        return 0;
    }
};
class GraduateStudent : public Student
{
```

```
  public:
    virtual double calcTuition()
    {
        return 1;
    }
};

double fn(Student& fs)
{
    // because calcTuition() is declared virtual this
    // call uses the run-time type of fs to resolve
    // the call
    return fs.calcTuition();
}



int main(int nArgc, char* pszArgs[])
{
    // the following expression calls
    // fn() with a Student object
    Student s;
    cout << "The value of s.calcTuition when\n"
         << "called virtually through fn() is "
         << fn(s)
         << "\n\n";

    // the following expression calls
    // fn() with a GraduateStudent object
    GraduateStudent gs;
    cout << "The value of gs.calcTuition when\n"
         << "called virtually through fn() is "
         << fn(gs)
         << "\n\n";
    return 0;
}
```

The keyword virtual added to the declaration of calcTuition() is a virtual member function. That is to say, calls to calcTuition() will be bound late if the run-time type of the object being used cannot be determined.

The LateBinding program contains the same call to fn() as shown in the two earlier versions. In this version, however, the call to calcTuition() goes to Student::calcTuition() when fs is a Student and to GraduateStudent:: calcTuition() when fs is a GraduateStudent.

The output from LateBinding is shown below. Declaring calcTuition() virtual tells fn() to resolve calls based on the run-time type.

```
The value of s.calcTuition when
called virtually through fn() is 0

The value of gs.calcTuition when
called virtually through fn() is 1
```

When defining the virtual member function, the virtual tag goes only with the declarations and not with the definition, as the following example illustrates:

```
class Student
{
  public:
    // declare function to be virtual here
    virtual double calcTuition()
    {
        return 0;
    }
};

// don't include the 'virtual' in the definition
double Student::calcTuition()
  {
      return 0;
  }
```

When Is a Virtual Function Not?

Just because you think a particular function call is bound late doesn't mean it is. C++ generates no indication at compile time of which calls it thinks are bound early and late.

The most critical thing to watch for is that all the member functions in question are declared identically, including the return type. If not declared with the same arguments in the subclasses, the member functions are not overridden polymorphically, whether or not they are declared virtual. Consider the following code snippet:

```cpp
#include <iostream.h>
class Base
{
  public:
    virtual void fn(int x)
    {
        cout << "In Base class, int x = " << x << "\n";
    }
};
class SubClass : public Base
{
  public:
    virtual void fn(float x)
    {
        cout << "In SubClass, float x = " << x << "\n";
    }
};

void test(Base &b)
{
    int i = 1;
    b.fn(i);            //this call not bound late
    float f = 2.0;
    b.fn(f);            //neither is this one
}
```

fn() in Base is declared as fn(int), whereas the SubClass version is declared fn(float). Because the functions have different arguments, there is no polymorphism. The first call is to Base::fn(int) — not surprising considering that b is of class Base and i is an int. However, the next call also goes to Base::fn(int) after converting the float to an int. No error is generated because this program is legal (other than a possible warning concerning the demotion of f. The output from calling test() shows no sign of polymorphism:

```
Calling test(bc)
In Base class, int x = 1
In Base class, int x = 2
Calling test(sc)
```

```
In Base class, int x = 1
In Base class, int x = 2
```

If the arguments don't match exactly, there is no late binding — with one exception: If the member function in the base class returns a pointer or reference to a base class object, an overridden member function in a subclass may return a pointer or reference to an object of the subclass. In other words, the following is allowed:

```
class Base
{
  public:
    Base* fn();
};

class Subclass : public Base
{
  public:
    Subclass* fn();
};
```

In practice, this is quite natural. If a function is dealing with Subclass objects, it seems natural that it should continue to deal with Subclass objects.

Virtual Considerations

Specifying the class name in the call forces the call to bind early. For example, the following call is to Base::fn() because that's what the programmer indicated, even if fn() is declared virtual:

```
void test(Base &b)
{
    b.Base::fn();            //this call is not bound late
}
```

A virtual function cannot be inlined. To expand a function inline, the compiler must know which function is intended at compile time. Thus, although the example member functions so far were declared in the class, all were outline functions.

Constructors cannot be virtual because there is no (completed) object to use to determine the type. At the time the constructor is called, the memory that the object occupies is just an amorphous mass. It's only after the constructor has finished that the object is a member of the class in good standing.

By comparison, the destructor normally should be declared virtual. If not, you run the risk of improperly destructing the object, as in the following circumstance:

```
class Base
{
  public:
    ~Base();
};
class SubClass : public Base
{
  public:
    ~SubClass();
};
void finishWithObject(Base *pHeapObject)
{
    //...work with object...
    //now return it to the heap
    delete pHeapObject;  // this calls ~Base() no matter
}                        // what the run-time type
                         // of pHeapObject is
```

If the pointer passed to finishWithObject() really points to a SubClass, the SubClass destructor is not invoked properly. Declaring the destructor virtual solves the problem.

So, when would you not want to declare the destructor virtual? There's only one instance. Earlier I said that virtual functions introduce a "little" overhead. Let me be more specific. When the programmer defines the first virtual function in a class, C++ adds an additional, hidden pointer — not one pointer per virtual function, just one pointer if the class has any virtual functions. A class that has no virtual functions (and does not inherit any virtual functions from base classes) does not have this pointer.

Now, one pointer doesn't sound like much, and it isn't unless the following two conditions are true:

- The class doesn't have many data members (so that one pointer represents a lot compared to what's there already).

- You intend to create a lot of objects of this class (otherwise, the overhead doesn't make any difference).

Done!

If both these conditions are met and your class doesn't already have any virtual member functions, you might not want to declare the destructor virtual.

Normally, you should declare the destructor virtual. If you don't declare the destructor virtual, document it!

REVIEW

By itself, inheritance is a nice but limited capability. Combined with polymorphism, inheritance is a powerful programming aid.

- Member functions in a class may be overridden by member functions defined in the base class. Calls to these functions are resolved at compile time based on the declared (compile-time) class. This is called early binding.

- A member function may be declared virtual, in which case calls are resolved based on the run-time class. This is called polymorphic or late binding.

- Calls in which the run-time and compile-time classes are known to be identical are bound early, regardless of whether the member function is declared virtual or not.

QUIZ YOURSELF

1. What is polymorphism? (See "Enter Polymorphism.")

2. What's another word for polymorphism? (See "Enter Polymorphism.")

3. What's the alternative and what is it called? (See "Overriding Member Functions.")

4. Name three reasons that C++ includes polymorphism? (See "Polymorphism and Object-Oriented Programming.")

5. What keyword is used to declare a member function polymorphic? (See "How Does Polymorphism Work?")

Abstract Classes and Factoring

Session Checklist

✔ Factoring common properties into a base class

✔ Using abstract classes to hold factored information

✔ Abstract classes and dynamic typing

**30 Min.
To Go**

So far we've seen how inheritance can be used to extend existing classes to new applications. Inheritance also affords the programmer the capability of combining common features from different classes in a process that is called *factoring*.

Factoring

To see how factoring works, let's look at the two classes used in a hypothetical banking system, Checking and Savings. These are shown graphically in Figure 23-1.

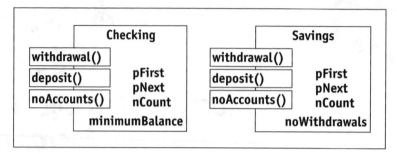

Figure 23-1
Independent classes Checking and Savings

To read this figure and the other figures that follow, remember that

- The big box is the class, with the class name at the top.
- The names in boxes are member functions.
- The names not in boxes are data members.
- The names that extend partway out of the boxes are publicly accessible members; those that do not extend outside the boxes are protected.
- A thick arrow represents the IS_A relationship.
- A thin arrow represents the HAS_A relationship.

Figure 23-1 shows that the Checking and Savings classes have a lot in common. Because they aren't identical, however, they must remain separate classes. Still, there should be a way to avoid this repetition.

We could have one of these classes inherit from the other. Savings has the extra members, so it makes more sense to let it inherit from Checking, as shown in Figure 23-2. The class is completed with the addition of data member noWithdrawals and the virtual overloading of member function withdrawal().

Although this solution is labor saving, it's not completely satisfying. The main problem is that it misrepresents the truth. This inheritance relationship implies that a Savings account is a special type of Checking account, which is not true.

"So what?" you say, "It works and it saves effort." True, but my reservations are more than stylistic trivialities. Such misrepresentations are confusing to the programmer, both today's programmer and tomorrow's programmer. Someday, a programmer unfamiliar with this program will have to read and understand what the code is doing. Misleading tricks are difficult to reconcile and understand.

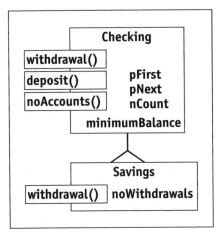

Figure 23-2
Savings implemented as a subclass of Checking

In addition, such misrepresentations can lead to problems down the road. Suppose, for example, that our bank changes its policies with respect to checking accounts. Let's say it decides to charge a service fee on checking accounts only if the minimum balance dips below a given value during the month.

A change like this can be easily handled with minimal changes to the class Checking. We'll have to add a new data member to the class Checking; let's call it minimumBalance.

But doing so creates a problem. Because Savings inherits from Checking, Savings gets this new data member as well. It has no use for this member because the minimum balance does not affect savings accounts. One extra data member may not be a big deal, but it does add confusion.

Changes such as this accumulate. Today it's an extra data member, tomorrow it's a changed member function. Eventually the Savings account class is carrying a lot of extra baggage that is applicable only to the Checking account class.

How do we avoid these problems? We can base both classes on a new class that is specially built for this purpose; let's call it Account. This class embodies all the features that a savings account and a checking account have in common, as shown in Figure 23-3.

How does this solve the problems? First, this is a more accurate description of the real world (whatever that is). In my concept of things, there really is something known as an account. Savings accounts and checking accounts are specializations of this more fundamental concept.

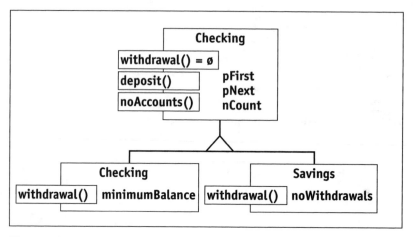

Figure 23-3
Basing Checking and Savings classes on a common Account class

In addition, the class Savings is insulated from changes to the class Checking (and vice versa). If the bank institutes a fundamental change to all accounts, we can modify Account and all subclasses will automatically inherit the change. But if the bank changes its policy only for checking accounts, the savings accounts remain insulated from the change.

This process of culling out common properties from similar classes is called factoring. This is an important feature of object-oriented languages for the reasons described so far, plus one more: reduction in redundancy.

In software, needless bulk is bad. The more code you generate, the more you have to debug. It's not worth staying up nights generating clever code just to save a few lines here or there — that type of cleverness usually boomerangs. But factoring out redundancy through inheritance can legitimately reduce the programming effort.

Factoring is legitimate only if the inheritance relationship corresponds to reality. Factoring together a class Mouse and Joystick because they're both hardware pointing devices is legitimate. Factoring together a class Mouse and Display because they both make low-level operating system calls is not — the mouse and the display share no real world proprerties.

Factoring can and usually does result in multiple levels of abstraction. For example, a program written for a more developed bank may have a class structure such as that shown in Figure 23-4.

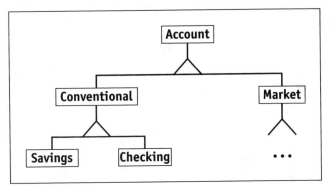

Figure 23-4
A more developed bank account hierarchy

Another class was inserted between Checking and Savings and the most general class, Account. This class, called Conventional, incorporates features common to conventional accounts. Other account types, such as stock market accounts, are also foreseen.

Such multitiered class structures are common and desirable as long as the relationships they express correspond to reality. There is, however, no one correct class hierarchy for any given set of classes.

Suppose that our bank enables account holders to access checking and stock market accounts remotely. Withdrawals from other account types can be made only at the bank. Although the class structure in Figure 23-4 seems natural, that shown in Figure 23-5 is also justifiable given this information. The programmer must decide which class structure best fits the data and leads to the cleanest, most natural implementation.

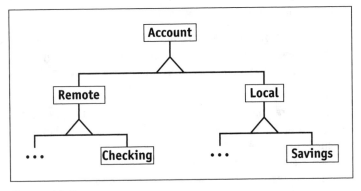

Figure 23-5
An alternate class hierarchy to that shown in Figure 23-4

Abstract Classes

As intellectually satisfying as factoring is, it introduces a problem of its own. Let's return one more time to the bank account classes, specifically the common base class Account. Let's think for a minute about how we might define the different member functions defined in Account.

Most Account member functions are no problem because both account types implement them in the same way. withdrawal() is different. The rules for withdrawing from a savings account are different than those for withdrawing from a checking account. Thus, we would expect Savings::withdrawal() to be implemented differently than Checking::withdrawal(). But the question is this: How do we implement Account::withdrawal()?

"No problem," you say. "Just go to your banker and ask, 'What are the rules for making a withdrawal from an account?' " The reply is, "What type of account? Savings or checking?" "From an account," you say, "just an account." Blank look.

The problem is that the question doesn't make sense. There's no such thing as "just an account." All accounts (in this example) are either checking accounts or savings accounts. The concept of an account is an abstract one that factors out properties common to the two concrete classes. It is incomplete, however, because it lacks the critical property withdrawal(). (After we get further into the details, we'll find other properties that a simple account lacks.)

Let me borrow an example from the animal kingdom. We can observe the different species of warm-blooded, baby-bearing animals and conclude that there is a concept *mammal*. We can derive classes from *mammal*, such as *canine, feline,* and *hominid*. It is impossible, however, to find anywhere on earth a pure mammal, that is, a mammal that isn't a member of some species. Mammal is a high-level concept that we have created — no instances of mammal exist.

The concept of mammal is fundamentally different than the concept of dog. "Dog" is a name we have given to an object that exists. There is no such thing as a mammal in the real world.

We don't want the programmer to create an object of class Account or class Mammal because we wouldn't know what to do with it. To address this problem, C++ allows the programmer to declare a class that cannot be instanced with an object. The only use for such a class is that it can be inherited.

A class that cannot be instanced is called an *abstract* class.

Declaring an abstract class

An abstract class is a class with one or more pure virtual functions. A *pure virtual function* is a virtual member function that is marked as having no implementation.

A pure virtual function has no implementation because we don't know how to implement it. For example, we don't know how to perform a withdrawal() in class Account. The concept doesn't make sense. However, we can't just not include a definition of withdrawal() because C++ will assume that we forgot to define the function and give us a link error stating that the function is missing (and presumed forgotten).

The syntax for declaring a function pure virtual — and letting C++ know that the function has no definition — is demonstrated in the following class Account:

```
// Account - this class is an abstract class describing
//           the base class for all bank accounts
class Account
{
  public:
    Account(unsigned nAccNo);

    //access functions
    int accountNo();
    Account* first();
    Account* next();

    //transaction functions
    virtual void deposit(float fAmount) = 0;
    virtual void withdrawal(float fAmount) = 0;

  protected:
    //keep Accounts in a linked list so there's no limit
    static Account* pFirst;
          Account* pNext;

    // all accounts have a unique account number
    unsigned    nAccountNumber;
};
```

The = 0 after the declaration of deposit() and withdrawal() indicates that the programmer does not intend to define these functions. The declaration is a placeholder for the subclasses. The subclasses of Account are expected to overload these functions with concrete functions.

A *concrete member function* is a function that is not pure virtual. All member functions prior to this Session have been concrete.

Although this notation of using the =0 to indicate that a member function is abstract is bizarre, it's here to stay. There is an obscure reason, if not exactly a justification, for this notation, but it's beyond the scope of this book.

An abstract class cannot be instanced with an object; that is, you can't make an object out of an abstract class. For example, the following declaration is not legal:

```
void fn()
{
    //declare an Account with 100 dollars
    Account acnt(1234);        // this is not legal
    acnt.withdrawal(50);       // what would this do?
}
```

If the declaration were allowed, the resulting object would be incomplete, lacking in some capability. For example, what should the preceding call acnt.withdrawal(50) do? There is no Account::withdrawal().

Abstract classes serve as base classes for other classes. An Account contains all the properties that we associate with a generic bank account including the capability to make a withdrawal and a deposit. It's just that we can't define how a generic account would do such a thing — that's left to the particular subclass to define. Said another way, an account is not an account unless the user can make deposits and withdrawals, even if such operations cannot be defined except in terms of particular types of accounts, such as savings and check accounts.

We can create other types of bank accounts by inheriting from Account, but they cannot be instanced with an object as long as they remain abstract.

Making a "concrete" class out of an abstract class

The subclass of an abstract class remains abstract until all pure virtual functions
are overloaded. The following class `Savings` is not abstract because it overloads
the pure virtual functions `deposit()` and `withdrawal()` with perfectly good
definitions.

```
// Account - this class is an abstract class describing
//           the base class for all bank accounts
class Account
{
  public:
    Account(unsigned nAccNo);

    //access functions
    int accountNo();
    Account* first();
    Account* next();

    //transaction functions
    virtual void deposit(float fAmount) = 0;
    virtual void withdrawal(float fAmount) = 0;

  protected:
    //keep Accounts in a linked list so there's no limit
    static Account* pFirst;
           Account* pNext;

    // all accounts have a unique account number
    unsigned    nAccountNumber;
};

// Savings - implement the Account concept
class Savings : public Account
{
```

```
public:
  // constructor - savings accounts are created
  //                with an initial cash balance
  Savings(unsigned nAccNo,
          float fInitialBalance)
      : Account(nAccNo)
  {
      fBalance = fInitialBalance;
  }

  // savings accounts know how to handle
  // these operations
  virtual void deposit(float fAmount);
  virtual void withdrawal(float fAmount);

protected:
  float fBalance;
};

// deposit and withdrawal - define the standard
//                account operations for savings accounts
void Savings::deposit(float fAmount)
{
    // ...some function...
}
void Savings::withdrawal(float fAmount)
{
    // ...some function...
}
```

An object of class `Savings` knows how to perform deposits and withdrawals when called on to do so. That is, the following makes sense:

```
void fn()
{
    Savings s(1234;
    s.deposit(100.0);
}
```

The class Account **has a constructor despite it being abstract. All accounts are created with an ID. The concrete** Savings **account class passes the account ID off to the** Account **base class while handling the initial balance itself. This is part of our object accountability concept — the Account class owns the account number field, so leave it to the Account class to initialize that field.**

**10 Min.
To Go**

When is a subclass abstract?

A subclass of an abstract class can remain abstract. Suppose we added an intermediate class to the account hierarchy. For example, suppose that my bank has something called a cash account.

Cash accounts are accounts in which assets are maintained as cash as opposed to securities. Both savings accounts and checking accounts are cash accounts. All deposits to cash accounts are handled the same in my bank; however, savings accounts charge after the first five withdrawals whereas checking accounts do not charge anything.

Using this definition, the class CashAccount can implement deposit()because that operation is well defined and common to all forms of cash account; however, CashAccount cannot implement the member function withdrawal() because different forms of cash account handle that operation differently.

In C++, the classes CashAccount and Savings appear as follows:

```
// CashAccount - a cash account holds all assets in cash
//                rather than securities. All cash accounts
//                require deposits in currency. All deposits
//                are handled the same. Withdrawals are
//                handled differently for different forms
//                of cash accounts
class CashAccount : public Account
{
  public:
    CashAccount(unsigned nAccNo,
                float fInitialBalance)
        : Account(nAccNo)
    {
        fBalance = fInitialBalance;
    }

    //transaction functions
```

```
    // deposit - all cash accounts accept deposits
    //           in currency
    virtual void deposit(float fAmount)
    {
        fBalance += fAmount;
    }

    // access functions
    float balance()
    {
        return fBalance;
    }

  protected:
    float fBalance;
};

// Savings - a savings account is a form of cash
//           account; the withdrawal operation is
//           well defined for savings accounts
class Savings : public CashAccount
{
  public:
    Savings(unsigned nAccNo,
            float fInitialBalance = 0.0F)
       :CashAccount(nAccNo, fInitialBalance)
    {
        // ...whatever else a savings account needs
        // to do that a cash account doesn't already...
    }

    // a savings account knows how to process
    // withdrawals as well
    virtual void withdrawal(float fAmount);
};

// fn - a test function
void fn()
{
    // open a savings account with $200 in it
```

```
        Savings savings(1234, 200);

        // deposit $100
        savings.deposit(100);

        // and withdraw $50 back out
        savings.withdrawal(50);
    }
```

The class `CashAccount` remains abstract because it overloads the `deposit()` but not the `withdrawal()` member functions. `Savings` is concrete because it overloads the final remaining pure virtual member function.

The test function `fn()` creates a `Savings` object, makes a deposit, and then makes a withdrawal.

 Originally, every pure virtual function in a subclass had to be overloaded, even if the function was overloaded with another pure virtual function. Eventually, people realized that this was as silly as it sounds and dropped the requirement. Neither Visual C++ nor GNU/C++ require it, but older compilers may.

Passing an abstract object to a function

Even though you can't instance an abstract class, it is possible to declare a pointer or a reference to an abstract class. With polymorphism, however, this isn't as crazy as it sounds. Consider the following code snippet:

```
    void fn(Account* pAccount){     //this is legal
    {
        pAccount->withdrawal(100.0);
    }

    void otherFn()
    {
        Savings s;

        //this is legitimate because Savings IS_A Account
        fn(&s);
    }
```

Here, pAccount is declared as a pointer to an Account. The function fn() is justified in calling pAccount->withdrawal() because all accounts know how to process their own withdrawals. However, it is understood that when the function is called, it will be passed the address of some nonabstract subclass object such as Savings.

It is important to note that, any object received by fn() will be of either class Savings or some other nonabstract subclass of Account. The function fn() is assured that we will never pass an actual object of class Account, because we could never create one to pass in the first place. That is, the following could never happen because C++ wouldn't allow it to happen:

```
void otherFn()
{
    // the following is not allowed because Account is
    // an abstract class
    Account a;

    fn(&a);
}
```

It is key that fn() was justified in calling withdrawal() with its abstract Account object because every concrete subclass of Account knows how to perform a withdrawal() operation.

A pure virtual function represents a promise to implement some feature in its concrete subclasses.

Why are pure virtual functions needed?

If withdrawal() can't be defined in the base class Account, why not leave it out? Why not define the function in Savings and keep it out of Account? In many object-oriented languages, you can do just that. But C++ wants to be capable of checking that you really know what you're doing.

C++ is a strongly typed language. When you refer to a member function, C++ insists that you prove that the member function exists in the class you specified. This avoids unfortunate run-time surprises when a referenced member function turns out to be missing.

Let's make the following minor changes to Account to demonstrate the problem:

```
class Account
{
    //just like before but without withdrawal() declared
};
class Savings : public Account
{
  public:
    virtual void withdrawal(float fAmount);
};

void fn(Account* pAcc)
{
    //withdraw some money
    pAcc->withdrawal(100.00F);  //this call is not allowed;
                                //withdrawal() is not a member
                                //of class Account
};
int otherFn()
{
    Savings s;     //open an Account
    fn(&s);
    //...continues on...
}
```

The otherFn() function operates the same as before. Just as before, the function fn() attempts to call withdrawal() with the Account object that it receives. Because the function withdrawal() is not a member of Account, however, the compiler generates an error.

In this case, the Account class has made no commitment to implement a withdrawal() member function. There could be a concrete subclass of Account that did not define a withdrawal() operation. In this case, the call to pAcc->withdrawal() would have no place to go — this is a possibility that C++ cannot accept.

Done!

REVIEW

Dividing classes of objects into taxonomies based on decreasing similarity is known as factoring. Factoring almost inevitably leads to classes that are conceptual rather than concrete. A Human is a Primate is a Mammal; however, the class Mammal is conceptual — there is no instance of Mammal that isn't some specific species.

You saw an example of this with the class Account. While there are savings accounts and checking accounts there is no object that is simply an account. In C++, we say that the class Account is abstract. A class becomes abstract as soon as one of its member functions does not have a firm definition. A subclass becomes concrete when it has defined all of the properties that were left dangling in the abstract base class.

- A member function that has no implementation is called a pure virtual function. Pure virtual functions are noted with an equal sign followed by a 0 in their declarations. Pure virtual functions have no definition.

- A class that contains one or more pure virtual functions is called an abstract class.

- An abstract class cannot be instanced.

- An abstract class may act as a base class for other classes.

- Subclasses of an abstract class become concrete (that is, nonabstract) when it has overridden all of the pure virtual functions that it inherits.

QUIZ YOURSELF

1. What is factoring? (See "Factoring.")

2. What is the one differentiating characteristic of an abstract class in C++? (See "Declaring an Abstract Class.")

3. How do you create a concrete class out of an abstract class? (See "Making a Concrete Class out of an Abstract Class.")

4. Why is it possible to declare a function fn(MyClass*) if MyClass is abstract? (See "Passing an Abstract Object to a Function.")

Multiple Inheritance

Session Checklist

✔ Introducing multiple inheritance

✔ Avoiding ambiguities with multiple inheritance

✔ Avoiding ambiguities with virtual inheritance

✔ Reviewing the ordering rules for multiple constructors

30 Min.
To Go

In the class hierarchies discussed so far, each class inherited from a single parent. This is the way things usually are in the real world. A microwave oven is a type of oven. One might argue that a microwave has things in common with a radar which also uses microwaves, but that's a real stretch.

Some classes, however, do represent the blending of two classes into one. An example of such a class is the sleeper sofa. As the name implies, it is a sofa and also a bed (although not a very comfortable bed). Thus, the sleeper sofa should be allowed to inherit bed-like properties as well as couch properties. To address this situation, C++ enables a derived class to inherit from more than one base class. This is called multiple inheritance.

How Does Multiple Inheritance Work?

Let's expand the sleeper sofa example to examine the principles of multiple inheritance. Figure 24-1 shows the inheritance graph for class SleeperSofa. Notice how this class inherits from class Sofa and from class Bed. In this way, it inherits the properties of both.

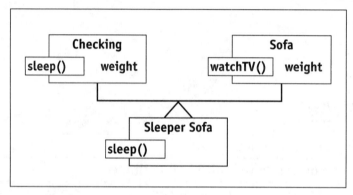

Figure 24-1
Class hierarchy of a sleeper sofa

The code to implement class SleeperSofa looks like the following:

```
// SleeperSofa - demonstrate how a sleeper sofa might work
#include <stdio.h>
#include <iostream.h>

class Bed
{
  public:
    Bed()
    {
        cout << "Building the bed part\n";
    }
    void sleep()
    {
        cout << "Trying to get some sleep over here!\n";
    }
    int weight;
};
```

```
class Sofa
{
  public:
    Sofa()
    {
        cout << "Building the sofa part\n";
    }
    void watchTV()
    {
        cout << "Watching TV\n";
    }
    int weight;
};

//SleeperSofa - is both a Bed and a Sofa
class SleeperSofa : public Bed, public Sofa
{
  public:
    // the constructor doesn't need to do anything
    SleeperSofa()
    {
        cout << "Putting the two together\n";
    }
    void foldOut()
    {
        cout << "Folding the bed out\n";
    }
};

int main()
{
    SleeperSofa ss;
    //you can watch TV on a sleeper sofa...
    ss.watchTV();          //Sofa::watchTV()
    //...and then you can fold it out...
    ss.foldOut();          //SleeperSofa::foldOut()
    //...and sleep on it (sort of)
    ss.sleep();            //Bed::sleep()
    return 0;
}
```

The names of both classes — Bed and Sofa — appear after the name SleeperSofa, indicating that SleeperSofa inherits the members of both base classes. Thus, both of the calls ss.sleep() and ss.watchTV() are legal. You can use the class SleeperSofa as either a Bed or a Sofa. Plus the class SleeperSofa can have members of its own, such as foldOut().

Executing the program generates the following output:

```
Building the bed part
Building the sofa part
Putting the two together
Watching TV
Folding the bed out
Trying to get some sleep over here!
```

The bed portion of the sleeper sofa is constructed first cbecause the class Bed appears first in the list of classes from which SleeperSofa inherits (it does not depend upon the order in which the classes are defined). Next the Sofa portion of the SleeperSofa is constructed. Finally, the SleeperSofa gets a crack at it.

Once the SleeperSofa object has been created, main() accesses each of the member functions in turn — first watching the TV on the sofa, then folding the sofa out and finally sleeping on the bed. (Obviously the member functions could have been called in any order.)

Inheritance Ambiguities

Although multiple inheritance is a powerful feature, it introduces several possible problems to the programmer. One is apparent in the preceding example. Notice that both Bed and Sofa contain a member weight. This is logical because both have a measurable weight. The question is, which weight does SleeperSofa inherit?

The answer is both. SleeperSofa inherits a member Bed::weight and a separate member Sofa::weight. Because they have the same name, unqualified references to weight are now ambiguous. The following snippet demonstrates the principle:

```
int main()
{
    // output the weight of the sleepersofa
    SleeperSofa ss;
    cout << "sofa weight = "
```

```
        << ss.weight    //this doesn't work!
        << "\n";
    return 0;
}
```

The program must indicate one of the two weights by specifying the desired base class. The following code snippet is correct:

```
#include <iostream.h>
void fn()
{
    SleeperSofa ss;
    cout << "sofa weight = "
        << ss.Sofa::weight    //specify which weight
        << "\n";
}
```

Although this solution corrects the problem, specifying the base class in the application function isn't desirable because it forces class information to leak outside the class into application code. In this case, fn() has to know that SleeperSofa inherits from Sofa.

These types of so-called name collisions were not possible with single inheritance, but are a constant danger with multiple inheritance.

**20 Min.
To Go**

Virtual Inheritance

In the case of SleeperSofa, the name collision on weight was more than a mere accident. A SleeperSofa doesn't have a bed weight separate from its sofa weight — it has only one weight. The collision occurred because this class hierarchy does not completely describe the real world. Specifically, the classes have not been completely factored.

Thinking about it a little more, it becomes clear that both beds and sofas are special cases of a more fundamental concept: furniture. (I suppose I could get even more fundamental and use something like object_with_mass, but furniture is fundamental enough.) Weight is a property of all furniture. This relationship is shown in Figure 24-2.

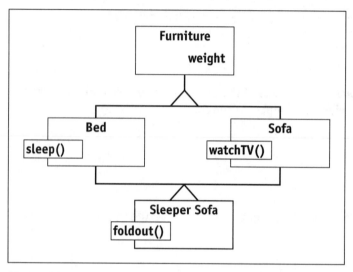

Figure 24-2
Further factoring of beds and sofas

Factoring out the class Furniture should relieve the name collision. With much relief and great anticipation of success, I generated the following C++ class hierarchy in the program AmbiguousInheritance:

```
// AmbiguousBaseClass- both Bed and Sofa can inherit from
//                     a common class Furniture
// This program does not compile!
#include <stdio.h>
#include <iostream.h>

class Furniture
{
  public:
    Furniture()
    {
        cout << "Creating the furniture concept";
    }
    int weight;
};

class Bed : public Furniture
{
```

```cpp
  public:
    Bed()
    {
        cout << "Building the bed part\n";
    }
    void sleep()
    {
        cout << "Trying to get some sleep over here!\n";
    }
};

class Sofa : public Furniture
{
  public:
    Sofa()
    {
        cout << "Building the sofa part\n";
    }
    void watchTV()
    {
        cout << "Watching TV\n";
    }
};

//SleeperSofa - is both a Bed and a Sofa
class SleeperSofa : public Bed, public Sofa
{
  public:
    // the constructor doesn't need to do anything
    SleeperSofa()
    {
        cout << "Putting the two together\n";
    }
    void foldOut()
    {
        cout << "Folding the bed out\n";
    }
};

int main()
```

```
{
    // output the weight of the sleepersofa
    SleeperSofa ss;
    cout << "sofa weight = "
         << ss.weight    //this doesn't work!
         << "\n";
    return 0;
}
```

Unfortunately, this doesn't help at all — weight is still ambiguous. "OK," I say (not really understanding why weight is still ambiguous), "I'll try casting ss to a Furniture."

```
#include <iostream.h>
void fn()
{
    SleeperSofa ss;
    Furniture *pF;
    pF = (Furniture*)&ss; //use a Furniture pointer...
    cout << "weight = "   //...to get at the weight
         << pF->weight
         << "\n";
};
```

Even this doesn't work. Now I get an error message indicating that the cast of SleeperSofa* to Furniture* is ambiguous. What's going on?

The explanation is straightforward. SleeperSofa doesn't inherit from Furniture directly. Both Bed and Sofa inherit from Furniture and then SleeperSofa inherits from them. In memory, a SleeperSofa looks like Figure 24-3.

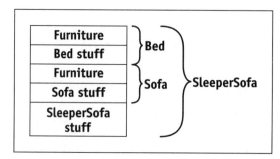

Figure 24-3
Memory layout of a SleeperSofa

You can see that a SleeperSofa consists of a complete Bed followed by a complete Sofa followed by some SleeperSofa unique stuff. Each of these subobjects in SleeperSofa has its own Furniture part, because each inherits from Furniture. Thus, a SleeperSofa contains two Furniture objects.

I haven't created the hierarchy shown in Figure 24-2 after all. The inheritance hierarchy I actually created is the one shown in Figure 24-4.

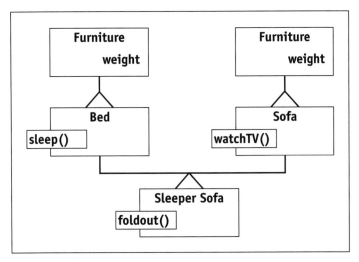

Figure 24-4
Actual result of my first attempt to factor out the Furniture class common to both Bed and Sofa

But this is nonsense. SleeperSofa needs only one copy of Furniture. I want SleeperSofa to inherit only one copy of Furniture, and I want Bed and Sofa to share that one copy.

C++ calls this *virtual inheritance* because it uses the virtual keyword.

 I hate this overloading of the term virtual because virtual inheritance has nothing to do with virtual functions.

I return to class SleeperSofa and implement it as follows:

```
// MultipleVirtual - base SleeperSofa on a single copy of
//                   Furniture
// This program does compile!
```

```
#include <stdio.h>
#include <iostream.h>

class Furniture
{
  public:
    Furniture()
    {
        cout << "Creating the furniture concept";
    }
    int weight;
};

class Bed : virtual public Furniture
{
  public:
    Bed()
    {
        cout << "Building the bed part\n";
    }
    void sleep()
    {
        cout << "Trying to get some sleep over here!\n";
    }
};

class Sofa : virtual public Furniture
{
  public:
    Sofa()
    {
        cout << "Building the sofa part\n";
    }
    void watchTV()
    {
        cout << "Watching TV\n";
    }
};

//SleeperSofa - is both a Bed and a Sofa
```

```
class SleeperSofa : public Bed, public Sofa
{
  public:
    // the constructor doesn't need to do anything
    SleeperSofa()
    {
        cout << "Putting the two together\n";
    }
    void foldOut()
    {
        cout << "Folding the bed out\n";
    }
};

int main()
{
    // output the weight of the sleepersofa
    SleeperSofa ss;
    cout << "sofa weight = "
        << ss.weight    //this doesn't work!
//        << ss.Sofa::weight // this does work
        << "\n";
    return 0;
}
```

Notice the addition of the keyword virtual in the inheritance of Furniture in Bed and Sofa. This says, "Give me a copy of Furniture unless you already have one somehow, in which case I'll just use that one." A SleeperSofa ends up looking like Figure 24-5 in memory.

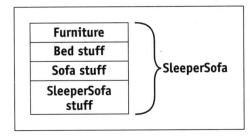

Figure 24-5
Memory layout of SleeperSofa with virtual inheritance

A SleeperSofa inherits Furniture, then Bed minus the Furniture part, followed by Sofa minus the Furniture part. Bringing up the rear are the members unique to SleeperSofa. (This may not be the order of the elements in memory, but that's not important for our purposes.)

The reference in main() to weight is no longer ambiguous because a SleeperSofa contains only one copy of Furniture. By inheriting Furniture virtually, you get the desired inheritance relationship as expressed in Figure 24-2.

If virtual inheritance solves this problem so nicely, why isn't it the norm? There are two reasons. First, virtually inherited base classes are handled internally much differently than normally inherited base classes, and these differences involve extra overhead. (Not that much extra overhead, but the makers of C++ were almost obsessively paranoid about overhead.) Second, sometimes you want two copies of the base class (although this is unusual).

I think virtual inheritance should be the norm.

As an example of a case in which you might not want virtual inheritance, consider a TeacherAssistant who is both a Student and a Teacher, both of which are subclasses of Academician. If the university gives its teaching assistants two IDs — a student ID and a separate teacher ID — class TeacherAssistant will need to contain two copies of class Academician.

10 Min.
To Go

Constructing the Objects of Multiple Inheritance

The rules for constructing objects need to be expanded to handle multiple inheritance. The constructors are invoked in this order:

- First, the constructor for any virtual base classes is called in the order in which the classes are inherited.

- Then the constructor for any nonvirtual base class is called in the order in which the classes are inherited.

- Next, the constructor for any member objects is called in the order in which the member objects appear in the class.

- Finally, the constructor for the class itself is called.

Base classes are constructed in the order in which they are inherited and not in the order in which they appear on the constructor line.

A Contrary Opinion

Not all object-oriented practitioners think that multiple inheritance is a good idea. In addition, many object-oriented languages don't support multiple inheritance. For example, Java does not support multiple inheritance — it is considered too dangerous and not really worth the trouble.

Multiple inheritance is not an easy thing for the language to implement. This is mostly the compiler's problem (or the compiler writer's problem) and not the programmer's problem. However, multiple inheritance opens the door to additional errors. First, there are the ambiguities mentioned in the section "Inheritance Ambiguities." Second, in the presence of multiple inheritance, casting a pointer from a subclass to a base class often involves changing the value of the pointer in sophisticated and mysterious ways, which can result in unexpected results. For example:

```
#include <iostream.h>
class Base1 {int mem;};
class Base2 {int mem;};
class SubClass : public Base1, public Base2 {};

void fn(SubClass *pSC)
{
    Base1 *pB1 = (Base1*)pSC;
    Base2 *pB2 = (Base2*)pSC;
    if ((void*)pB1 == (void*)pB2)
    {
        cout << "Members numerically equal\n";
    }
}
int main()
{
    SubClass sc;
    fn(&sc);
    return 0;
}
```

Done!

pB1 and pB2 are not numerically equal even though they came from the same original value, pSC, and the message "Members numerically equal" doesn't appear. (Actually, fn() is passed a zero because C++ doesn't perform these transmigrations on null. See how strange it gets?)

REVIEW

I suggest that you avoid using multiple inheritance until you are comfortable with C++. Single inheritance provides enough expressive power to get used to. Later, you can study the manuals until you're sure that you understand exactly what's going on when you use multiple inheritance. One exception is the use of commercial libraries such as Microsoft's Foundation Classes (MFC), which use multiple inheritance quite a bit. These classes have been checked out and are safe. (You are generally not even aware that you are using multiply inherited base classes when using libraries such as MFC.)

- A class can inherit from more than one class by stringing class names, separated by commas, after the :. Although the examples in this base class only used two base classes, there is no reasonable limitation to the number of base classes. Inheritance from more than two base classes is extremely unusual.

- Members that the base classes share are ambiguous to the subclass. That is, if both `BaseClass1` and `BaseClass2` contain a member function `f()`, then `f()` is ambiguous in `Subclass`.

- Ambiguities in the base classes can be resolved by using a class indicator, thus the subclass might refer to `BaseClass1::f()` and `BaseClass2::f()`.

- Having both base classes inherit from a common base class of their own in which common properties have been factored out can solve the problem if the classes inherit virtually.

QUIZ YOURSELF

1. What might we use as the base classes for a class like `CombinationPrinterCopier`? (A printer-copier is a laser printer that can also serve as a copy machine.) (See the introduction section.)

2. Complete the following class description by replacing the question marks:

```
class Printer
{
  public:
    int nVoltage;
    // ....other stuff...
}
class Copier
```

```
{
  public:
    int nVolatage;
    // ....other stuff...
}
class CombinationPinterCopier ?????
{
    // ....other stuff...
}
```

3. What is the main problem that might arise in accessing the voltage of a CombinationPrinterCopier object? (See "Inheritance Ambiguities.")

4. Given that both a Printer and a Copier are ElectronicEquipment, what could be done to solve the voltage problem? (See "Virtual Inheritance.")

5. What are some of the reasons why multiple inheritance might not be a good thing? (See "A Contrary Opinion.")

Session Checklist

✔ Separating programs into multiple modules

✔ Using the #include-directive

✔ Adding files to a Project

✔ Other preprocessor commands

**30 Min.
To Go**

All of the programs to this point have been small enough to contain in a single .cpp source file. This is fine for the examples contained in a book such as *C++ Weekend Crash Course,* but this would be a severe limitation in real-world application programming. This session examines how to divide a program into parts through the clever use of project and include files.

Why Divide Programs?

The programmer can divide a single program into separate files sometimes known as *modules*. These individual source files are compiled separately and then combined during the build process to generate a single program.

The process of combining separately compiled modules into a single executable is called *linking*.

There are a number of reasons to divide programs into more manageable pieces. First, dividing a program into modules results in a higher level of encapsulation. Classes wall off their internal members in order to provide a certain degree of safety. Programs can wall off functions to do the same thing.

Remember that encapsulation was one of the advantages of object-oriented programming.

Second, it is easier to comprehend and, therefore, easier to write and debug a program that consists of a number of well-thought-out modules than a single source file full of all of the classes and functions that the program uses.

Next comes reuse. I used the reuse argument to help sell object-based programming. It is extremely difficult to keep track of a single class reused among multiple programs when a separate copy of the class is kept in each program. It is much better if a single class module is automatically shared among programs.

Finally, there is the argument of time. It doesn't take a compiler such as Visual C++ or GNU C++ very long to build the examples contained in this book using a high-speed computer like yours. Commercial programs sometimes consist of millions of source lines of code. Rebuilding a program of that size can take more than 24 hours. (Almost as long as it's taking you to get through this book!) A programmer would not tolerate rebuilding a program like that for every single change. However, the majority of the time is spent compiling the source file into object files. The link process is much quicker.

Separating Class Definition from Application Program

This section begins with the EarlyBinding example from Session 22 and separates the definition of the class Student from the remainder of the application. To avoid confusion, let's call the result SeparatedClass.

Dividing the program

We begin by deciding what the logical divisions of SeparatedClass should be. Clearly the application functions fn() and main() can be separated from the class definition. These functions are not reusable nor do they have anything to do with the definitions of the class Student. Similarly, the Student class does not refer to the fn() or main() functions at all.

I store the application portion of the program in a file called SeparatedClass.cpp. So far the program appears as follows:

```
// SeparatedClass - demonstrate an application separated
//                  from the class definition
#include <stdio.h>
#include <iostream.h>

double fn(Student& fs)
{
    // because calcTuition() is declared virtual this
    // call uses the run-time type of fs to resolve
    // the call
    return fs.calcTuition();
}

int main(int nArgc, char* pszArgs[])
{
    // the following expression calls
    // fn() with a Student object
    Student s;
    cout << "The value of s.calcTuition when\n"
         << "called virtually through fn() is "
         << fn(s)
         << "\n\n";

    // the following expression calls
    // fn() with a GraduateStudent object
    GraduateStudent gs;
    cout << "The value of gs.calcTuition when\n"
         << "called virtually through fn() is "
         << fn(gs)
         << "\n\n";
    return 0;
}
```

Unfortunately, this module does not compile successfully because nothing in SeparatedClass.cpp defines the class Student. We could, of course, insert the definition of Student back into SeparatedClass.cpp, but doing so defeats our purpose; it puts us back where we started.

The #include directive

What is needed is some method for including the declaration Student in SeparatedClass.cpp programmatically. The #include directive does exactly that. The #include directive includes the contents of the file named in the source code exactly at the point of the #include directive. This is harder to explain than it is to do in practice.

First, I create the file student.h, which contains the definition of the Student and GraduateStudent classes:

```
// Student - define the properties of a Student
class Student
{
  public:
    virtual double calcTuition()
    {
        return 0;
    }

  protected:
    int nID;
};
class GraduateStudent : public Student
{
  public:
    virtual double calcTuition()
    {
        return 1;
    }

  protected:
    int nGradId;
};
```

The target file of the #include **directive is known as an** *include* **file. By convention include files carry the name of the base class they contain with a lower case first letter and the extension .h. You may also see C++ include files with extensions such as .hh, .hpp, and .hxx. Theoretically, the C++ compiler doesn't care.**

The new version of the application source file SeparatedClass.cpp appears as follows:

```
// SeparatedClass - demonstrates an application separated
//                  from the class definition
#include <stdio.h>
#include <iostream.h>

#include "student.h"

double fn(Student& fs)
{
    // ...identical to earlier version from here down...
```

The #include directive was added.

The #include **directive must start in column one. The ". . ." portion must be on the same line as the** #include**.**

If you were to physically include the contents of student.h in the file SeparatedClass.cpp, you would end up with exactly the same LateBinding.cpp file that we started with. This is exactly what happens during the build process — C++ adds student.h to SeparatedClass.cpp and compiles the result.

The #include **directive does not have the same syntax as other C++ commands. This is because it is not a C++ directive at all. A preprocessor makes a first pass over your C++ program before the C++ compiler executes. It is this preprocessor which interprets the** #include **directive.**

Dividing application code

The SeparatedClass program successfully divided the class definition from the application code, but suppose that this was not enough — suppose that we wanted to separate the function fn() from main(). I could, of course, use the same approach of creating an include file fn.h to include from the main source file.

The include file solution does not address the problem of creating programs that take forever to build. In addition, this solution introduces all sorts of problems concerning which function can call which function based on the order of inclusion. A better solution is to divide the sources into separate compilation units.

During the compilation phase of the build operation, C++ converts the .cpp source code into the equivalent machine instructions. This machine code information is saved in a file called the object file with either the extension .obj (Visual C++) or .o (GNU C++). In a subsequent phase, known as the link phase, the object file is combined with the C++ standard library code to create the executable .exe program.

Let's use this capability to our own advantage. We can separate the SeparatedClass.cpp file into a SeparatedFn.cpp file and a SeparatedMain.cpp file. We begin by creating the two files.

The SeparatedFn.cpp file appears as follows:

```
// SeparatedFn - demonstrates an application separated
//               into two parts - the fn() part
#include <stdio.h>
#include <iostream.h>

#include "student.h"

double fn(Student& fs)
{
    // because calcTuition() is declared virtual this
    // call uses the run-time type of fs to resolve
    // the call
    return fs.calcTuition();
}
```

The remaining SeparatedMain() program might appear as:

```
// SeparatedMain - demonstrates an application separated
//                 into two parts - the main() part
#include <stdio.h>
#include <iostream.h>

#include "student.h"
```

```
int main(int nArgc, char* pszArgs[])
{
    // the following expression calls
    // fn() with a Student object
    Student s;
    cout << "The value of s.calcTuition when\n"
         << "called virtually through fn() is "
         << fn(s)
         << "\n\n";

    // the following expression calls
    // fn() with a GraduateStudent object
    GraduateStudent gs;
    cout << "The value of gs.calcTuition when\n"
         << "called virtually through fn() is "
         << fn(gs)
         << "\n\n";
    return 0;
}
```

Both source files include the same .h files. This is because both files need access to the definition of the Student class as well as to the C++ Standard Library functions.

Project file

Full of expectation, I open the SeparatedMain.cpp file in the compiler and click Build.

10 Min. To Go

If you're trying this at home, make sure that you have closed the SeparatedClass project file.

The error message "undeclared identifier" appears. C++ does not know what a fn() is when compiling SeparatedMain.cpp. That makes sense, because the definition of fn() is in a different file.

Clearly I need to add a prototype declaration for fn() to the SeparatedMain.cpp source file:

```
double fn(Student& fs);
```

The resulting source file passes the compile step, but generates an error during the link step that it could not find the function fn(Student) among the .o object files.

I could (and probably should) add a prototype declaration for main() **to the SeparatedFn.cpp file; however, it isn't necessary because** fn() **does not call** main().

What is needed is a way to tell C++ to bind the two source files into the same program. Such a file is called the *project file*.

Creating a project file under Visual C++

There are several ways to create a project file. The techniques differ between the two compilers. In Visual C++, execute these steps:

1. Make sure that you close any project files created during previous attempts to create the program by clicking Close Workspace in the File menu. (A workspace is Microsoft's name for a collection of project files.)

2. Open the SeparatedMain.cpp source file. Click compile.

3. When Visual C++ asks you if would like to create a Project file, click Yes. You now have a project file containing the single source file SeparatedMain.cpp.

4. If not already open, open the Workspace window (click Workspace under View).

5. Switch to File view. Right click on SeparatedMain files, as shown in Figure 25-1. Select Add Files to Project. From the menu, open the SeparatedFn.cpp source file. Both SeparatedMain.cpp and SeparatedFn.cpp should now appear in the list of functions that make up the project.

6. Click Build to successfully build the program. (The first time that both source files are compiled is when performing a Build All.)

I did not say that this was the most elegant way, just the easiest.

Figure 25-1
Right click the Project in the Workspace Window to add files to the project.

The SeparatedMain project file on the accompanying CD-ROM contains both source files already.

Creating a project file under GNU C++

Use these steps to create a project file under rhide, the GNU C++ environment.

1. Without any files open, click Open Project in the Project menu.

2. Type in the name SeparatedMainGNU.gpr (the name isn't actually important — you can choose any name you want). A project window with the single entry, <empty>, opens along the bottom of the display.

3. Click Add Item under Project. Open the file SeparatedMain.cpp.

4. Repeat for SeparatedFn.cpp.

5. Select Make in the Compile menu to successfully create the program SeparatedMainGNU.exe. (Make rebuilds only those files that have changed; Build All rebuilds all source files whether changed or not.)

Figure 25-2 shows the contents of the Project Window alongside the Message Window displayed during the make process.

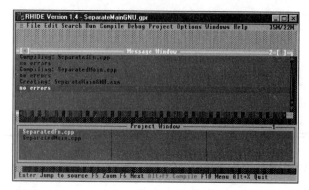

Figure 25-2
The rhide environment displays the files compiled and the program linked during the project build process.

Reexamining the standard program template

Now you can see why we have been including the directives #include <stdio.h> and #include <iostream.h> in our programs. These include files contain the definitions for the functions and classes that we have been using, such as strcat() and cin>>.

The standard C++-defined .h files are included using the <> brackets, whereas locally defined .h files are defined using the quote commands. The only difference between the two is that C++ looks for files contained in quotes starting with the *current* directory (the directory containing the project file), whereas C++ begins the search for bracketed files in the C++ include file directories. Either way, the programmer controls the directories searched via project file settings.

In fact, it is the very concept of separate compilation that makes the include file critical. Both SeparatedFn and SeparatedMain knew of Student because student.h was included. We could have typed in this definition in both source files, but this would have been very dangerous. The same definition in two different places enhances the possibility that the two could get out of synch — one could get changed without the other.

Including the definition of Student in a single student.h file and including that file in the two modules makes it impossible for the definitions to differ.

Handling outline member functions

The example Student and GraduateStudent classes defined their functions within the class; however, the member functions should have been declared outside of the class (only the Student class is shown — the GraduateStudent class is identical).

```cpp
// Student - define the properties of a Student
class Student
{
  public:
    // declare the member function
    virtual double calcTuition();

  protected:
    int nID;
};

// define the code separate from the class
 double Student::calcTuition();
 {
     return 0;
 }
```

A problem arises if the programmer tries to include both the class and the member functions in the same .h file. The function Student::calcTuition() becomes a part of both SeparatedMain.o and SeparatedFn.o. When these two files are linked, the C++ linker complains that calcTuition() is defined twice.

 When the member function is defined within the class, C++ takes special pains to avoid defining the function twice. C++ can't avoid the problem when the member function is defined outside of the class.

External member functions must be defined in their own .cpp source file as in the following Student.cpp:

```cpp
#include "student.h"
// define the code separate from the class
 double Student::calcTuition();
 {
     return 0;
 }
```

Done!

REVIEW

This session demonstrated how the programmer can divide programs into multiple source files. Smaller source files save build time because the programmer need only compile those source modules that have actually changed.

- Separately compiled modules increase the encapsulation of packages of similar functions. As you have already seen, separate, encapsulated packages are easier to write and debug. The standard C++ library is one such encapsulated package.

- The build process actually consists of two phases. During the first, the compile phase, the C++ source statements are converted into a machine readable, but incomplete object files. During the final, link phase, these object files are combined into a single executable.

- Declarations, including class declarations, must be compiled along with each C++ source file that uses the function or class declared. The easiest way to accomplish this is to place related declarations in a single .h file, which is then included in source .cpp files using the #include directive.

- The project file lists the modules that make up a single program. The project file also contains certain program-specific settings which affect the way the C++ environment builds the program.

QUIZ YOURSELF

1. What is the act of converting a C++ source file into a machine-readable object file called? (See "Why Divide Programs?")

2. What is the act of combining these object files into a single executable called? (See "Why Divide Programs?")

3. What is the project file used for? (See "Project File.")

4. What is the primary purpose of the #include directive? (See "The #include Directive.")

C++ Preprocessor

Session Checklist

✔ Assigning names to commonly used constants

✔ Defining compile-time macros

✔ Controlling the compilation process

**30 Min.
To Go**

The programs in Session 25 used the #include preprocessor directive to include the definition of classes in the multiple source files that made up our programs. In fact, all of the programs that you have seen so far have included the stdio.h and iostream.h file to define the functions that make up the standard C++ library. This session examines the #include directive along with other preprocessor commands.

The C++ Preprocessor

As a C++ programmer, you and I click the Build command to instruct the C++ compiler to convert our source code into an executable program. We don't typically worry about the details of how the compiler works. In Session 25, you learned that the build process consists of two parts, a compile step that converts each of our .cpp files into machine-language object code and a separate link step that combines these object files with those of the standard C++ library to create an .exe executable file. What still isn't clear is that the compile step itself is divided into multiple phases.

The compiler operates on your C++ source file in multiple passes. Generally, a first pass finds and identifies each of the variables and class definitions, while a subsequent pass generates the object code. However, a given C++ compiler makes as many or as few passes as it needs — there is no C++ standard.

Even before the first compiler pass, however, the C++ preprocessor gets a chance. The C++ processor scans through the .cpp file looking for lines that begin with a pound (#) sign in the first column. The output from the preprocessor, itself a C++ program, is fed to the compiler for subsequent processing.

The C language uses the same preprocessor so that anything said here about the C++ preprocessor is also true of C.

The #include Directive

The #include directive includes the contents of the named file at the point of the insertion. The preprocessor makes no attempt to process the contents of the .h file.

The include file does not have to end in .h, but it can confuse both the programmer and the preprocessor if it does not.

The name following the #include command must appear within either quotes (" ") or angle brackets (< >). The preprocessor assumes that files contained in quotes are user defined and, therefore, appear in the current directory. The preprocessor searches for files contained in angle brackets in the C++ compiler directories.

The include file should not include any C++ functions because they will be expanded and compiled separately by the modules that include the file. The contents of the include file should be limited to class definitions, global variable definitions, and other preprocessor directives.

The #define Directive

**20 Min.
To Go**

The #define directive defines a constant or macro. The following example shows how the #define is used to define a constant.

```
#define MAX_NAME_LENGTH 256

void fn(char* pszSourceName)
{
    char szLastName[MAX_NAME_LENGTH];

    if (strlen(pszSourceName) >= MAX_NAME_LENGTH)
    {
        // ...source string too long error processing...
    }

    // ...and so it goes...
}
```

The preprocessor directive defines a parameter MAX_NAME_LENGTH to be replaced at compile time by the constant value 256. The preprocessor replaces the name MAX_NAME_LENGTH with the constant 256 everywhere that it is used. Where we see MAX_NAME_LENGTH, the C++ compiler sees 256.

This example demonstrates the naming convention for #define constants. Names are all uppercase with underscores used to divide words.

When used this way, the #define directive enables the programmer to assign meaningful names to constant values; MAX_NAME_LENGTH has greater meaning to the programmer than 256. Defining constants in this fashion also makes programs easier to modify. For example, the maximum number characters in a name might be embedded throughout a program. However, changing this maximum name length from 256 characters to 128 is simply a matter of modifying the #define no matter how many places it is used.

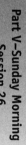

Defining macros

The #define directive also enables definitions macros — a compile-time directive that contains arguments. The following demonstrates the definition and use of the macro square(), which generates the code necessary to calculate the square of its argument.

```
#define square(x) x * x
void fn()
{
    int nSquareOfTwo = square(2);
    // ...and so forth...
}
```

The preprocess turns this into the following:

```
void fn()
{
    int nSquareOfTwo = 2 * 2;
    // ...and so forth...
}
```

Common errors using macros

The programmer must be very careful when using #define macros. For example, the following does not generate the expected results:

```
#define square(x) x * x
void fn()
{
    int nSquareOfTwo = square(1 + 1);
}
```

The preprocessor expands the macro into the following:

```
void fn()
{
    int nSquareOfTwo = 1 + 1 * 1 + 1;
}
```

Because multiplication takes precedence over addition, the expression is interpreted as if it had been written as follows:

```
void fn()
{
    int nSquareOfTwo = 1 + (1 * 1) + 1;
}
```

The resulting value of nSquareOfTwo is 3 and not 4.

Fully qualifying the macro using a liberal dosage of parentheses helps because parentheses control the order of evaluation. There would not have been a problem had square been defined as follows:

```
#define square(x) ((x) * (x))
```

However, even this does not solve the problem in every case. For example, the following cannot be made to work:

```
#define square(x) ((x) * (x))
void fn()
{
    int nV1 = 2;
    int nV2;
    nV2 = square(nV1++);
}
```

You might expect the resulting value of nV2 to be 4 rather than 6 and of nV1 to be 3 rather than 4 caused by the following macro expansion:

```
void fn()
{
    int nV1 = 2;
    int nV2;
    nV2 = nV1++ * nV1++;
}
```

Macros are not type safe. This can cause confusion in mixed-mode expressions such as the following:

```
#define square(x) ((x) * (x))
void fn()
{
    int nSquareOfTwo = square(2.5);
}
```

Because nSquareOfTwo is an int, you might expect the resulting value to be 4 rather than the actual value of 6 (2.5 * 2.5 = 6.25).

C++ inline functions avoid the problems of macros:

```
inline int square(int x) {return x * x}
void fn()
{
    int nV1 = square(1 + 1); // value is two
    int nV2;
    nV2 = square(nV1++)    // value of nV2 is 4, nV1 is 3
    int nV3 = square(2.5) // value of nV3 is 4
}
```

The inline version of square() does not generate any more code than macros nor does it suffer from the traps and pitfalls of the preprocessor version.

Compile Controls

The preprocessor also provides compile-time decision-making capabilities.

**10 Min.
To Go**

The #if directive

The most C++-like of the preprocessor control directives is the #if statement. If the constant expression following an #if is nonzero, any statements up to an #else are passed on to the compiler. If the constant expression is zero, the statements between the #else and an #endif are passed through. The #else clause is optional. For example, the following:

```
#define SOME_VALUE 1
#if SOME_VALUE
int n = 1;
#else
int n = 2;
#endif
```

is converted to

```
int n = 1;
```

A few operators are defined for the preprocessor. For example:

```
#define SOME_VALUE 1
#if SOME_VALUE - 1
int n = 1;
#else
int n = 2;
#endif
```

is converted to the following:

```
int n = 2;
```

Remember that these are compile-time decisions and not run-time decisions. The expressions following the #if **involve constants and** #define **directives — variables and function calls are not allowed.**

The #ifdef directive

Another preprocessor control directive is the #ifdef. The #ifdef is true if the constant next to it is defined. Thus, the following:

```
#define SOME_VALUE 1
#ifdef SOME_VALUE
int n = 1;
#else
int n = 2;
#endif
```

is converted to the following:

```
int n = 1;
```

However, the directive

```
#ifdef SOME_VALUE
int n = 1;
#else
int n = 2;
#endif
```

is converted to the following:

```
int n = 2;
```

The #ifndef is also defined with the exact opposite definition.

Using the #ifdef/#ifndef directives for inclusion control

The most common use for the #ifdef is inclusion control. A symbol cannot be defined twice. The following is illegal:

```
class MyClass
{
    int n;
};
class MyClass
{
    int n;
};
```

If MyClass is defined in the include file myclass.h, it would be erroneous to include that file twice in the same .cpp source file. You might think that this problem is easily avoided; however, it is not uncommon for one include file to include another include file, such as in the following example:

```
#include "myclass.h"
class mySpecialClass : public MyClass
{
    int m;
}
```

An unsuspecting programmer might easily include both mycl ass.h and myspecial-class.h in the same source file leading to a doubly defined compiler error.

```
// the following does not compile
#include "myclass.h"
#include "myspecialclass.h"
void fn(MyClass& mc)
{
    // ...might be an object of class MyClass or MySpecialClass
}
```

This particular example is easily fixed; however, in a large application the relationships between the numerous include files can be bewildering.

Judicious use of the #ifdef directive avoids this problem by defining the myclass.h include file as follows:

```
#ifndef MYCLASS_H
#define MYCLASS_H
class MyClass
{
    int n;
};
#endif
```

When myclass.h is included the first time, MYCLASS_H is not defined and #ifndef is true. However, the constant MYCLASS_H is defined within myclass.h. The next time that myclass.h is encountered during compilation MYCLASS_H is defined and the class definition is avoided.

Using the #ifdef to include debug code

Another common use for the #ifdef clause is compile-time inclusion of debug code. Consider, for example, the following debug function:

```
void dumpState(MySpecialClass& msc)
{
    cout << "MySpecialClass:"
        << "m = " << msc.m
        << "n = " << msc.n;
}
```

Each time this function is called, dumpState() prints the contents of the MySpecialClass object to standard output. I can insert calls throughout my program to keep track of the MySpecialClass objects. After the program is ready for release, I need to remove each of these calls. Not only is this tiresome, but it runs the risk of reintroducing errors to the system. In addition, I might be forced to reinsert these calls in the program should I need to debug the program again.

I could define some type of flag that controls whether the program outputs the state of the program's MySpecialClass objects, but the calls themselves introduce overhead that slows the function. A better approach is the following:

```
#ifdef DEBUG
void dumpState(MySpecialClass& msc)
{
```

```
        cout << "MySpecialClass:"
            << "m = " << msc.m
            << "n = " << msc.n;
    }
#else
inline dumpState(MySpecialClass& mc)
{
}
#endif
```

Done!

If the parameter `DEBUG` is defined, then the debug function `dumpState()` is compiled. If `DEBUG` is not defined, then a do-nothing inline version of `dumpState()` is compiled instead. The C++ compiler converts each call to this inline version to nothing.

If the inline version of the function doesn't work, perhaps because the compiler does not support inline functions, then use the following macro definition:

```
#define dumpState(x)
```

Both Visual C++ and GNU C++ support this approach. Constants may be defined from the project settings without adding a `#define` directive to the source code. In fact, `_DEBUG` is automatically defined when compiling in debug mode, the constant.

REVIEW

The most common use for the preprocessor is to include the same class definitions and function prototypes in multiple .cpp source files using the `#include` directive. The `#if` and `#ifdef` preprocessor directives enable control over which lines of code are compiled and which are not.

- The name of the file included via the `#include` directive should end in .h. To do otherwise confuses other programmers and might even confuse the compiler. Filenames included in quotes (" ") are assumed to be in the current (or some other user specified) directory, whereas filenames included in brackets (< >) are assumed to reference one of the standard C++-defined include files.

- If the constant expression after an `#if` directive is nonzero, then the C++ commands that follow are passed to the compiler; otherwise, they are not passed. The `#ifdef` x directive is true if the `#define` constant x is defined.

- All preprocessor directives control which C++ statements the compiler "sees." All are interpreted at compile time and not at execution time.

Quiz Yourself

1. What is the difference between #include "file.h" and #include <file.h>? (See "The #include Directive.")

2. What are the two types of #define directive? (See "The #define Directive.")

3. Given the macro definition #define square(x) x * x, what is the value of square(2 + 3)? (See "The #define Directive.")

4. Name a benefit of an inline function compared to the equivalent macro definition. (See "Common Errors Using Macros.")

5. What is a common use for the #ifndef directive? (See "Using the #ifdef/#ifndef Directives for Inclusion Control.")

PART

V

Sunday Morning

1. What is the output of the program shown in the listing below?

```cpp
// ConstructionTest - demonstrate the order that
//                    objects are constructed
#include <stdio.h>
#include <iostream.h>
#include <string.h>

// Advisor - let's provide an empty class
//           for now
class Advisor
{
  public:
    Advisor(char* pszName)
    {
        cout << "Advisor:"
             << pszName
             << "\n";
    }
};

class Student
{
  public:
    Student() : adv("student data member")
    {
```

```
            cout << "Student\n";
            new Advisor("student local");
        }
        Advisor adv;
    };

    class GraduateStudent : public Student
    {
      public:
        GraduateStudent() : adv("graduate data member")
        {
            cout << "Graduate Student\n";
            new Advisor("graduate student local");
        }

      protected:
        Advisor adv;
    };

    int main(int nArgc, char* pszArgs[])
    {
        GraduateStudent gs;
        return 0;
    }
```

2. Given that graduate students must make a grade of 2.5 or better to pass and that regular students can get by with a 1.5, write a function pass() using the classes defined earlier in this session that accepts a grade and returns a 0 to students who fail and a 1 to students who pass.

3. Create a class Checking that inherits from the CashAccount and Account as shown above. A checking account is similar to a savings account except that it charges an extra dollar for each withdrawal. Don't worry about overdrafts.

If you want to save time, you can find the classes Account, CashAccount, **and** Savings **in the directory ExerciseClasses on the accompanying CD-ROM. You can use these as a starting point.**

Execute your class against the following:

```
void fn(Account* pAccount)
{
    pAccount->deposit(100);
    pAccount->withdrawal(50);
}

int main(int nArgc, char* pszArgs[])
{
    // open a savings account
    Savings savings(1234, 0);
    fn(&savings);

    // now a checking account
    Checking checking(5678, 0);
    fn(&checking);

    // output result
    cout << "Resulting savings account balance is "
        << savings.balance()
        << "\n";
    cout << "Resulting checking account balance is "
        << checking.balance()
        << "\n";

    return 0;
}
```

Hint: The output to this program should be as follows:

```
Resulting savings account balance is 50
Resulting checking account balance is 49
```

4. Create a program that creates a multiple inheritance object pc of class CombinationPrinterCopier. This program should print using pc. In addition, the program should output the voltage of pc.

Hints:

a. Look for help for words in quotes.

b. You will not be able to pass the voltage up through the constructors; instead, set the voltage in the constructor for CombinationPrinterCopier.

PART

VI

*Sunday
Afternoon*

Overloading Operators

Session Checklist

✔ Overview of overloading operators in C++

✔ Discussion of operator format versus function format

✔ Implementing operators as a member function versus as a nonmember function

✔ The return value from an overloaded operator

✔ A special case: the cast operator

30 Min. To Go

essions 6 and 7 discussed the mathematical and logical operators that C++ defines for the intrinsic data types.

The *intrinsic* data types are those that are built in the language, such as int, float, double, and so forth, plus the various pointer types.

In addition to these intrinsic operators, C++ enables the programmer to define the operators for classes that the programmer has created. This is called *operator overloading*.

Normally, operator overloading is optional and usually not attempted by beginning C++ programmers. A lot of experienced C++ programmers don't think operator overloading is such a great idea either. However, there are three operators that you need to learn how to overload: assignment (=), left shift (<<), and right shift (>). They are important enough that they have been granted their own chapters, which immediately follow this one.

Operator overloading can introduce errors that are very difficult to find. Be sure you know how operator overloading works before attempting to use it.

Why Do I Need to Overload Operators?

C++ considers user-defined types, such as Student and Sofa, to be just as valid as intrinsic types, such as int and char. Because operators are defined for the intrinsic types, why not allow them to be defined for user-defined types?

This is a weak argument, but I admit that operator overloading has its uses. Consider the class USDollar. Some of the operators make no sense at all when applied to dollars. For example, what would it mean to invert a USDollar? On the other hand, some operators definitely are applicable. For example, it makes sense to add a USDollar to or subtract a USDollar from a USDollar, with the result being a USDollar. It also makes sense to multiply or divide a USDollar by a double. However, multiplying a USDollar by a USDollar does not make much sense.

Operator overloading can improve readability. Consider the following, first without overloaded operators:

```
//expense - calculate the amount of money paid
//          (including both principal and simple interest)
USDollar expense(USDollar principal, double rate)
{
    //calculate the interest expense
USDollar interest = principal.interest(rate);

    //now add this to the principal and return the result
    return principal.add(interest);
}
```

With the proper overloaded operators, the same function looks like the following:

```
//expense - calculate the amount of money paid
//          (including both principal and simple interest)
```

```
USDollar expense(USDollar principal, double rate)
{
    USDollar interest = principal * rate;
    return principal + interest;
}
```

Before we investigate how to overload an operator, we need to understand the relationship between an operator and a function.

What Is the Relationship Between Operators and Functions?

An operator is nothing more than a built-in function with a peculiar syntax. For example, the operator + could just as well have been written add().

C++ gives each operator a function-style name. The functional name of an operator is the operator symbol preceded by the keyword operator and followed by the appropriate argument types. For example, the + operator that adds an int to an int generating an int is called int operator+(int, int).

The programmer can overload all operators, except ., ::, * (dereference), and &, by overloading their functional name with these restrictions:

- The programmer cannot invent new operators. You cannot invent the operation x $ y.

- The format of the operators cannot be changed. Thus, you could not define an operation %i because % is a binary operator.

- The operator precedence cannot change. A program cannot force operator+ to be evaluated before operator*.

- Finally, the operators cannot be redefined when applied to intrinsic types. Existing operators can only be overloaded for newly defined types.

How Does Operator Overloading Work?

Let's see operator overloading in action. Listing 27-1 shows a class USDollar with an addition operator and an increment operator defined.

Listing 27-1
USDollar with Overloaded Addition and Increment Operators

```cpp
// USDollarAdd - demonstrate the definition and use
//               of the addition operator for the class
//               USDollar
#include <stdio.h>
#include <iostream.h>

// USDollar - represent the greenback
class USDollar
{
    // make sure that the user-defined operations have
    // access to the protected members of the class
    friend USDollar operator+(USDollar&, USDollar&);
    friend USDollar& operator++(USDollar&);

  public:
    // construct a dollar object with an initial
    // dollar and cent value
    USDollar(int d = 0, int c = 0);

    // rationalize - normalize the number of cents by
    //               adding a dollar for every 100 cents
    void rationalize()
    {
        dollars += (cents / 100);
        cents   %= 100;
    }

    // output- display the value of this object
    //         to the standard output object
    void output()
    {
        cout << "$"
             << dollars
             << "."
             << cents;
    }
```

```
   protected:
     int dollars;
     int cents;
};

USDollar::USDollar(int d, int c)
{
    // store of the initial values locally
    dollars = d;
    cents = c;

    rationalize();
}

//operator+ - add s1 to s2 and return the result
//             in a new object
USDollar operator+(USDollar& s1, USDollar& s2)
{
   int cents   = s1.cents   + s2.cents;
   int dollars = s1.dollars + s2.dollars;
   return USDollar(dollars, cents);
}

//operator++ - increment the specified argument;
//             change the value of the provided object
USDollar& operator++(USDollar& s)
{
    s.cents++;
    s.rationalize();
    return s;
}

int main(int nArgc, char* pszArgs[])
{
   USDollar d1(1, 60);
   USDollar d2(2, 50);
   USDollar d3(0, 0);
```

Continued

Listing 27-1 *Continued*

```
// first demonstrate a binary operator
d3 = d1 + d2;
        d1.output();
cout << " + ";
        d2.output();
cout << " = ";
        d3.output();
cout << "\n";

// now check out a unary operator
++d3;
cout << "After incrementing it equals ";
        d3.output();
cout << "\n";
return 0;
}
```

The class USDollar is defined as having an integer number of dollars and an integer number of cents less than 100. Starting from the beginning of the class and working our way down, the functions operator+() and operator++() are declared in the USDollar to be friends of the class.

Remember that a class friend is a function that has access to the protected members of the class. Because operator+() **and** operator++() **are implemented as conventional nonmember functions, they must be declared as friends to be granted access to the protected members.**

The constructor for USDollar creates an object from an integer number of dollars and an integer number of cents, both of which may be defaulted. Once stored, the constructor calls the rationalize() function which normalizes the amount by adding the number of cents greater than 100 into the dollar amount. The output() function displays the USDollar to cout.

The operator+() has been defined with two arguments because addition is a binary operator (that is, it has two arguments). The operator+() starts by adding the dollar and cents values of both of its USDollar arguments. It then creates a new USDollar with these values and returns it to the caller.

Any operation on the value of a USDollar object should call rationalize() to make sure that number of cents does not exceed 100. The operation+() function calls rationalize() in the USDollar constructor.

The increment operator operator++() has only one argument. This function increments the number of cents in object s. The function then returns a reference to the object it just incremented.

The main() function displays the sum of two dollar amounts. It then increments the result of the addition and displays that. The results of executing USDollarAdd are shown below.

```
$1.60 + $2.50 = $4.10
After incrementing it equals $4.11
```

In use, the operators appear very natural. What could be simpler than d3 = d1 + d2 and ++d3?

Special considerations

There are a few special considerations to consider when overloading operators. First, C++ does not infer anything about the relationships between operators. Thus, operator+=() has nothing to do with either operator+() or operator=().

In addition, nothing forces operator+(USDollar&, USDollar&) to perform addition. You could have operator+() do anything you like; however, doing anything else besides addition is a REALLY BAD IDEA. People are accustomed to their operators performing in certain ways. They don't like them performing other operations.

Originally, there was no way to overload the prefix operator ++x separately from the postfix version x++. Enough programmers complained that the rule was made that operator++(ClassName) refers to the prefix operator and operator++(ClassName, int) refers to the postfix operator. A zero is always passed as the second argument. The same rule applies to operator--().

If you provide only one operator++() or operator--(), it is used for both the prefix and postfix versions. The standard for C++ says that a compiler doesn't have to do this, but most compilers do.

A More Detailed Look

Why does operator+() return by value, but operator++() returns by reference? This is not an accident, but a very important difference.

20 Min. To Go

The addition of two objects changes neither object. That is, a + b changes neither a nor b. Thus, operator+() must generate a temporary object in which it can store the result of the addition. This is why operator+() constructs an object and returns this object by value to the caller.

Specifically, the following would not work:

```
// this doesn't work
USDollar& operator+(USDollar& s1, USDollar& s2)
{
    s1.cents   += s2.cents;
    s1.dollars += s2.dollars;
    return s1;
}
```

because it modifies s1. Thus, after the addition s1 + s2, the value of s1 would be different. In addition, the following does not work:

```
// this doesn't work either
USDollar& operator+(USDollar& s1, USDollar& s2)
{
    int cents = s1.cents + s2.cents;
    int dollars = s1.dollars + s2.dollars;
    USDollar result(dollars, cents);
    return result;
}
```

Although this compiles without complaint, it generates incorrect results. The problem is that the returned reference refers to an object, result, whose scope is local to the function. Thus, result is out of scope by the time it can be used by the calling function.

Why not allocate a block of memory from the heap, as follows?

```
// this sort of works
USDollar& operator+(USDollar& s1, USDollar& s2)
{
    int cents = s1.cents + s2.cents;
    int dollars = s1.dollars + s2.dollars;
    return *new USDollar(dollars, cents);
}
```

This would be fine except that there is no mechanism to return the allocated block of memory to the heap. Such memory leaks are hard to trace. Memory slowly drains from the heap each time an addition is performed.

Returning by value forces the compiler to generate a temporary object of its own on the caller's stack. The object generated in the function is then copied to the object as part of the return from operator+(). But how long does the temporary returned from operator+() hang around? A temporary must remain valid until the "extended expression" in which it appears is complete. The extended expression is everything up to the semicolon.

For example, consider the following snippet:

```
SomeClass f();
LotsAClass g();
void fn()
{
    int i;
    i = f() + (2 * g());

    // ...both the temporary object which f() returns
    // and the temporary which g() returns are invalid here...
}
```

The temporary object returned by f() remains in existence while g() is invoked and while the multiplication is performed. This object becomes invalid at the semicolon.

To return to our USDollar example, were the temporary not retained, the following would not work:

```
d1 = d2 + d3 + ++d4;
```

The temporary created by the addition of d2 to d3 must remain valid while d4 is incremented or vice versa.

 C++ does not specify the order in which operators are performed. Thus, you do not know whether d2 + d3 or ++d4 is performed first. You must write your functions so that it doesn't matter.

Unlike operator+(), the unary operator++() does modify its argument. Thus, there is no need to create a temporary or to return by value. The argument provided can be returned to the caller by reference. In fact, the following function, which returns by value, has a subtle bug:

```
// this isn't 100% reliable either
USDollar operator++(USDollar& s)
{
    s.cents++;
    s.rationalize();
    return s;
}
```

By returning s by value, the function forces the compiler to generate a copy of the object. Most of the time, this is OK. But what happens in an admittedly unusual but legal expression such as ++(++a)? We would expect a to be incremented by 2. With the preceding definition, however, a is incremented by 1 and then a copy of a — not a itself — is incremented a second time.

The general rule is this: If the operator changes the value of its argument, accept the argument by reference so that the original may be modified and return the argument by reference in case the same object is used in a subsequent operation. If the operator does not change the value of either argument, create a new object to hold the results and return that object by value. The input arguments can always be referential to save time in a binary argument, but neither argument should be modified.

 There are binary operators that change the value of their arguments such as the special operators +=, *=, and so forth.

Operators as Member Functions

An operator can be a member function in addition to being implemented as a non-member function. Implemented in this way, our example USDollar class appears as shown in Listing 27-2. (Only the germane portions are shown.)

 The complete version of the program shown in Listing 27-2 is contained in the file USDollarMemberAdd found on the accompanying CD-ROM.

Listing 27-2
Implementing an Operator as a Member Function

```cpp
// USDollar - represent the greenback
class USDollar
{
  public:
    // construct a dollar object with an initial
    // dollar and cent value
    USDollar(int d = 0, int c = 0)
    {
        // store of the initial values locally
        dollars = d;
        cents = c;

        rationalize();
    }

    // rationalize - normalize the number of cents by
    //               adding a dollar for every 100 cents
    void rationalize()
    {
        dollars += (cents / 100);
        cents    %= 100;
    }

    // output- display the value of this object
    //         to the standard output object
    void output()
    {
        cout << "$"
             << dollars
             << "."
             << cents;
    }

    //operator+ - add the current object to s2 and
    //            return in a new object
```

Continued

Listing 27-2 *Continued*

```
    USDollar operator+(USDollar& s2)
    {
        int cents   = this->cents   + s2.cents;
        int dollars = this->dollars + s2.dollars;
        return USDollar(dollars, cents);
    }

    //operator++ - increment the current object
    USDollar& operator++()
    {
        cents++;
        rationalize();
        return *this;
    }

protected:
    int dollars;
    int cents;
};
```

The nonmember function operator+(USDollar, USDollar) has been rewritten as the member function USDollar::operator+(USDollar). At first glance, it appears that the member version has one fewer argument than the non-member version. If you think back, however, you'll remember that this is the hidden first argument to all member functions.

This difference is most obvious in USDollar::operator+() itself. Here I show the non-member and member versions in sequence.

```
// operator+ - the nonmember version
USDollar operator+(USDollar& s1, USDollar& s2)
{
    int cents   = s1.cents   + s2.cents;
    int dollars = s1.dollars + s2.dollars;
    USDollar t(dollars, cents);
    return t;
}
//operator+ - the member version
```

```
USDollar USDollar::operator+(USDollar& s2)
{
    int c = this->cents   + s2.cents;
    int d = this->dollars + s2.dollars;
    USDollar t(d, c);
    return t;
}
```

We can see that the functions are nearly identical. However, where the non-member version adds s1 and s2, the member version adds the "current object" — the one pointed at by this — to s2.

The member version of an operator always has one less argument than the non-member version — the left-hand argument is implicit.

10 Min. To Go

Yet Another Overloading Irritation

Just because you have overloaded operator*(double, USDollar&), that doesn't mean you have overloaded operator*(USDollar&, double). Because these two operators have different arguments, they have to be overloaded separately. This doesn't have to be as big a deal as it would at first appear.

First, there is nothing that keeps one operator from referring to the other. In the case of operator*(), we would probably do something similar to the following:

```
USDollar operator*(USDollar& s, double f)
{
    // ...implementation of function here...
}
inline USDollar operator*(double f, USDollar& s)
{
    //use the previous definition
    return s * f;
}
```

The second version merely calls the first version with the order of the operators reversed. Making it inline even avoids any extra overhead.

When Should an Operator be a Member?

There isn't much difference between implementing an operator as a member or as a nonmember with these exceptions:

1. The following operators must be implemented as member functions:

    = Assignment
    ( ) Function call
    [ ] Subscript
    -> Class membership

2. An operator such as the following could not be implemented as a member function.

    ```
    // operator*(double, USDollar&) - define in terms of
    //                        operator*(USDollar&, double)
    USDollar operator*(double factor, USDollar& s)
    {
        return s * factor;
    }
    ```

    To be a member function, operator(float, USDollar&) needs to be a member of class double. As noted earlier, we cannot add operators to the intrinsic classes. Thus, an operator in which the class name is the right-hand argument must be a nonmember function.

3. Operators that modify the object on which they operate, such as operator++(), should be made a member of the class.

Cast Operator

The cast operator can be overloaded as well. The USDollarCast program in Listing 27-3 demonstrates the definition and use of a cast operator that converts a USDollar object to and from a double value.

Listing 27-3
Overloading the Cast Operator

```
// USDollarCast - demonstrate how to write a cast
//                operator; in this case, the
//                cast operator converts a USDollar
```

```
//               to a double and the constructor
//               converts it back
#include <stdio.h>
#include <iostream.h>

class USDollar
{
  public:
    // constructor to build a dollar from a double
    USDollar(double value = 0.0);

    //the following function acts as a cast operator
    operator double()
    {
        return dollars + cents / 100.0;
    }

    // display - simple debug member function
    void display(char* pszExp, double dV)
    {
        cout << pszExp
            << " = $" << dollars << "." << cents
            << " (" << dV << ")\n";
    }

  protected:
    int dollars;
    int cents;
};

// constructor - divide the double value into its
//               integer and fractional parts
USDollar::USDollar(double value)
{
    dollars = (int)value;
    cents = (int)((value - dollars) * 100 + 0.5);
}
```

Continued

Listing 27-3 *Continued*

```
int main()
{
    USDollar d1(2.0), d2(1.5), d3, d4;

    //invoke cast operator explicitly...
    double dVal1 = (double)d1;
    d1.display("d1", dVal1);

    double dVal2 = (double)d2;
    d2.display("d2", dVal2);

    d3 = USDollar((double)d1 + (double)d2);
    double dVal3 = (double)d3;
    d3.display("d3 (sum of d1 and d2 w/ casts)", dVal3);

    //...or implicitly
    d4 = d1 + d2;
    double dVal4 = (double)d3;
    d4.display("d4 (sum of d1 and d2 w/o casts)", dVal4);

    return 0;
}
```

A cast operator is the word `operator` followed by the desired type. The member function `USDollar::operator double()` provides a mechanism for converting an object of class `USDollar` into a `double`. (For reasons that are beyond me, cast operators have no return type.) The `USDollar(double)` constructor provides the conversion path from a `double` back to a `USDollar` object.

As the preceding example shows, conversions using the cast operator can be invoked either explicitly or implicitly. Let's look at the implicit case carefully.

To make sense of the expression `d4 = d1 + d2` in the `USDollarCast` program, C++ goes through these gyrations:

1. First, C++ looks for a member function `USDollar::operator+(USDollar)`.

2. If that can't be found, it looks for the nonmember version of the same thing, `operator+(USDollar, USDollar)`.

3. Lacking that as well, it looks for an operator+() that it could use by
    converting one or the other arguments to a different type. Finally, it
    finds a match: If it converted both d1 and d2 to double, it could use the
    intrinsic operator+(double, double). Of course, it then has to convert
    the resulting double back to USDollar using the constructor.

The output from USDollarCast appears below. The USDollar::cast() function
enables the programmer to convert freely from USDollar objects to double values
and back.

```
d1 = $2.0 (2)
d2 = $1.50 (1.5)
d3 (sum of d1 and d2 w/ casts) = $3.50 (3.5)
d4 (sum of d1 and d2 w/o casts = $3.50 (3.5)
```

This demonstrates both the advantage and disadvantage of providing a cast
operator. Providing a conversion path from USDollar to double relieves programmers of the need to provide a complete set of operators. USDollar can just piggy-
back on the operators defined for double.

On the other hand, it also removes the ability of programmers to control which
operators are defined. By providing a conversion path to double, USDollar gets all
of double's operators whether they make sense or not. For example, I could just as
well have written d4 = d1 * d2. In addition, the extra conversions may not be the
most efficient process in the world. For example, the simple addition just noted
involves three type conversions with all of the attendant function calls, multipli-
cations, divisions, and so on.

Be careful not to provide two conversion paths to the same type. For example,
the following is asking for trouble:

```
class A
{
  public:
    A(B& b);
};
class B
{
  public:
    operator A();
};
```

Done!

If asked to convert an object of class B to an object of class A, the compiler will not know whether to use B's cast operator B:operatorA() or A's constructor A::A(B&), both of which start out with a B and end up making an A out of it.

Perhaps the result of the two conversion paths would be the same, but the compiler doesn't know that. C++ must know which conversion path you intend it to use. The compiler spits out an error if it can't determine this unambiguously,

REVIEW

Overloading a new class with the proper operators can lead to some simple and elegant application code. In most cases, however, operator overloading is not necessary. The following sessions examine two cases in which operator overloading is critical.

- Operator overloading enables the programmer to redefine the existing operators for the programmer's classes. However, the programmer cannot add new operators to nor change the syntax of existing operators.

- There is a significant difference between passing and returning an object by value and by reference. Depending on the operator, this difference may be critical.

- Operators that modify the object should be implemented as member functions. In addition, certain operators must be member functions. Operators in which the left-hand argument is an intrinsic type and not a user-defined class cannot be implemented as member functions. Otherwise, it doesn't make a lot of difference.

- The cast operator enables the programmer to inform C++ how a user-defined class object can be converted into an intrinsic type. For example, casting a Student to an int might return the student ID number (I didn't say that this conversion was a good idea, only that it is possible.) Having done so, user classes may be mixed with intrinsics in expressions, for example.

- User-defined operators offer the programmer the opportunity to create programs that are easier to read and maintain; however, custom operators can be tricky and should be used carefully.

Quiz Yourself

---

1. It is important that you be able to overload three operators for any given class. Which operators are they? (See the introduction.)

2. How could the following code ever make sense?

   ```
   USDollar dollar(100, 0);
   DM& mark = !dollar;
   ```

   (See "Why Do I Need to Overload Operators?")

3. Is there another way that I could have written the above without the use of programmer-defined operators, just using "normal" function calls. (See "Why Do I Need to Overload Operators?")

The Assignment Operator

Session Checklist

✔ Introduction to the assignment operator

✔ Why and when the assignment operator is necessary

✔ Similarities between the assignment operator and the copy
constructor

**30 Min.
To Go**

Whether or not you start out overloading operators, you need to learn to
overload the assignment operator fairly early. The assignment operator
can be overloaded for any user-defined class. By following the pattern
provided in this session, you will be generating your own version of operator=()
in no time.

Why Is Overloading the Assignment Operator Critical?

C++ provides a default definition for operator=() for all user-defined classes. This
default definition performs a member-by-member copy, like the default copy constructor. In the following example, each member of source is copied over the corresponding member in destination.

```
void fn()
{
   MyStruct source, destination;
   destination = source;
}
```

However, this default definition is not correct for classes that allocate resources, such as heap memory. The programmer must overload `operator=()` to handle the transfer of resources.

Comparison with copy constructor

The assignment operator is much like the copy constructor. In use, the two look almost identical:

```
void fn(MyClass &mc)
{
    MyClass newMC(mc);   // of course, this uses the
                         // copy constructor
    MyClass newerMC = mc;// less obvious, this also invokes
                         // the copy constructor
    MyClass newestMC;    // this creates a default object
    newestMC = mc;       // and then overwrites it with
                         // the argument passed
}
```

The creation of newMC follows the standard pattern of creating a new object as a mirror image of the original using the copy constructor `MyClass(MyClass&)`. Not so obvious is that C++ allows the second format in which newerMC is created using the copy constructor.

However, newestMC is created using the default (void) constructor and then overwritten by mc using the assignment operator. The difference is that when the copy constructor was invoked on newerMC, the object newerMC did not already exist. When the assignment operator was invoked on newestMC, it was already a MyClass object in good standing.

The rule is this: The copy constructor is used when a new object is being created. The assignment operator is used if the left-hand object already exists.

Like the copy constructor, an assignment operator should be provided whenever a shallow copy is not appropriate. (Session 20 has a full discussion of shallow versus deep constructors.) It suffices to say that a copy constructor and an assignment operator should be used when the class allocates and saves resources within the class so that you don't end up with two objects pointing to the same resource.

20 Min. To Go

How Do I Overload the Assignment Operator?

Overloading the assignment operator is similar to overloading any other operator. For example, Listing 28-1 is the program DemoAssign, which includes both a copy constructor and an assignment operator.

Remember that the assignment operator must be a member function of the class.

Listing 28-1
Overloading the Assignment Operator

```
// DemoAssign - demonstrate the assignment operator
#include <stdio.h>
#include <string.h>
#include <iostream.h>

// Name - a generic class used to demonstrate
//        the assignment and copy constructor
//        operators
class Name
{
  public:
    Name(char *pszN = 0)
    {
        copyName(pszN);
    }
    Name(Name& s)
    {
        copyName(s.pszName);
```

Continued

Part VI–Sunday Afternoon
Session 28

Listing 28-1 *Continued*

```
    }
    ~Name()
    {
        deleteName();
    }
    //assignment operator
    Name& operator=(Name& s)
    {
        //delete existing stuff...
        deleteName();
        //...before replacing with new stuff
        copyName(s.pszName);
        //return reference to existing object
        return *this;
    }

    // display - output the current object
    //           the default output object
    void display()
    {
        cout << pszName;
    }

  protected:
    void copyName(char *pszN);
    void deleteName();
    char *pszName;
};

// copyName() - allocate heap memory to store name
void Name::copyName(char *pszName)
{
    this->pszName = 0;
    if (pszName)
    {
        this->pszName = new char[strlen(pszName) + 1];
        strcpy(this->pszName, pszName);
    }
```

```
}

// deleteName() - return heap memory
void Name::deleteName()
{
    if (pszName)
    {
        delete pszName;
        pszName = 0;
    }
}

// displayNames - output function to reduce the
//                number of lines in main()
void displayNames(Name& pszN1, char* pszMiddle,
                  Name& pszN2, char* pszEnd)
{
    pszN1.display();
    cout << pszMiddle;
    pszN2.display();
    cout << pszEnd;
}

int main(int nArg, char* pszArgs[])
{
    // create two objects
    Name n1("Claudette");
    Name n2("Greg");
    displayNames(n1, " and ",
                 n2, " are newly created objects\n");

    // now make a copy of an object
    Name n3(n1);
    displayNames(n3, " is a copy of ",
                 n1, "\n");

    // make a copy of the object from the
    // address
```

Continued

Listing 28-1 *Continued*

```
        Name* pN = &n2;
        Name n4(*pN);
        displayNames(n4, " is a copy using the address of ",
                     n2, "\n");

        // overwrite n2 with n1
        n2 = n1;
        displayNames(n1, " was assigned to ",
                     n2, "\n");
        return 0;
}
```

Output:

```
Claudette and Greg are newly created objects
Claudette is a copy of Claudette
Greg is a copy using the address of Greg
Claudette was assigned to Claudette
```

The class Name retains a person's name in memory, which it allocates from the heap in the constructor. The constructors and destructor for class Name are similar to those presented in Sessions 19 and 20. The constructor Name(char*) copies the name given it to the pszName data member. This constructor also serves as the default constructor. The copy constructor Name(&Name) copies the name of the object passed to the name stored in the current object by calling copyName(). The destructor returns the pszName character string to the heap by calling deleteName().

The function main() demonstrates each of these member functions. The output from DemoAssign is shown at the end of Listing 28-1 above.

Take an extra look at the assignment operator. The function operator=() looks to all the world like a destructor immediately followed by a copy constructor. This is typical. Consider the assignment in the example n2 = n1. The object n2 already has a name associated with it ("Greg"). In the assignment, the memory that the original name occupies must be returned to the heap by calling deleteName() before new memory can be allocated into which to store the new name ("Claudette") by calling copyName().

The copy constructor did not need to call deleteName() because the object didn't already exist. Therefore, memory had not already been assigned to the object when the constructor was invoked.

In general, an assignment operator has two parts. The first part resembles a destructor in that it deletes the assets that the object already owns. The second part resembles a copy constructor in that it allocates new assets.

Two more details about the assignment operator

There are two more details about the assignment operator of which you need to be aware. First, the return type of operator=() is Name&. I didn't go into detail at the time, but the assignment operator is an operator like all others. Expressions involving the assignment operator have both a value and a type, both of which are taken from the final value of the left-hand argument. In the following example, the value of operator=() is 2.0 and the type is double.

```
double d1, d2;
void fn(double );
d1 = 2.0;
```

This is what enables the programmer to write the following:

```
d2 = d1 = 2.0
fn(d2 = 3.0);    // performs the assignment and passes the
                 // resulting value to fn()
```

The value of the assignment d1 = 2.0, 2.0, and type, double, are passed to the next assignment operator. In the second example, the value of the assignment d2 = 3.0 is passed to the function fn().

I could have made void the return type of Name::operator=(). However, if I did, the above example would no longer work:

```
void otherFn(Name&);
void fn()
{
   Name n1, n2, n3;

   // the following is only possible if the assignment
   // operator returns a reference to the current object
   n1 = n2 = n3;
   otherFn(n1 = n2);
}
```

The results of the assignment n1 = n2 is void, the return type of operator=(), which does not match the prototype of otherFn(). Declaring operator=() to return a reference to the "current" object and returning *this retains the semantics of the assignment operator for intrinsic types.

The second detail is that operator=() was written as a member function. Unlike other operators, the assignment operator cannot be overloaded with a non-member function. The special assignment operators, such as += and *=, have no special restrictions and can be nonmember functions.

An Escape Hatch

Providing your class with an assignment operator can add considerable flexibility to the application code. However, if this is too much for you, or if you can't make copies of your object, overloading the assignment operator with a protected function will keep anyone from accidentally making an unauthorized shallow copy. For example:

```
class Name
{
  //...just like before...
  protected:
    //assignment operator
    Name& operator=(Name& s)
    {
        return *this;
    }
};
```

With this definition, assignments such as the following are precluded:

```
void fn(Name &n)
{
    Name newN;
    newN = n;        //generates a compiler error -
                     //function has no access to op=()
}
```

This copy protection for classes saves you the trouble of overloading the assignment operator but reduces the flexibility of your class.

If your class allocates resources such as memory off of the heap you *must* either write a satisfactory assignment operator and copy constructor or make both protected to preclude the default provided by C++ from being used.

REVIEW

Assignment is the only operator that you must overload and then only under certain conditions. Fortunately, defining assignment for your class isn't too difficult if you follow the pattern laid out for you in this session.

- C++ provides a default assignment operator that performs member-by-member copies. This version of assignment is fine for many class types; however, classes that can be allocated resources must include a copy constructor and an overloaded assignment operator.

- The semantics of the assignment operator is generally similar to a destructor immediately followed by a copy constructor. The destructor removes whatever resources might already be in the class, while the copy constructor makes a deep copy of the resources assigned it.

- Declaring the assignment operator protected removes the danger but limits the class by precluding assignment to your class.

QUIZ YOURSELF

1. When do you need to include an assignment operator in your class? (See "Why is Overloading the Assignment Operator Critical?")

2. The return type of the assignment operator should always match the class type. Why? (See "Two More Details About the Assignment Operator.")

3. How can you avoid the need to write an assignment operator? (See "An Escape Hatch.")

Session Checklist

✔ Rediscovering stream I/O as an overloaded operator

✔ Using stream file I/O

✔ Using stream buffer I/O

✔ Writing your own inserters and extractors

✔ Behind the scenes with manipulators

**30 Min.
To Go**

S o far, our programs have performed all input from the `cin` input object and output through the `cout` output object. Perhaps you haven't really thought about it much, but this input/output technique is a subset of what is known as stream I/O.

This session explains stream I/O in more detail. I must warn you that stream I/O is too large a topic to be covered completely in a single session — entire books are devoted to this one topic. I can get you started, though, so that you can perform the main operations.

How Does Stream I/O Work?

Stream I/O is based on overloaded versions of operator>>() and operator<<().
The declaration of these overloaded operators is found in the include file iostream.h,
which we have included in our programs since Session 2. The code for these functions is included in the standard library, which your C++ program links with.

The following shows just a few of the prototypes appearing in iostream.h:

```
//for input we have:
istream& operator>>(istream& source, char *pDest);
istream& operator>>(istream& source, int  &dest);
istream& operator>>(istream& source, char &dest);
//...and so forth...

//for output we have:
ostream& operator<<(ostream& dest, char *pSource);
ostream& operator<<(ostream& dest, int   source);
ostream& operator<<(ostream& dest, char  source);
//...and so it goes...
```

When overloaded to perform I/O, operator>>() is called the *extractor* and
operator<<() is called the *inserter*.

Let's look in detail at what happens when I write the following:

```
#include <iostream.h>
void fn()
{
    cout << "My name is Randy\n";
}
```

The cout is an object of class ostream (more on this later). Thus, C++ determines
that the best match is the operator<<(ostream&, char*) function. C++ generates
a call to this function, the so-called char* inserter, passing the function the
ostream object cout and the string "My name is Randy\n" as arguments. That is, it
makes the call operator<<(cout, "My name is Randy\n"). The char* inserter
function, which is part of the standard C++ library, performs the requested output.

The ostream and istream classes form the base of a set of classes that connect
the application code with the outside world including input from and output to
the file system. How did the compiler know that cout is of class ostream? This
and a few other global objects are also declared in iostream.h. A list is shown in

Table 29-1. These objects are constructed automatically at program startup, before `main()` gets control.

Table 29-1
Standard Stream I/O Objects

Object	Class	Purpose
cin	istream	Standard input
cout	ostream	Standard output
cerr	ostream	Standard error output
clog	ostream	Standard printer output

Subclasses of `ostream` and `istream` are used for input and output to files and internal buffers.

The fstream Subclasses

The subclasses `ofstream`, `ifstream`, and `fstream` are defined in the include file fstream.h to perform stream input and output to a disk file. These three classes offer a large number of member functions. A complete list is provided with your compiler documentation, but let me get you started.

Class `ofstream`, which is used to perform file output, has several constructors, the most useful of which is the following:

```
ofstream::ofstream(char *pszFileName,
                   int mode = ios::out,
                   int prot = filebuff::openprot);
```

The first argument is a pointer to the name of the file to open. The second and third arguments specify how the file will be opened. The legal values for `mode` are listed in Table 29-2 and those for `prot` in Table 29-3. These values are bit fields that are ORed together (the classes `ios` and `filebuff` are both parent classes of `ostream`).

The expression `ios::out` **refers to a static data member of the class** `ios`.

Table 29-2

Constants Defined in ios to Control How Files Are Opened

Flag	Meaning
ios::ate	Append to the end of the file, if it exists
ios::in	Open file for input (implied for istream)
ios::out	Open file for output (implied for ostream)
ios::trunc	Truncate file if it exists (default)
ios::nocreate	If file doesn't already exist, return error
ios::noreplace	If file does exist, return error
ios::binary	Open file in binary mode (alternative is text mode)

Table 29-3

Values for prot in the ofstream Constructor

Flag	Meaning
filebuf::openprot	Compatibility sharing mode
filebuf::sh_none	Exclusive; no sharing
filebuf::sh_read	Read sharing allowed
filebuf::sh_write	Write sharing allowed

For example, the following program opens the file MYNAME and then writes some important and absolutely true information to that file:

```
#include <fstream.h>
void fn()
{
    //open the text file MYNAME for writing - truncate
    //whatever's there now
    ofstream myn("MYNAME");
    myn << "Randy Davis is suave and handsome\n"
        << "and definitely not balding prematurely\n";
}
```

The constructor ofstream::ofstream(char*) expects only a filename and provides defaults for the other file modes. If the file MYNAME already exists, it is truncated; otherwise, MYNAME is created. In addition, the file is opened in compatibility sharing mode.

Referring to Table 29-2, if I wanted to open the file in binary mode and append to the end of the file if the file already exists, I would create the ostream object as follows. (In binary mode, newlines are not converted to carriage returns and line feeds on output nor are carriage returns and line feeds converted back to newlines on input.)

```
void fn()
{
   //open the binary file BINFILE for writing; if it
   //exists, append to end of whatever's already there

   ofstream bfile("BINFILE", ios::binary | ios::ate);
   //...continue on as before...
}
```

The stream objects maintain state information about the I/O process. The member function bad() returns an error flag which is maintained within the stream classes. This flag is nonzero if the file object has an error.

Stream output predates the exception-based error-handling technique explained in Session 30.

To check whether the MYNAME and BINFILE files were opened properly in the earlier examples, I would have coded the following:

```
#include <fstream.h>
void fn()
{
   ofstream myn("MYNAME");
   if (myn.bad())         //if the open didn't work...
   {
      cerr << "Error opening file MYNAME\n";
      return;            //...output error and quit
   }
```

```
   myn << "Randy Davis is suave and handsome\n"
       << "and definitely not balding prematurely\n";
}
```

All attempts to output to an `ofstream` object that has an error have no effect until the error has been cleared by calling the member function `clear()`.

This last paragraph is meant quite literally — no output is possible as long as the error flag is nonzero.

The destructor for class `ofstream` automatically closes the file. In the preceding example, the file was closed when the function exited.

Class `ifstream` works much the same way for input, as the following example demonstrates:

```
#include <fstream.h>
void fn()
{
   //open file for reading; don't create the file
   //if it isn't there

   ifstream bankStatement("STATEMNT", ios::nocreate);
   if (bankStatement.bad())
   {
      cerr << "Couldn't find bank statement\n";
      return;
   }
   while (!bankStatement.eof())
   {
      bankStatement >> nAccountNumber >> amount;
      //...process this withdrawal
   }
}
```

The function opens the file **STATEMNT** by constructing the object `bankStatement`. If the file does not exist, it is not created. (We assume that the file has information for us, so it wouldn't make much sense to create a new, empty file.) If the object is bad (for example, if the object was not created), the function outputs an error message and exits. Otherwise, the function loops, reading the `nAccountNumber` and withdrawal `amount` until the file is empty (end-of-file is true).

An attempt to read an ifstream object that has the error flag set, indicating a previous error, returns immediately without reading anything.

Let me warn you one more time. Not only is nothing returned from reading an input stream that has an error, but the buffer comes back unchanged. This program can easily come to the false conclusion that it has just read the same value as previously. Further, eof() will never return a true on an input stream which has an error.

The class fstream is like an ifstream and an ofstream combined (in fact, it inherits from both). An object of class fstream can be created for input or output, or both.

**20 Min.
To Go**

The strstream Subclasses

The classes istrstream, ostrstream, and strstream are defined in the include file strstrea.h. (The file name appears truncated on the PC because MS-DOS allowed no more than 8 characters for a file name; GNU C++ uses the full file name strstream.h.) These classes enable the operations defined for files by the fstream classes to be applied to buffers in memory.

For example, the following code snippet parses the data in a character string using stream input:

```
#include <strstrea.h>
//Change to <strstream.h> for GNU C++
char* parseString(char *pszString)
{
    //associate an istrstream object with the input
    //character string
    istrstream inp(pszString, 0);

    //now input from that object
    int nAccountNumber;
    float dBalance;
    inp >> nAccountNumber >> dBalance;

    //allocate a buffer and associate an
    //ostrstream object with it
```

```
char* pszBuffer = new char[128];
ostrstream out(pszBuffer, 128);

//output to that object
out << "account number = " << nAccountNumber
    << ", dBalance = $" << dBalance
    << ends;

return pszBuffer;
}
```

This function appears to be much more complicated than it needs to be, however, parseString() is easy to code but very robust. The parseString() function can handle any type of messing input that the C++ extractor can handle and it has all of the formatting capability of the C++ inserter. In addition, the function is actually simple once you understand what it's doing.

For example, let's assume that pszString pointed to the following string:

"1234 100.0"

The function parseString() associates the object inp is with the input string by passing that value to the constructor for istrstream. The second argument to the constructor is the length of the string. In this example, the argument is 0, which means "read until you get to the terminating NULL."

The extractor statement inp >> first extracts the account number, 1234, into the int variable nAccountNumber exactly as if it were reading from the keyboard or a file. The second half extracts the value 100.0 into the variable dDBalance.

On the output side, the object out is associated with the 128 character buffer pointed to by pszBuffer. Here again, the second argument to the constructor is the length of the buffer — this value cannot be defaulted because ofstrstream has no way of determining the size of the buffer (there is no terminating NULL at this point). A third argument, which corresponds to the mode, defaults to ios::out. You can set this argument to ios::ate, however, if you want the output to append to the end of whatever is already in the buffer rather than overwrite it.

The function then outputs to the out object - this generates the formatted output in the 128 character buffer. Finally, the parseString() function returns the buffer. The locally defined inp and out objects are destructed when the function returns.

The constant ends **tacked on to the end of the inserter command is necessary to add the** null **terminator to the end of the buffer string.**

The buffer returned in the preceding code snippet given the example input contains the string.

"account number = 1234, dBalance = $100.00"

Comparison of string-handling techniques

The string stream classes represent an extremely powerful concept. This becomes clear in even a simple example. Suppose I have a function whose purpose is to create a descriptive string from a USDollar object.

My solution without using ostrstream appears in Listing 29-1.

Listing 29-1
Converting USDollar to a String for Output

```
// ToStringWOStream - convert USDollar to a string
//                    displaying the amount

#include <stdio.h>
#include <iostream.h>
#include <stdlib.h>
#include <string.h>

// USDollar - represent the greenback
class USDollar
{
  public:
    // construct a dollar object with an initial
    // dollar and cent value
    USDollar(int d = 0, int c = 0);

    // rationalize - normalize the number of nCents by
    //               adding a dollar for every 100 nCents
void rationalize()
```

Continued

Listing 29-1 *Continued*

```
    {
        nDollars += (nCents / 100);
        nCents   %= 100;
    }

// output- return as description of the
    //          current object
    char* output();

  protected:
    int nDollars;
    int nCents;
};

USDollar::USDollar(int d, int c)
{
    // store of the initial values locally
    nDollars = d;
    nCents = c;

    rationalize();
}

// output- return as description of the
//          current object
char* USDollar::output()
{
    // allocate a buffer
    char* pszBuffer = new char[128];

    // convert the nDollar and nCents values
    // into strings
    char cDollarBuffer[128];
    char cCentsBuffer[128];
    ltoa((long)nDollars, cDollarBuffer, 10);
    ltoa((long)nCents,   cCentsBuffer,  10);

    // make sure that the cents uses 2 digits
```

```
    if (strlen(cCentsBuffer) != 2)
        {
            char c = cCentsBuffer[0];
            cCentsBuffer[0] = '0';
            cCentsBuffer[1] = c;
cCentsBuffer[2] = '\0';
        }

    // now tack the strings together

    strcpy(pszBuffer, "$");
    strcat(pszBuffer, cDollarBuffer);
    strcat(pszBuffer, ".");
    strcat(pszBuffer, cCentsBuffer);

    return pszBuffer;
}

int main(int nArgc, char* pszArgs[])
{
    USDollar d1(1, 60);
    char* pszD1 = d1.output();
    cout << "Dollar d1 = " << pszD1 << "\n";
    delete pszD1;

    USDollar d2(1, 5);
    char* pszD2 = d2.output();
    cout << "Dollar d2 = " << pszD2 << "\n";
    delete pszD2;

    return 0;
}
```

Output

```
Dollar d1 = $1.60
Dollar d2 = $1.05
```

The ToStringWOStream program does not rely on stream routines to generate the text version of a USDollar object. The function USDollar::output() makes heavy use of the ltoa() function, which converts a long into a string, and of the strcpy() and strcat() functions to perform the direct string manipulation. The function must itself handle the case in which the number of cents is less than 10 and, therefore, occupies only a single digit. The output from this program is shown at the end of the listing.

The following represents a version of USDollar::output() that does use the ostrstream class.

This version is included in the ToStringWStreams program on the accompanying CD-ROM.

```
char* USDollar::output()
{
    // allocate a buffer
    char* pszBuffer = new char[128];

    // attach an ostream to the buffer
    ostrstream out(pszBuffer, 128);

    // convert into strings (setting the width
    // insures that the number of cents digit is
    // no less than 2
    out << "$" << nDollars << ".";
    out.fill('0');out.width(2);
    out << nCents << ends;

    return pszBuffer;
}
```

This version associates the output stream object out with a locally defined buffer. It then writes the necessary values using the common stream inserter and returns the buffer. Setting the width to 2 insures that the number of cents uses 2 digits when its value is less than 10. The output from this version is identical to the output shown in Listing 29-1. The out object is destructed when control exits the output() function.

I find the stream version of output()much easier to follow and less tedious than the earlier nonstream version.

Manipulators

So far, we have seen how to use stream I/O to output numbers and character strings using default formats. Usually the defaults are fine, but sometimes they don't cut it. True to form, C++ provides two ways to control the format of output.

First, invoking a series of member functions on the stream object can control the format. You saw this in the earlier `display()` member function where `fill('0')` and `width(2)` set the minimum width and left fill character of `ostrstream`.

The argument out **represents an ostream object. Because** ostream **is a base class for both** ofstream **and** ostrstream, **this function works equally well for output to a file or to a buffer maintained within the program!**

A second approach is through *manipulators*. Manipulators are objects defined in the include file iomanip.h to have the same effect as the member function calls. The only advantage to manipulators is that the program can insert them directly in the stream rather than having to resort to a separate function call.

The `display()` function rewritten to use manipulators appears as follows:

```
char* USDollar::output()
{
    // allocate a buffer
    char* pszBuffer = new char[128];

    // attach an ostream to the buffer
    ostrstream out(pszBuffer, 128);

    // convert into strings; this version uses
    // manipulators to set the fill and width
    out << "$" << nDollars << "."
        << setfill('0') << setw(2)
        << nCents << ends;

    return pszBuffer;
}
```

The most common manipulators and their corresponding meanings are listed in Table 29-4.

Table 29-4

Common Manipulators and Stream Format Control Functions

Manipulator	Member function	Description
dec	flags(10)	Set radix to 10
hex	flags(16)	Set radix to 16
Oct	flags(8)	Set radix to 8
setfill(c)	fill(c)	Set the fill character to c
setprecision(c)	precision(c)	Set display precision to c
setw(n)	width(n)	Set width of field to n characters *

Watch out for the width parameter (width() function and setw() manipulator). Most parameters retain their value until they are specifically reset by a subsequent call, but the width parameter does not. The width parameter is reset to its default value as soon as the next output is performed. For example, you might expect the following to produce two eight-character integers:

```
#include <iostream.h>
#include <iomanip.h>
void fn()
{
   cout << setw(8)        //width is 8...
        << 10             //...for the 10, but...
        << 20             //...default for the 20
        << "\n";
}
```

What you get, however, is an eight-character integer followed by a two-character integer. To get two eight-character output fields, the following is necessary:

```
#include <iostream.h>
#include <iomanip.h>
void fn()
{
   cout << setw(8)        //set the width...
        << 10
        << setw(8)        //...now reset it
<< 20
```

```
            << "\n";
    }
```

Which way is better, manipulators or member function calls? Member functions provide a bit more control because there are more of them. In addition, the member functions always return the previous setting so you know how to restore it (if you want). Finally, each function has a version without any arguments to return the current value, should you want to restore the setting later.

Even with all these features, the manipulators are the more common, probably because they look neat. Use whichever you prefer, but be prepared to see both in other people's code.

Custom Inserters

**10 Min.
To Go**

The fact that C++ overloads the left-shift operator to perform output is neat because you are free to overload the same operator to perform output on classes you define.

Consider the USDollar class once again. The following version of the class includes an inserter that generates the same output as the display() versions prior:

```
// Inserter - provide an inserter for USDollar

#include <stdio.h>
#include <iostream.h>
#include <iomanip.h>

// USDollar - represent the greenback
class USDollar
{
    friend ostream& operator<<(ostream& out, USDollar& d);
  public:
    // ...no change...
};

// inserter - output a string description
//            (this version handles the case of cents
//             less than 10)
ostream& operator<<(ostream& out, USDollar& d)
{
```

```
     char old = out.fill();
     out << "$"
         << d.nDollars
         << "."
         << setfill('0') << setw(2)
         << d.nCents;

     // replace the old fill character
     out.fill(old);

     return out;
}


int main(int nArgc, char* pszArgs[])
{
   USDollar d1(1, 60);
   cout << "Dollar d1 = " << d1 << "\n";

   USDollar d2(1, 5);
   cout << "Dollar d2 = " << d2 << "\n";

   return 0;
}
```

The inserter performs the same basic operations as the earlier `display()` functions outputting this time directly to the `ostream out` object passed to it. However, the `main()` function is even more straightforward than the earlier versions. This time the `USDollar` object can be inserted directly into the output stream.

You may wonder why the `operator<<()` returns the `ostream` object passed to it. This is what enables the insertion operations to be chained. Because `operator<<()` binds from left to right, the following expression

```
     USDollar d1(1, 60);
     cout << "Dollar d1 = " << d1 << "\n";
```

is interpreted as

```
     USDollar d1(1, 60);
     ((cout << "Dollar d1 = ") << d1) << "\n";
```

The first insertion outputs the string "Dollar d1 = " to cout. The result of this expression is the object cout, which is then passed to operator<<(ostream&,

USDollar&). It is important that this operator return its ostream object so that the object can be passed to the next inserter, which outputs the newline character "\n".

Smart Inserters

We often would like to make the inserter smart. That is, we would like to say cout << baseClassObject and let C++ choose the proper subclass inserter in the same way that it chooses the proper virtual member function. Because the inserter is not a member function, we cannot declare it virtual directly.

We can easily sidestep the problem by making the inserter depend on a virtual display() member function as demonstrated by the VirtualInserter program in Listing 29-2.

Listing 29-2
VirtualInserter Program

```
// VirtualInserter - base USDollar on the base class
//                   Currency. Make the inserter virtual
//                   by having it rely on a virtual
//                   display() routine

#include <stdio.h>
#include <iostream.h>
#include <iomanip.h>

// Currency - represent any currency
class Currency
{
    friend ostream& operator<<(ostream& out, Currency& d);
  public:
    Currency(int p = 0, int s = 0)
    {
        nPrimary = p;
        nSecondary = s;
    }

    // rationalize - normalize the number of nCents by
    //               adding a dollar for every 100 nCents
```

Continued

Listing 29-2 *Continued*

```cpp
    void rationalize()
    {
        nPrimary   += (nSecondary / 100);
        nSecondary %= 100;
    }

    // display - display the object to the
    //           given ostream object
    virtual ostream& display(ostream&) = 0;

  protected:
    int nPrimary;
    int nSecondary;
};

// inserter - output a string description
//            (this version handles the case of cents
//            less than 10)
ostream& operator<<(ostream& out, Currency& c)
{
    return c.display(out);
}

// define dollar to be a subclass of currency
class USDollar : public Currency
{
  public:
    USDollar(int d, int c) : Currency(d, c)
    {
    }

    // supply the display routine
    virtual ostream& display(ostream& out)
    {
        char old = out.fill();
        out << "$"
            << nPrimary
            << "."
```

```
            << setfill('0') << setw(2)
            << nSecondary;

        // replace the old fill character
        out.fill(old);

        return out;
    }
};

void fn(Currency& c, char* pszDescriptor)
{
    cout << pszDescriptor << c << "\n";
}

int main(int nArgc, char* pszArgs[])
{
    // invoke USDollar::display() directly
    USDollar d1(1, 60);
    cout << "Dollar d1 = " << d1 << "\n";

    // invoke the same function virtually
    // through the fn() function
    USDollar d2(1, 5);
    fn(d2, "Dollare d2 = ");

    return 0;
}
```

The class Currency defines a nonmember, and therefore nonpolymorphic, inserter function. However, rather than perform any real work, this inserter relies on a virtual member function display() to perform all the real work. The subclass USDollar need only provide the display() function to complete the task. This version of the program produces the same output shown at the bottom of Listing 29-1.

That the insertion operation is, indeed, polymorphic is demonstrated by creating the output function fn(Currency&, char*). The fn() function does not know what type of currency it is receiving and, yet, displays the currency passed it using the rules for a USDollar. main() outputs d1 directly and d2 through this added function fn(). The virtual output from fn() appears the same as its nonpolymorphic brethren.

Other subclasses of `Currency`, such as `DMMark` or `FFranc`, can be created even though they have different display rules by simply providing the corresponding `display()` function. The base code could continue to use `Currency` with impunity.

But Why the Shift Operators?

You might ask, "Why use the shift operators for stream I/O? Why not use another operator?"

The left-shift operator was chosen for several reasons. First, it's a binary operator. This means the `ostream` object can be made the left-hand argument and the output object the right-hand argument. Second, left shift is a very low priority operator. Thus, expressions such as the following work as expected because addition is performed before insertion:

```
cout << "a + b" << a + b << "\n";
```

Third, the left-shift operator binds from left to right. This is what enables us to string output statements together. For example, the previous function is interpreted as follows:

```
#include <iostream.h>
void fn(int a, int b)
{
    ((cout << "a + b") << a + b) << "\n";
}
```

Done!

But having said all this, the real reason is probably just that it looks really neat. The double less than, <<, looks like something moving out of the code, and the double greater than, >, looks like something coming in. And, hey, why not?

REVIEW

I began this session warning you that stream I/O is too complex to cover in a single chapter of any book, but this introduction should get you started. You can refer to your compiler documentation for a complete listing of the various member functions you can call. In addition, the relevant include files, such as iostream.h and iomanip.h, contain prototypes with explanatory comments for all the functions.

- Stream output is based on the classes `istream` and `ostream`.
- The include file iostream.h overloads the left-shift operator to perform output to `ostream` and overloads the right-shift operator to perform input from `istream`.
- The `fstream` subclass is used to perform file I/O.
- The `strstream` subclass performs I/O to internal memory buffers using the same insertion and extraction operators.
- The programmer may overload the insertion and extraction operators for the programmer's own classes. These operators can be made polymorphic through the use of intermediate functions.
- The manipulator objects defined in iomanip.h may be used to invoke `stream` format functions.

QUIZ YOURSELF

1. What are the two operators << and >> called when used for stream I/O? (See "How Does String I/O Work?")
2. What is the base class of the two default I/O objects `cout` and `cin`? (See "How Does String I/O Work?")
3. What is the class `fstream` used for? (See "The fstream Subclasses.")
4. What is the class `strstream` used for? (See "The strstream Subclasses.")
5. What manipulator sets numerical output into hexadecimal mode? What is the corresponding member function? (See "Manipulators.")

Session Checklist:

✔ Returning error conditions

✔ Using exceptions, a new error-handling mechanism

✔ Throwing and catching exceptions

✔ Overloading an exception class

I n addition to the ubiquitous error-message approach to error reporting, C++
includes an easier and far more reliable error-handling mechanism. This
technique, known as exception handling, is the topic of this session.

**30 Min.
To Go**

Conventional Error Handling

An implementation of the common example factorial function appears as follows.

**This factorial function appears on the accompanying CD-ROM in a
program called FactorialProgram.cpp.**

```
// factorial - calculate the factorial of nBase which
//              is equal to nBase * (nBase - 1) *
//              (nBase - 2) * ...
int factorial(int nBase)
{
    // begin with an "accumulator" of 1
    int nFactorial = 1;

    // loop from nBase down to one, each time
    // multiplying the previous accumulator value
    // by the result
    do
    {
        nFactorial *= nBase;
    } while (--nBase > 1);

    // return the result
    return nFactorial;
}
```

While simple enough, this function is lacking a critical feature: the factorial of zero is known to be 1, while the factorial of negative numbers is not defined. The above function should include a test for a negative argument and, if so, indicate an error.

The classic way to indicate an error in a function is to return some value that cannot otherwise be returned by the function. For example, it is not possible for the returned value from factorial to be negative. Thus, if passed a negative number, the factorial function could return a –1. The calling function can check the returned value — if it's a negative, the calling function knows that an error occurred and can take the appropriate action (whatever that may be).

This is the way that error processing has been done ever since the early days of FORTRAN. Why change it now?

Why Do I Need a New Error Mechanism?

There are several problems with the error-return approach to error reporting. First, while it's true that the result of a factorial cannot be negative, other functions are not so lucky. Take logarithm for example. You can't take the log of a negative number either, but logarithms can be either negative or positive — there is no value that could be returned from a `logarithm()` function that isn't a legal logarithm.

Second, there's just so much information you can store in an integer. Maybe –1 for "argument is negative" and –2 for "argument too large," but if the argument is too large, there is no way to store the value passed. Knowing that value might help to debug the problem. There's no place to store any more than the single error-return value.

Third, the processing of error returns is optional. Suppose someone writes `factorial()` so that it dutifully checks the argument and returns a negative number if the argument is out of range. If the code that calls that function doesn't check the error return, it doesn't do any good. Sure, we make all kinds of menacing threats such as, "You will check your error returns or else . . . " but we all know that the language (and our boss) can't do anything to us if we don't.

Even if I do check the error return from `factorial()` or any other function, what can my function do with the error? Probably nothing more than output an error message of its own and return another error indication to its calling function. Soon the code looks like this:

```
// call some function, check the error return,
// handle it, and return
int nErrorRtn = someFunc();
if (nErrorRtn)
{
    errorOut("Error on call to someFunc()");
    return MY_ERROR_1;
}

nErrorRtn = someOtherFunc();
if (nErrorRtn )
{
    errorOut("Error on call to someOtherFunc()");
    return MY_ERROR_2;
}
```

This mechanism has several problems:

- It's highly repetitive;
- It forces the user to invent and keep track of numerous error return indications; and
- It mixes the error-handling code in the normal code flow, thereby obscuring both.

These problems don't seem so bad in this simple example, but the complexity rises rapidly as the complexity of the calling code increases. After a while, there's actually more code written to handle errors, checking pesky codes, than the "real" code.

The net result is that error-handling code doesn't get written to handle all the conditions it should.

How Do Exceptions Work?

20 Min. To Go

C++ introduces a totally new mechanism for capturing and handling errors. Called *exceptions,* this mechanism is based on the keywords try, throw, and catch. In outline, it works like this: a function tries (try) to get through a piece of code. If the code detects a problem, it throws an error indication that the function can catch.

Listing 30-1 demonstrates how exceptions work.

Listing 30-1
Exceptions in Action

```
// FactorialExceptionProgram - output the factorial
//                             function with exception-
//                             based error handling
#include <stdio.h>
#include <iostream.h>

// factorial - calculate the factorial of nBase which
//             is equal to nBase * (nBase - 1) *
//             (nBase - 2) * ...
int factorial(int nBase)
{
    // if nBase < 0...
    if (nBase <= 0)
    {
        // ...throw an error
        throw "Illegal argument exception";
    }

    int nFactorial = 1;
    do
    {
        nFactorial *= nBase;
```

```
        } while (--nBase > 1);

        // return the result
        return nFactorial;
    }

    int main(int nArgc, char* pszArgs[])
    {
        // call factorial in a loop. Catch any exceptions
        // that the function might generate
        try
        {
            for (int i = 6; ; i--)
            {
                cout << "factorial("
                     << i
                     << ") = "
                     << factorial(i)
                     << "\n";
            }
        }
        catch(char* pErrorMsg)
        {
            cout << "Detected an error of:"
                 << pErrorMsg
                 << "\n";
        }
        return 0;
    }
```

The main() function begins with a block marked by the keyword try. One or more catch blocks appear immediately after the try block. The try keyword is followed by a single argument that looks similar to a function definition.

Within the try block, main() can do whatever it wants. In this case, main() enters a loop that calculates the factorial of progressively smaller numbers. Eventually the program passes a negative number to the factorial() function.

When our clever factorial() function detects a bogus request, it throws a character string containing a description of the error using the keyword throw. At that point, C++ begins looking for a catch block whose argument matches the object thrown. It does not finish the remainder of the try block. If C++ doesn't find a `catch` in the current function, it returns to the point of the call and continues the search there. This process is repeated until a matching catch block is found or control passes out of `main()`.

In this example, the thrown error message is caught by the phrase at the bottom of `main()`, which outputs the message. The next statement executed is the return command, which terminates the program.

Why is the exception mechanism an improvement?

The exception mechanism addresses the problems inherent in the error-return mechanism by removing the error-processing path from the normal code path. Further, exceptions make error handling obligatory. If your function doesn't handle the thrown exception, then control passes up the chain of called functions until C++ finds a function that does handle the thrown exception. This also gives you the flexibility to ignore errors that you can't do anything about anyway. Only the functions that can actually correct the problem need to catch the exception. So how does this work?

Trying to Catch the Details Thrown at You

Let's take a closer look at the steps that the code goes through to handle an exception. When a throw occurs, C++ first copies the thrown object to some neutral place. It then looks for the end of the current `try` block. C++ then looks for a matching `catch` somewhere up the chain of function calls. The process is called *unwinding the stack*.

An important feature of stack unwinding is that as each stack is unwound any objects that go out of scope are destructed just as if the function had executed a return statement. This keeps the program from losing assets or leaving objects dangling.

Listing 30-2 is an example program that unwinds the stack.

Listing 30-2
Unwinding the Stack

```
#include <iostream.h>
class Obj
{
  public:
    Obj(char c)
```

```
    {
        label = c;
        cout << "Constructing object " << label << endl;
    }
  ~Obj()
    {
        cout << "Destructing object "  << label << endl;
    }

  protected:
    char label;
};

void f1();
void f2();

int main(int, char*[])
{
    Obj a('a');
    try
    {
        Obj b('b');
        f1();
    }
    catch(float f)
    {
        cout << "Float catch" << endl;
    }
    catch(int i)
    {
        cout << "Int catch" << endl;
    }
    catch(...)
    {
        cout << "Generic catch" << endl;
    }
    return 0;
}
```

Continued

Listing 30-2 *Continued*

```
void f1()
{
    try
    {
        Obj c('c');
        f2();
    }
    catch(char* pMsg)
    {
        cout << "String catch" << endl;
    }
}

void f2()
{
    Obj d('d');
    throw 10;
}
```

Output:

```
Constructing object a
Constructing object b
Constructing object c
Constructing object d
Destructing object d
Destructing object c
Destructing object b
Int catch
Destructing object a
```

First, are the four objects a, b, c, and d being constructed as control passes through each declaration before f2() throws the int 10. Because there is no try block defined within f2(), C++ unwinds f2()'s stack, causing object d to be destructed. f1() defines a try block, but it's only catch phrase is designed to handle char*, which does not match the int thrown, so C++ continues looking. This unwinds f1()'s stack resulting in object c being destructed.

Back in main(), C++ finds another try block. Exiting that block causes object |b to go out of scope. The first catch phrase is designed to catch float, which is skipped because it doesn't match our `int`. The next catch phrase matches our `int` exactly, so control stops there. The final catch phrase, which would catch any type of object thrown, is skipped because a matching catch phrase was already found.

> **A function declared as** `fn(...)` **accepts any number of any type of arguments. The same applies to** `catch` **phrases; a** `catch(...)` **catches anything thrown at it.**

**10 Min.
To Go**

What kinds of things can I throw?

A C++ program can throw just about any type of object it wants. C++ uses simple rules for finding the appropriate catch phrase.

C++ searches the `catch` phrase that appears after the first `try` block that it finds. Each `catch` phrase is searched in order, looking for one that matches the object thrown. A "match" is defined using the same rules as used to define an argument match in an overloaded function. If no matching catch phrase is found, then the code continues to the next higher-level `try` block in an ever-outward spiral, until an appropriate catch is found. If no catch phrase is found, the program terminates.

The earlier `factorial()` function threw a character string; that is, it threw an object of type `char*`. The corresponding catch declaration matched by promising to process an object of type `char*`. However, a function can throw just about any type of object it wants to throw.

A program may throw the result of any expression. This means that you can throw as much information as you want. Consider the following class definition:

```cpp
#include <iostream.h>
#include <string.h>

// Exception - generic exception-handling class
class Exception
{
  public:
    // construct an exception object with a description
    // of the problem along with the file and line #
    // where the problem occurred
    Exception(char* pMsg, char* pFile, int nLine)
    {
        this->pMsg = new char[strlen(pMsg) + 1];
```

```
        strcpy(this->pMsg, pMsg);

        strncpy(file, pFile, sizeof file);
        file[sizeof file - 1] = '\0';
        lineNum = nLine;
    }

    // display - output the contents of the
    //           current object to the output stream
    virtual void display(ostream& out)
    {
        out << "Error <" << pMsg << ">\n";
        out << "Occured on line #"
            << lineNum
            << ", file "
            << file
            << endl;
    }

protected:
    // error message
    char* pMsg;

    // file name and line number where error occurred
    char file[80];
    int lineNum;
};
```

The corresponding throw looks like this:

```
throw Exception("Negative argument to factorial",
                __FILE__,
                __LINE__);
```

FILE__ and __LINE__ are intrinsic #defines that are set to the name of the source file and the current line number within that file, respectively.

The corresponding catch is straightforward:

```
void myFunc()
{
    try
    {
        //...whatever calls
    }

    // catch an Exception object
    catch(Exception x)
    {
        // use the built-in display member function
        // to display the object contents to the
        // error stream
        x.display(cerr);
    }
}
```

The catch snags the Exception object and then uses the built-in display() member function to display the error message.

 The version of factorial using the Exception class is contained on the accompanying CD-ROM as FactorialThrow.cpp.

The output from executing the factorial program is shown below.

```
factorial(6) = 720
factorial(5) = 120
factorial(4) = 24
factorial(3) = 6
factorial(2) = 2
factorial(1) = 1
Error <Negative argument to factorial>
Occurred on line #59,
        file C:\wecc\Programs\lesson30\FactorialThrow.cpp
```

The Exception class represents a generic error-reporting class. However, this class can be extended by subclassing from it. For example, I might define an InvalidArgumentException class that stores off the value of the invalid argument, in addition to the message and location of the error:

```cpp
class InvalidArgumentException : public Exception
{
  public:
    InvalidArgumentException(int arg, char* pFile, int nLine)
      : Exception("Invalid argument", pFile, nLine)
    {
        invArg = arg;
    }

    // display - output the contents of the current
    //           object to the specified output object
    virtual void display(ostream& out)
    {
        // rely on the base class to output its information
        Exception::display(out);

        // now output our portion
        out << "Argument was "
            << invArg
            << "\n";
    }

  protected:
    int invArg;
};
```

The calling function automatically handles the new InvalidArgumentException because an InvalidArgumentException is an Exception and the display() member function is polymorphic.

The InvalidArgumentException::display() **relies on the base class** Exception **to output that portion of the object.**

Chaining Catch Phrases

A program may extend its error-handling flexibility by attaching multiple catch phrases to the same try block. The following code snippet demonstrates the concept:

```
void myFunc()
{
    try
    {
        //...whatever calls
    }
    // catch a simple character string
    catch(char* pszString)
    {
        cout << "Error:" << pszString << "\n";
    }
    // catch an Exception object
    catch(Exception x)
    {
        x.display(cerr);
    }

    // ...execution continues here...
}
```

In this example, if the thrown object is a simple string, it is captured by the first catch phrase, which outputs the string to the console. If the object is not a character string, it is compared to the Exception class. If the object is an Exception or any subclass of Exception, it is processed by the second phrase.

Because this process continues serially, the programmer must start with the more specific object type and continue to the more general. Thus, to do the following is a mistake:

```
void myFunc()
{
    try
    {
        //...whatever calls
    }
    catch(Exception x)
```

```
    {
        x.display(cerr);
    }
    catch(InvalidArgumentException x)
    {
        x.display(cerr);
    }
}
```

Done!

Because an `InvalidArgumentException` is an `Exception`, control will never reach the second catch phrases.

The compiler does not catch this coding mistake.

Even if `display()` were a virtual function, it wouldn't make any difference in the above example. The `Exception` catch phrase would call the `display()` function to match the object's run-time class.

Because the generic `catch(...)` phrase catches any exception passing its way, it must appear last in the list of `catch` phrases. Any `catch` appearing after a generic `catch` is unreachable.

REVIEW

The C++ exception mechanism provides a simple, controlled, and extensible mechanism for handling errors. It avoids the logical complexity that can occur using the standard error-return mechanism. It also makes certain that objects are destructed properly as they go out of scope.

- The conventional error-handling technique of returning an otherwise illegal value to indicate the type of error has severe limitations. First, there is a limited amount of information that can be encoded. Second, the calling function is forced to handle the error, either by processing it or by returning the error, whether it can do anything about the error or not. Finally, many functions have no illegal value that can be returned.

- The exception-error technique enables functions to return a virtually unlimited amount of data. In addition, if a calling function chooses to ignore an error, the exception continues to propagate up the chain of functions until it finds one that can handle the error.
- Exceptions can be subclasses, giving the programmer increased flexibility.
- Catch phrases may be chained to enable the calling function to handle different types of errors differently.

QUIZ YOURSELF

1. Name three limitations of the error-return technique. (See "Conventional Error Handling.")
2. Name the three new keywords used by the exception handling technique. (See "How Do Exceptions Work.")

PART

VI

Sunday Afternoon

1. Supply the appropriate copy con-
    structor and assignment operator

for the `AssignProblem` module. A resource must be opened with the
`nValue` stored in the `MyClass` object and that resource object must

- Be opened before it is valid

- Be closed after it is opened

- Be closed before it can be reopened

Assume that the prototyped functions are defined somewhere else.

```
// AssignProblem - demonstrate the assignment operator
#include <stdio.h>
#include <iostream.h>

class MyClass;

// Resource - the function open() prepares
//            the object for use while the
//            function close() "puts it away";
//            a resource must be closed before
//            it can be reopened
class Resource
{
  public:
    Resource();
    void open(int nValue);
    void close();
};
```

```cpp
// MyClass - should be opened before use and closed
//            after use
class MyClass
{
  public:
    MyClass(int nValue)
    {
        resource.open(nValue);
    }

    ~MyClass()
    {
        resource.close()
    }

    //supply copy constructor and assignment operator
    MyClass(MyClass& mc)
    {
        // ...what goes here?
    }
    MyClass& operator=(MyClass& s)
    {
        // ...and what goes here?
    }

  protected:
    Resource resource;

    // the value to pass to resource.open()
    int nValue;
};
```

2. Write an inserter for the following program, which outputs lastname, firstname (student ID) for the following Student class.

```
// StudentInserter -

#include <stdio.h>
#include <iostream.h>
#include <string.h>

// Student - your typical beer-swilling undergraduate
class Student
{
  public:
    Student(char* pszFName, char* pszLName, int nSSNum)
    {
        strncpy(szFName, pszFName, 20);
        strncpy(szLName, pszLName, 20);
        this->nSSNum = nSSNum;
    }

  protected:
    char szLName[20];
    char szFName[20];
    int  nSSNum;
};

int main(int nArgc, char* pszArgs[])
{
    Student student("Kinsey", "Lee", 1234);
    cout << "My friend is " << student << "\n";
    return 0;
}
```

APPENDIX

A

Answers to Part Reviews

Friday Evening Review Answers

1.
```
1.  Grab jack handle
2.  While car not on ground
3.      Move jack handle down
4.      Move jack handle up
5.  Release jack handle
```

This solution is simpler than the program presented for removing wheels. There is no need to begin by grabbing the jack. Because the car is already in the air, being held up by the jack, we can assume that we know where the jack is.

The loop in steps 2 through 4 moves the jack handle up and down until the car has been lowered to the ground. Step 5 completes the program by releasing the handle of the jack so that the processor's hand is available for the next steps.

2. Removing the minus sign between the 212 and 32 causes Visual C++ to generate the incorrect "missing ;" error message.

3. I fixed the problem by adding a semicolon after the 212 and rebuilt. Visual C++ built the "corrected" program without complaint.

4. The resulting corrected program calculates a Fahrenheit temperature of 244, which is obviously incorrect.

5. Apparently both "nFactor = 212;" and "32;" are legal commands. However, the resulting incorrect value for *nFactor* results in an incorrect conversion calculation.

6. Forgetting a minus sign is an understandable mistake for a poor typist such as I. Had Visual C++ corrected what it thought was a simple missing semicolon, the program would have compiled and executed without complaint. I would have had to search through the program to find the error in my calculations. Such an error would have thrown suspicion on the formula used to convert Celsius degrees to Fahrenheit when a simple typo is the real problem. This represents a waste of time when the error message generated by Visual C++, although incorrect, vectors my attention directly to the problem.

7. Rebuilding Conversion.cpp after removing the quote symbol generates this error message:

```
Conversion.cpp(29) Error: unterminated string or character
constant
```

This error message indicates that GNU C++ thinks that the error occurred on line 29. (That's the significance of the "29" in the error message itself.)

8. Because GNU C++ didn't see a quote symbol to terminate the string on line 26, it thought that the string continued to the next quote that it saw, which was on line 29. (This quote is actually the beginning of another string, but GNU C++ doesn't know that.)

9. If GNU C++ were to try to fix the quote problem on its own, it might do one of two things. It could add an extra quote at the point that it detected the problem, which is the open quote on line 29, thinking that the open quote should be terminated. Alternatively, it could remove the quote that it found there thinking that it was put there in error. Both solutions "fix" the problem to the extent that rebuilding the resulting program generates no build errors. Try it: add an extra quote to line 29 or remove the open quote that is there and rebuild. As it turns out, both solutions work.

10. With an input of 100 degrees Celsius, the program generates the completely nonsensical output shown below.

```
C:\wecc\Programs\lesson3>exit
Enter the temperature in Celsius:100
Fahrenheit value is::
```

```
                 cout << nFahrenheit;

                 cout << Time to return_
```

11. The GNU C++ solution masks the real problem. The resulting output from the program is nonsensical and, therefore, gives no hint as to the real problem. With such output, it is difficult to even get started fixing the problem unless the programmer knows that there is a syntax error in the source code that was "fixed" by the compiler.

    (Fortunately, the output from this program does lead the knowledgeable programmer in the direction of the problem; however, not nearly as well as an error message during the build.)

12. In general, when a compiler attempts to fix a problem automatically it ends up creating a new problem that is more difficult to trace back to the original problem.

13. **a.** Yes

    b. No — variables must begin with a letter.

    c. No — variable names may not contain spaces.

    d. Yes — variable names may contain digits.

    e. No — variables cannot begin with an ampersand.

14.
```
// Sum      - output the sum of three integers
//            input from the user
#include <stdio.h>
#include <iostream.h>

int main(int nArg, char* nArgs[])
{
    int nValue1;
    int nValue2;
    int nValue3;
    cout << "Input three numbers (follow each with newline)";
    cout << "#1:";
    cin  >> nValue1;

    cout << "#2:";
    cin  >> nValue2;

    cout << "#3:";
```

```
    cin  >> nValue3;

    cout << "The sum is:";
    cout << nValue1 + nValue2 + nValue3;

    cout << "\n";
    return 0;
}
```

Extra credit:

replace

```
 cout << nValue1 + nValue2 + nValue3;
```

with

```
 cout << (nValue1 + nValue2 + nValue3)/3;
```

Saturday Morning Review Answers

1. **a.** Dividing nTons by 1.1 causes a rounding-off error.

    b. 2/1.1 equals 1.8 which rounds off to 1. The function returns 1000 kg.

    c. The result of dividing 2 by 1.1 is a double-precision floating point. Assigning this value to the integer nLongTons results in a demotion that the compiler should note.

    Bonus: "Assign double to int. Possible loss of significance." or words to that effect.

2. The following function suffers much less from rounding off than its predecessor:

    ```
    int ton2kg(int nTons)
    {
    return (nTons * 1000) / 1.1;
    }
    ```

3. **a.** 80 tons converts to roughly 4,500,000,000 g. This is beyond the range of an int on an Intel-based PC.

    b. The only possible solution is to return a float or a double instead of an int. The range of a float is much larger than that of an int.

4. **a.** false

   b. true

   c. true

   d. indeterminate but probably true

   You cannot depend on two independently calculated floating-point variables to be equal.

   e. false

   The value of n4 is 4. Because the left hand side of the && is false, the right hand side is not evaluated and the == is never executed (see section on short circuit evaluation)

5. **a.** 0x5D

   b. 93

   c. 1011 1010$_2$

   It's easiest to perform the addition in binary. Just remember the rules:

   1. 0+0 → 0

   2. 1+0 → 1

   3. 0 + 1 → 1

   4. 1 + 1 → 0 carry the 1.

   Alternatively convert 93 * 2 = 186 back to binary.

   Bonus: 0101 1101$_2$ * 2 has the same bit pattern shifted to the left one position and a 0 shoved into the empty position on the right.

   d. 0101 1111$_2$

   Convert 2 into binary 0000 0010$_2$ and OR the two numbers together.

   e. true

   The 0000 0010$_2$ bit is not set; thus, ANDing the two together results in a 0.

6. Remember that C++ ignores all white space, including tabs. Thus, while the else clause appears to belong to the outer if statement, it actually belongs with the inner if statement, as if it had been written:

```
int n1 = 10;
if (n1 > 11)
{
    if (n1 > 12)
```

```
    {
        n1 = 0;
    }
    else
    {
        n1 = 1;
    }
}
```

The outer if statement has no else clause and, thus, n1 remains unchanged.

7. Because the n1 is not less than 5, the body of the while() control is never executed. In the case of the do...while() control, the body is executed once even though n1 is no less than 5. In this case, n1 ends up with a value of 11.

The difference between the two loops is that the do...while() always executes its body at least once, even if the conditional clause is false from the beginning.

8.  ```
    double cube(double d)
    {
        return d * d * d;
    }
    ```

Because the Intel processor in your PC handles integers and floating-point variables differently, the machine code generated by the two functions cube(int) and cube(double) are completely different.

9. The expression cube(3.0) matches the function cube(double); thus, cube(double) is passed the double value 3.0 and returns the double value 9.0, which is demoted to 9 and assigned to the variable n. Although the result is the same, how you got there is different.

10. The compiler generates an error because the first cube(int) function and the final function have identical names. Remember that the return type is not part of the function's full name.
    ```

Saturday Afternoon Review Answers

1.
```cpp
class Student
{
    public:
        char szLastName[128];
        int nGrade; // 1->first grade, 2->second grade, etc.
        double dGPA;
}
```

2.
```cpp
void readAndDisplay()
{
    Student s;

    // input student information
    cout << "Enter the student's name:";
    cin.getline(s.szLastName);
    cout << "Grade (1-> first grade, 2->second...)\n";
    cin  >> s.nGrade;
    cout << "GPA:";
    cin  >> s.dGPA;

    // output student info
    cout << "\nStudent information:\n";
    cout << s.szLastName << "\n";
    cout << s.nGrade << "\n";
    cout << s.dGPA << "\n";
}
```

3.
```cpp
void readAndDisplayAverage()
{
    Student s;

    // input student information
    cout << "Enter the student's name:";
    cin.getline(s.szLastName);
    cout << "Grade (1-> first grade, 2->second...)\n";
    cin  >> s.nGrade;
    cout << "GPA:";
```

```
// enter in three GPAs to be averaged:
double dGrades[3];
cin >> dGrade[0];
cin >> dGrade[1];
cin >> dGrade[2]
s.dGPA = (dGrade[0] + dGrade[1] + dGrade[2]) / 3;

// output student info
cout << "\nStudent information:\n";
cout << s.szLastName << "\n";
cout << s.nGrade << "\n";
cout << s.dGPA << "\n";
}
```

4. **a.** 16 bytes (4 + 4 + 8)

    b. 80 bytes (4 * 20)

    c. 8 (4 + 4) Remember that the size of a pointer is 4 bytes irrespective of what it points at.

5. **a.** Yes.

    b. It allocates memory from the heap but doesn't return it before exiting (this is known as a memory leak).

    c. Every time the function is called, another piece of memory is lost until the heap is exhausted.

    d. It may take quite awhile for the memory to be consumed. Such a small memory leak may require executing the program for many hours just to detect the problem.

6. dArray[0] is at 0x100, dArray[1] is at 0x108, and dArray[2] is at 0x110. The array stretches from 0x100 up to 0x118.

7. Assignment 1 has the same effect as dArray[1] = 1.0;. The second assignment destroys the floating point value stored in dArray[2], but is otherwise not fatal because a 4-byte integer value fits within the 8 bytes allocated for a double.

8.
```
LinkableClass* removeHead()
{
    LinkableClass* pFirstEntry;
    pFirstEntry = pHead;
    if (pHead != 0)
```

```
    {
        pHead = pHead->pNext;
    }
    return pFirstEntry;
}
```

The removeHead() function first checks whether the head pointer is null. If it is, then the list is already empty. If it is not, then removeHead() stores the first entry locally in pFirstEntry. It then moves pHead down to the next entry. Finally, the function returns pFirstEntry.

9.
```
LinkableClass* returnPrevious(LinkableClass* pTarget)
{
    // return a null if the list is empty
    if (pHead == 0)
    {
        return 0;
    }

    // now iterate through the list
    LinkableClass* pCurrent= pHead;
    while(pCurrent->pNext)
    {
        // if the next pointer of the current
        // entry is equal to pTarget...
        if (pCurrent->pNext == pTarget)
        {
            // ...then return pCurrent
            return pCurrent;
        }
    }

    // if we make it through the entire list without
    // finding pTarget then return a null
    return 0;
}
```

The returnPrevious() function returns the address of the entry in the list immediately prior to *pTarget. The function begins by checking that the linked list is not empty. If it is, then there is no previous entry and the function returns a null.

returnPrevious() then iterates through the list each time saving the address of the current entry in the variable pCurrent. On each pass through the loop, the function checks whether pCurrent's next pointer points to pTarget. If it does, then the function returns pCurrent.

If returnPrevious() makes it all the way through the list without finding pTarget, then it returns a null.

10.
```
LinkableClass* returnTail()
{
    // return the entry immediately prior to the
    // end; i.e., return the entry whose next
    // pointer is null.
    return returnPrevious(0);
}
```

The entry immediately prior to the null is the last entry in the list.

Extra credit:

```
LinkableClass* removeTail()
{
    // find the last entry in the list; if it's null
    // then the list is empty
    LinkableClass* pLast = returnPrevious(0);
    if (pLast == 0)
    {
        return 0;
    }

    // now find the entry that points to this last
    // entry
    LinkableClass* pPrevious = returnPrevious(pLast);

    // if pPrevious is null...
    if (pPrevious == 0)
    {
        // ...then pLast is the only entry;
        // set the head pointer to null
        pHead = 0;
    }
    else
    {
```

```
            // ...otherwise, remove pLast from pPrevious
            pPrevious->pNext = 0;
        }

        // either way, return the last pointer
        return pLast;
    }
```

The removeTail() function removes the last entry in a linked list. It begins by finding the address of the last entry by calling returnPrevious(0). It stores this address in pLast. If pLast is null, then the list is empty and the function returns a null immediately.

Finding the last entry is not enough. To remove the last entry, removeTail() must find the entry prior to pLast so that it can unlink the two.

removeTail() finds the address of the entry prior to pLast by calling returnPrevious(pLast). If there is no previous entry, then the list must have only one entry. removeTail() zeros the appropriate next pointer before returning pLast.

11. To demonstrate this solution, I used Visual C++ as a comparison to rhide.

I begin by executing the program just to see what happens. If the program appears to work, I don't stop there, but I would like to know what I'm up against. The results of entering the standard "this is a string" and "THIS IS A STRING" inputs are shown below.

```
This program concatenates two strings
<this version doesn't work.>

Enter string #1:This is a string
Enter string #2:THIS IS A STRING

THI
Press any key to continue
```

Because I'm reasonably sure that the problem is in concatString(), I set a breakpoint at the beginning of the function and start over. After encountering the breakpoint, the target and source strings seem correct as shown in Figure A-1.

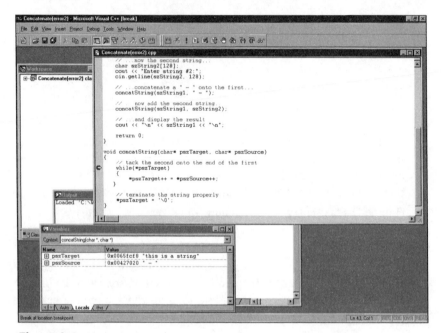

Figure A-1
The initial Variables window displays both the source and destination strings.

From the breakpoint, I begin to single-step. At first the local variables demonstrated in the Variables window seem correct. As I head into the `while` loop, however, it becomes immediately clear that the source string is about to overwrite the target string; that is, the `concatString()` function is more of an overwrite function.

The `concatString()` should have started by moving the `pszTarget` pointer to the end of the target string before starting the transfer process. This problem is not easily fixed in the debugger, so I go back and add the extra code to move the pointer to the end of the target string.

Actually, it is possible to fix this problem with a little debugger sleight-of-hand. In the locals display, click the value of the pointer in the right hand column next to `pszTarget`**. Whatever value is there, add 0x10 (there are 16 characters in "this is a string"). The** `pszTarget` **pointer now points to the end of the target string and you can proceed with the transfer.**

The updated concatString() is as follows:

```
void concatString(char* pszTarget, char* pszSource)
{
    // move pszTarget to the end of the source string
    while(*pszTarget)
    {
        pszTarget++;
    }

    // tack the second onto the end of the first
    while(*pszTarget)
    {
        *pszTarget++ = *pszSource++;
    }

    // terminate the string properly
    *pszTarget = '\0';
}
```

Replacing the breakpoint on the second while, the one that performs the copy, I start the program over with the same "this is a string" inputs. The local variables shown in Figure A-2 now appear correct.

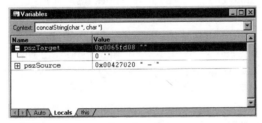

Figure A-2
pszTarget should point at a null before the copy takes place.

The pszTarget **variables should point at the null at the end of the source string before the program can copy the source string.**

With confidence I attempt to step through the transfer `while` loop. As soon as I press Step Over, however, the program steps over the loop entirely. Apparently, the `while` condition is not true even on the first pass through the loop. Reflecting for a moment, I realize that the condition is wrong. Rather than stop when `pszTarget` points to `null`, I should be stopping when `pszSource` points to a `null`. Updating the `while` condition as follows solves the problem:

```
while(*pszSource)
```

I start over again with the same inputs , and the debugger reveals that all seems to be OK. At completion, the program displays the proper output as well.

Saturday Evening Review Answers

1. I find shirts and pants, which are subclasses garments, which are clothing. Also in the clothing chain are shoes and pairs of socks. The pairs of socks can be further divided into pairs that match and those that don't match and so on.

2. Shoes have at least one hole for the insertion of a foot. Shoes have some type of restraint device to hold them on the foot. Shoes have some type of covering on the bottom to protect the foot from the ground. That's about all you can say about my shoes.

3. I have dress shoes and biking shoes. You can wear biking shoes to work, but it is extremely difficult to walk in them. However, they do cover your feet, and work would not come to a grinding halt.

   By the way, I also have a special pair of combination shoes. These have connections for bike pedals while retaining a conventional sole. Going to work in these hybrid shoes wouldn't be that bad at all.

4. The constructor for a linked list object should make sure that the next link points to a null when the object is constructed. It is not necessary to do anything to the static data member.

```
class Link
{
    static Link* pHead;
    Link* pNextLink;
```

```
        Link()
        {
            pNextLink = 0;
        }
    };
```

The point is that the static element pHead cannot be initialized in the constructor lest it be reinitialized each time a LinkedList object is created.

5. The following is my version of the destructor and copy constructor.

```
// destructor - remove the object and
//              remove the entry
~LinkedList()
{
    // if the current object is in a list...
    if (pNext)
    {
        // ...then remove it
        removeFromList();
    }

    // if the object has a block of memory...
    if (pszName)
    {
        // ...return it to the heap
        delete pszName;
    }
    pszName = 0;
}

// copy constructor - called to create a copy of
//                    an existing object
LinkedList(LinkedList& l)
{
    // allocate a block of the same size
    // off of the heap
    int nLength = strlen(l.pszName) + 1;
    this->pszName = new char[nLength];

    // now copy the name into this new block
```

```
        strcpy(this->pszName, l.pszName);

        // zero out the length as long as the object
        // is not in a linked list
        pNext = 0;
    }
```

If the object is a member of a linked list, then the destructor must remove it before the object is reused and the pNext pointer is lost. In addition, if the object "owns" a block of heap memory, it must be returned as well. Similarly the copy constructor performs a deep copy by allocating a new block of memory off of the heap to hold the object name. The copy constructor does not add the object onto the existing linked list (though it could).

Sunday Morning Review Answers

1. The output sequence is:

```
Advisor:student data member
Student
Advisor:student local
Advisor:graduate data member
Graduate Student
Advisor:graduate student local
```

Let's step through the sequence slowly:

Control passes to the constructor for GraduateStudent and from there to the constructor for the base class Student.

The data member Student::adv is constructed.

Control passes to the body of the Student constructor.

A local object of class Advisor is created from the heap.

Control returns to the GraduateStudent constructor which constructs the data member GraduateStudent::adv.

Control enters the constructor for GraduateStudent which subsequently allocates an Advisor object off of the heap.

2.

```
// PassProblem - use polymorphism to decide whether
//                a student passes using different
//                criteria for pass or fail
#include <stdio.h>
#include <iostream.h>

class Student
{
  public:
    virtual int pass(double dGrade)
    {
        // if passing grade...
        if (dGrade > 1.5)
        {
            // ...return a pass
            return 1;
        }
        // ...otherwise return a fail
        return 0;
    }
};
class GraduateStudent : public Student
{
  public:
    virtual int pass(double dGrade)
    {
        if (dGrade > 2.5)
        {
            return 1;
        }
        return 0;
    }
};
```

3. My version of the Checking class is as follows:

```
// Checking - same as a savings account except that
//            withdrawals cost a dollar
class Checking : public CashAccount
{
  public:
```

```
        Checking(unsigned nAccNo,
                float fInitialBalance = 0.0F)
            : CashAccount(nAccNo, fInitialBalance)
        {
        }

        // a savings account knows how to process
        // withdrawals as well (don't worry about overdrafts)
        virtual void withdrawal(float fAmount)
        {
            // take out withdrawal
            fBalance -= fAmount;

            // now take out charge
            fBalance -= 1;
        }
    };
```

The entire program is on the CD-ROM under the name AbstractProblem.

4. My solution to the problem is:

```
// MultipleVirtual - create a PrinterCopier class by
//                   inheriting a class Sleeper and
//                   a class Copier
#include <stdio.h>
#include <iostream.h>
class ElectronicEquipment
{
  public:
    ElectronicEquipment()
    {
        this->nVoltage = nVoltage;
    }
    int nVoltage;
};
class Printer : virtual public ElectronicEquipment
```

```
{
  public:
    Printer() : ElectronicEquipment()
    {
    }
    void print()
    {
       cout << "print\n";
    }
};
class Copier : virtual public ElectronicEquipment
{
  public:
    Copier() : ElectronicEquipment()
    {
    }
    void copy()
    {
       cout << "copy\n";
    }
};
class PrinterCopier : public Printer, public Copier
{
  public:
    PrinterCopier(int nVoltage) : Copier(), Printer()
    {
       this->nVoltage = nVoltage;
    }
};

int main(int nArgs, char* pszArgs)
{
   PrinterCopier ss(220);

   // first let's print
   ss.print();

   // now let's copy
   ss.copy();
```

```
   // now let's output the voltage
   cout << "voltage = " << ss.nVoltage << "\n";

   return 0;
}
```

Sunday Afternoon Review Answers

1. My version of the two functions are as follows:

```
MyClass(MyClass& mc)
{
    nValue = mc.nValue;
    resource.open(nValue);
}
MyClass& operator=(MyClass& s)
{
resource.close();

    nValue = s.nValue;
    resource.open(nValue);
}
```

The copy constructor opens the current object with the value of the source object.

The assignment operator first closes the current resource because it was opened with a different value. It then reopens the resource object with the new value assigned it.

2. My class and inserter are as follows:

```
// Student - your typical beer-swilling undergraduate
class Student
{
    friend ostream& operator<<(ostream& out, Student& d);
  public:
    Student(char* pszFName, char* pszLName, int nSSNum)
    {
        strncpy(szFName, pszFName, 20);
        strncpy(szLName, pszLName, 20);
```

```
            this->nSSNum = nSSNum;
    }

  protected:
    char szLName[20];
    char szFName[20];
    int  nSSNum;
};

// inserter - output a string description
//            (this version handles the case of cents
//            less than 10)
ostream& operator<<(ostream& out, Student& s)
{
    out << s.szLName
        << ", "
        << s.szFName
        << "("
        << s.nSSNum
        << ")";
    return out;
}
```

APPENDIX

B

Supplemental Problems

This appendix contains supplemental problems from different parts of the book to give you additional practice in working with C++ and honing your new skills. The problems are given below in one section divided by part number; following is another section with answers to the problems.

Problems

Saturday Morning

1. Which of the following statements *should*:
   a. generate no messages?
   b. generate warnings?
   c. generate errors?
      1. int n1, n2, n3;
      2. float f1, f2 = 1;
      3. double d1, d2;
      4. n1 = 1; n2 = 2; n3 = 3; f2 = 1;
      5. d1 = n1 * 2.3;
      6. n2 = n1 * 2.3;
      7. n2 = d1 * 1;

         8. n3 = 100; n3 = n3 * 1000;

         9. f1 = 200 * f2;

2. Given that n1 is equal to 10, evaluate the following:

     a. n1 / 3

     b. n1 % 3

     c. n1++

     d. ++n1

     e. n1 %= 3

     f. n1 -= n1

     g. n1 = -10; n1 = +n1; what is n1?

3. What is the difference between the following for loops?

```
for(int i = 0; i < 10; i++)
{
    // ...
}
for (int i = 0; i < 10; ++i)
{
    // ...
}
```

4. Write the function int cube(int n), which calculates the n * n * n of n.

5. Describe exactly what happens in the following case using the function written in problem 1?

```
int n = cube(3.0);
```

6. The following program demonstrates a very crude function that calculates the integer square root of a number by repetitively comparing the square to the actual value. In other words, 4 * 4 = 16, therefore the square root of 16 is 4. This function reckons that 3 is the square root of 15 because 3 * 3 is less than 15 but 4 * 4 is greater than 15.

   However, the program generates unexpected results. Fix it!

```
// Lesson - this function demonstrates a crude but
//          effective method for calculating a
//          square root using only integers.
//          This version does not work.
#include <stdio.h>
#include <iostream.h>
```

```cpp
// squareRoot - given a number n, return its square
//              root by calculating nRoot * nRoot
//              for ever increasing values of
//              nRoot until n is surpassed.
void squareRoot(int n)
{
    // start counting at 1
    int nRoot = 1;

    // loop forever
    for(;;)
    {
        // check the square of the current
        // value (and increment to the next)
        if ((nRoot++ * nRoot) > n)
        {
            // close as we can get, return
            // what we've got
            return nRoot;
        }
    }

    // shouldn't be able to get here
    return 0;
}

// test the function squareRoot() with a
// single value (a much more thorough test
// would be required except that this already
// doesn't work)
int main(int argc, char* pszArgs[])
{
    cout << "This program doesn't work!\n";

    cout << "Square root of "
         << 16
         << " is "
         << squareRoot(16)
         << "\n";
```

```
    return 0;
}
```

Hint: Be very wary of the autoincrement feature, as well as the postincrement feature.

Saturday Afternoon

1. The C++ library function strchr() returns the index of a given character in a string. For example, strchr("abcdef", 'c') returns 2. strchr() returns a –1 if the character does not exist anywhere within the string.

   Write myStrchr() which works the same as strchr().

   When you think that your function is ready, execute it against the following:

```
// MyStrchr - search a given character within
//            a string. Return the index of
//            of the result.
#include <stdio.h>


#include <iostream.h>

// myStrchr - return the index of a test
//            character in a string. Return
//            a -1 if the character not found.
int myStrchr(char target[], char testChar);

// test the myStrchr function with different
// string combinations
void testFn(char szString[], char cTestChar)
{
    cout << "The offset of "
         << cTestChar
         << " in "
         << szString
         << " is "
         << myStrchr(szString, cTestChar)
         << "\n";
}
```

```
int main(int nArgs, char* pszArgs[])
{
    testFn("abcdefg", 'c');
    testFn("abcdefg", 'a');
    testFn("abcdefg", 'g');
    testFn("abcdefc", 'c');
    testFn("abcdefg", 'x');

    return 0;
}
```

Hint: Make sure that you do not run off the end of the string in the event that you don't find the desired character.

2. Although the following is bad programming, this mistake may not cause problems. Please explain why problems might not be caused.

```
void fn(void)
{
    double d;
    int*   pnVar = (int*)&d;
    *pnVar = 10;
}
```

3. Write a pointer version of the following displayString(). Assume that this is a null terminated string (don't pass the length as an argument to the function).

```
void displayCharArray(char sArray[], int nSize)
{
    for(int i = 0; i< nSize; i++)
    {
        cout << sArray[i];
    }
}
```

4. Compile and execute the following program. Explain the results:

```
#include <stdio.h>
#include <iostream.h>

// MyClass - a meaningless test class
class MyClass
{
```

```
    public:
        int n1;
        int n2;
};

int main(int nArg, char* nArgs[])
{
    MyClass* pmc;
    cout << "n1  = " << pmc->n1
         << ";n2 = " << pmc->n2
         << "\n";
    return 0;
}
```

Sunday Morning

1. Write a class Car that inherits from the class Vehicle and that has a Motor. The number of wheels is specified in the constructor to the class Vehicle and the number of cylinders specified in the constructor for Motor. Both of these values are passed to the constructor for the class Car.

Answers

Saturday Morning

1.
   1. No problem.
   2. No warning: you can initialize however you like.
   3. Nope.
   4. Nothing here.
   5. No problem: n1 is automatically promoted to a double in order to perform the multiplication. Most compilers will not note this conversion.
   6. n1 * 2.3 results in a double. Assigning this back to an int results in a demotion warning.

7. Similar to 6. Although 1 is an `int`, d1 is a `double`. The result is a `double` that must be demoted.

8. No warning but it doesn't work. The result is beyond the range of an `int`.

9. This should generate a warning (it does under Visual C++ but not under GNU C++). The result of multiplying an `int` times a `float` is a `double` (all calculations are performed in double precision). This must be demoted to be assigned to a `float`.

2. **a.** 3

Round off error as described in Session 5 converts the expected 3.3 to 3.

b. 1

The closest divisor to 10 / 3 is 3 (same as 1a). 10 – (3 * 3) is 1, the remainder after division.

c. 10

n1++ evaluates to the value of the variable before it is incremented. After the expression is evaluated, n1 = 11.

d. 11

++n increments the value of the variable before it is returned.

e. 1

This is the same as n1 = n1 % 3

f. 0

This is the same as n1 = n1 - n1. n1 - n1 is always zero.

g. –10

The unary plus (+) operator has no effect. In particular, it does not change the sign of a negative number.

3. No difference.

The increment clause of the `if` statement is considered a separate expression. The value of i after a preincrement or a postincrement is the same (it's only the value of the expression itself that is different).

4.
```
int cube(int n)
{
    return n * n * n;
}
```

5. The double 3.0 is demoted to the integer 3 and the result is returned from cube(int) as the integer 9.

6. Error #1: The program doesn't compile properly because the function squareRoot() has been declared as returning a void. Change the return type to int and rebuild.

   Error #2: The program now figures that the square root of 16 is 6! To sort out the problem, I break the compound if in two so that I can output the resulting value:

```
// loop forever
for(;;)
{
    // check the square of the current
    // value (and increment to the next)
    int nTest = nRoot++ * nRoot;
    cout << "Test root is "
        << nRoot
        << " square is "
        << nTest
        << "\n";
    if (nTest > n)
    {
        // close as we can get, return
        // what we've got
        return nRoot;
    }
}
```

The result of executing the program is shown below.

```
This program doesn't work!
Test root is 2 square is 1
Test root is 3 square is 4
Test root is 4 square is 9
Test root is 5 square is 16
Test root is 6 square is 25
Square root of 16 is 6
```

The program output is not correct at all; however, careful examination reveals that the left side is one off. Thus, the square of 3 is 9, but the displayed value of nRoot is 4. The square of 4 is 16 but the displayed value of nRoot is 5. By incrementing nRoot in expression, nRoot is one more than the nRoot actually used in the calculation. Thus, nRoot needs to be incremented after the if statement.

The new squareRoot() function becomes

```
// loop forever
for(;;)
{
    // check the square of the current
    // value (and increment to the next)
    int nTest = nRoot * nRoot;
    cout << "Test root is "
         << nRoot
         << " square is "
         << nTest
         << "\n";
    if (nTest > n)
    {
        // close as we can get, return
        // what we've got
        return nRoot;
    }

    // try the next value of nRoot
    nRoot++;
}
```

The autoincrement has been moved until after the test (the autoincrement always looked fishy where it was). The output of the new, improved program is shown below.

```
This program doesn't work!
Test root is 1 square is 1
Test root is 2 square is 4
Test root is 3 square is 9
Test root is 4 square is 16
Test root is 5 square is 25
Square root of 16 is 5
```

The square is being calculated, but for some reason the function doesn't stop when nRoot is equal to 4. After all, 4 * 4 == 16. This is exactly the problem — the comparison is for nTest > n when it should be nTest >= n. The corrected program generates the desired result as shown below.

```
This program works!
Test root is 1 square is 1
Test root is 2 square is 4
Test root is 3 square is 9
Test root is 4 square is 16
Square root of 16 is 4
```

After checking several other values, I convince myself that the function does work and I remove the output statements.

Saturday Afternoon

1. The following MyStrchr represents my solution to the problem:

```
// myStrchr - return the index of a test
//            character in a string. Return
//            a -1 if the character not found.
int myStrchr(char target[], char testChar)
{
    // loop through the character string;
    // stop if we hit the end of the string
    int index = 0;
    while(target[index])
    {
        // if the current member of the
        // string matches the target
        // character...
        if (target[index] == testChar)
        {
            // ...then exit
            break;
        }

        // skip to the next character
        index++;
    }

    // if we ended up at the end of the
    // string without encountering the
    // character...
```

```
    if (target[index] == '\0')
    {
        // ...return a -1 rather than
        // the length of the array
        index = -1;
    }

    // return the index calculated
    return index;
}
```

The actual myStrchr() function begins by iterating through the string target stopping when the current character, referenced by target[index], is equal to 0 meaning that the program has reached the end of the string. This test safeguards that the function doesn't go too far if the test character is not encountered.

Within this loop, the program compares the current character to the desired character contained in testChar. If the character is found, the function exits the loop prematurely.

Once outside the loop, the program terminated either because the end of the string was encountered or because it found the desired character. If the end of the string was the reason for exit then target[index] will equal 0, or '\0' to use the character equivalent. In that case, index is forced to –1.

The resulting index is returned to the caller.

The result of executing this program is shown below.

```
The offset of c in abcdefg is 2
The offset of a in abcdefg is 0
The offset of g in abcdefg is 6
The offset of c in abcdefg is 2
The offset of x in abcdefg is -1
Press any key to continue
```

The above program could have been simplified by simply exiting from within the loop if the character were found:

```
int myStrchr(char target[], char testChar)
{
    // loop through the character string;
    // stop if we hit the end of the string
    int index = 0;
```

```
    while(target[index])
    {
        // if the current member of the
        // string matches the target
        // character...
        if (target[index] == testChar)
        {
            // ...then return the index
            return index;
        }

        // skip to the next character
        index++;
    }

    // if we exited the loop then we must
    // have encountered the end without
    // finding the desired character
    return -1;
}
```

If the target character is found, the index value is returned immediately. If control exits the loop, it can only mean that the end of the string was encountered without finding the desired character.

Personally, I find this style more straightforward; however, some organizations have a rule against multiple returns in a single function.

2. A double occupies 8 bytes whereas an int occupies only 4 bytes. It's entirely possible that C++ would use 4 of the 8 bytes to store the integer 10, leaving the other 4 bytes unused. This would not cause an error; however, you should not assume that your compiler would work this way.

3.
```
void displayString(char* pszString)
{
    while(*pszString)
    {
        cout << *pszString;
        pszString++;
    }
}
```

4. The output of `pmc->n1` and `pmc->n2` are garbage because the pointer `pmc` was not initialized to point to anything. In fact, the program might abort without generating any output due to a bad pointer.

Sunday Morning

1.
```cpp
class Vehicle
{
  public:
    Vehicle(int nWheels)
    {
    }
};

class Motor
{
  public:
    Motor(int nCylinders)
    {
    }
};

class Car : pubic Vehicle
{
  public:
    Car(int nCyliners, int nWheels)
      : Vehicle(nWheels), motor(nCylinders)
    {
    }

    Motor motor;
};
```

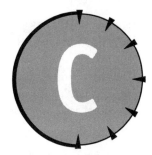

What's On the CD-ROM

The CD-ROM that accompanies this book contains materials to help you work through the sessions and learn C++ in a weekend:

- Installation files for the GNU C++ compiler
- The C++ Weekend Crash Course Self-Assessment Test
- A complete set of all the programs from the book

GNU C++

The installation files for GNU C++ that you'll find on this CD-ROM were taken from the Delorie Web site mentioned in Session 3. Here we've provided complete sets of install files for Windows 95, 98 and NT/2000.

To install GNU C++ from these files, follow these steps:

1. Create a folder named \DJGPP.
2. Copy the complete set of Zip files from the appropriate folder on the CD-ROM for your version of Windows into the DJGPP folder.
3. Unzip the files into the DJGPP folder itself.
4. Add the following commands to AUTOEXEC.BAT:

```
set PATH=C:\DJGPP\BIN;%PATH%
set DJGPP=C:\DJGPP\DJGPP.ENV
```

Note: the above command lines assume your DJGPP folder is directly under C:\. If you've placed your DJGPP folder somewhere else, substitute that path in the commands above.

5. Reboot to complete the installation.

The \BIN folder, created when you unzip the files, includes the actual GNU tool executables. The DJGPP.ENV file sets a series of options to describe the Windows GNU C++ "environment."

 Before you begin using GNU C++ check the DJGPP.ENV file to make sure that Long File Name support is enabled. Disabling Long File Name support is the most common GNU C++ installation error.

Open the DJGPP.ENV file using a text file editor such as Microsoft Notebook. Don't worry if you see one long string of text punctuated by little black boxes — Unix uses a different newline character than Windows. Look for the phrase "LFN=y" or "LFN=Y" (the case is not important). If you find "LFN=n" instead (or if you don't find "LFN" at all), change the "n" to a "y". Save the file. (Make sure that you save the file as an ASCII text file and not in some other format such as a Word .DOC file.)

C++ Weekend Crash Course Self-Assessment Test

The C++ Weekend Crash Course Self-Assessment Test provides you with a way to check your knowledge and skills once you've completed the book. Its fifty questions cover the entire range of basic C++ concepts.

Sample Programs

The \Programs folder contains the source code for each of the programs found in the book. I suggest that you copy the entire folder and all its subfolders to your hard disk; however, you may copy individual source files if you prefer.

The programs are separated by session. Each session's folder includes the .CPP source file plus executables; the latter are present only as a convenience to the reader. You may execute the programs directly from the CD-ROM. The .EXE executable found in the folder itself was generated by GNU C++. The Visual C++ .EXE is present in a subfolder named DEBUG.

Session 2 contains directions for building a program using Visual C++. Session 3 contains similar instructions for GNU C++.

Note: Two source files are slightly modified from that appearing in the book:

1. The function ltoa() has been replaced with a call to the functionally equivalent function itoa() in ToStringWOStream.cpp in Session 29.

2. GNU C++ uses the full name strstream.h while Visual C++ uses the 8.3 format of strstrea.h. The reference to this include file in ToStringWStream.cpp must be adjusted accordingly. The source code appearing here uses an #ifdef to decide automatically which include file name to use. The source code in the book indicates the problem via a comment.

Index

SYMBOLS

Continued

Continued

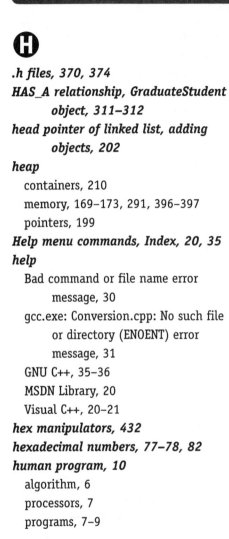

Continued

Continued

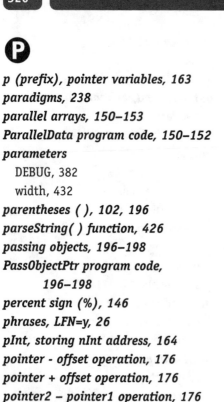

Hungry Minds, Inc.
End–User License Agreement

READ THIS. You should carefully read these terms and conditions before opening the software packet(s) included with this book ("Book"). This is a license agreement ("Agreement") between you and Hungry Minds, Inc. ("HMI"). By opening the accompanying software packet(s), you acknowledge that you have read and accept the following terms and conditions. If you do not agree and do not want to be bound by such terms and conditions, promptly return the Book and the unopened software packet(s) to the place you obtained them for a full refund.

1. **License Grant.** HMI grants to you (either an individual or entity) a non-exclusive license to use one copy of the enclosed software program(s) (collectively, the "Software") solely for your own personal or business purposes on a single computer (whether a standard computer or a work-station component of a multi-user network). The Software is in use on a computer when it is loaded into temporary memory (RAM) or installed into permanent memory (hard disk, CD-ROM, or other storage device). HMI reserves all rights not expressly granted herein.

2. **Ownership.** HMI is the owner of all right, title, and interest, including copyright, in and to the compilation of the Software recorded on the disk(s) or CD-ROM ("Software Media"). Copyright to the individual programs recorded on the Software Media is owned by the author or other authorized copyright owner of each program. Ownership of the Software and all proprietary rights relating thereto remain with HMI and its licensers.

3. **Restrictions On Use and Transfer.**

    (a) You may only (i) make one copy of the Software for backup or archival purposes, or (ii) transfer the Software to a single hard disk, provided that you keep the original for backup or archival purposes. You may not (i) rent or lease the Software, (ii) copy or reproduce the Software through a LAN or other network system or through any computer subscriber system or bulletin-board system, or (iii) modify, adapt, or create derivative works based on the Software.

    (b) You may not reverse engineer, decompile, or disassemble the Software. You may transfer the Software and user documentation on a permanent basis, provided that the transferee agrees to accept the terms and conditions of this Agreement and you retain no copies. If the Software is an update or has been updated, any transfer must include the most recent update and all prior versions.

4. **Restrictions on Use of Individual Programs.** You must follow the individual requirements and restrictions detailed for each individual program in Appendix C of this Book. These limitations are also contained in the individual license agreements recorded on the Software Media. These limitations may include a requirement that after using the program for a specified period of time, the user must pay a registration fee or discontinue use. By opening the Software packet(s), you will be agreeing to abide by the licenses and restrictions for these individual programs that are detailed in Appendix C and on the Software Media. None of the material on this Software Media or listed in this Book may ever be redistributed, in original or modified form, for commercial purposes.

5. **Limited Warranty.**

   (a) HMI warrants that the Software and Software Media are free from defects in materials and workmanship under normal use for a period of sixty (60) days from the date of purchase of this Book. If HMI receives notification within the warranty period of defects in materials or workmanship, HMI will replace the defective Software Media.

   (b) HMI AND THE AUTHOR OF THE BOOK DISCLAIM ALL OTHER WARRANTIES, EXPRESS OR IMPLIED, INCLUDING WITHOUT LIMITATION IMPLIED WARRANTIES OF MERCHANTABILITY AND FITNESS FOR A PARTICULAR PURPOSE, WITH RESPECT TO THE SOFTWARE, THE PROGRAMS, THE SOURCE CODE CONTAINED THEREIN, AND/OR THE TECHNIQUES DESCRIBED IN THIS BOOK. HMI DOES NOT WARRANT THAT THE FUNCTIONS CONTAINED IN THE SOFTWARE WILL MEET YOUR REQUIREMENTS OR THAT THE OPERATION OF THE SOFTWARE WILL BE ERROR FREE.

   (c) This limited warranty gives you specific legal rights, and you may have other rights that vary from jurisdiction to jurisdiction.

6. **Remedies.**

   (a) HMI's entire liability and your exclusive remedy for defects in materials and workmanship shall be limited to replacement of the Software Media, which may be returned to HMI with a copy of your receipt at the following address: Software Media Fulfillment Department, Attn.: *C++ Weekend Crash Course,* Hungry Minds, Inc., 10475 Crosspoint Blvd., Indianapolis, IN 46256, or call 1-800-762-2974. Please allow four to six weeks for delivery. This Limited Warranty is void if failure of the Software Media has resulted from accident, abuse, or misapplication. Any replacement Software Media will be warranted for the remainder of the original warranty period or thirty (30) days, whichever is longer.

(b) In no event shall HMI or the author be liable for any damages whatsoever (including without limitation damages for loss of business profits, business interruption, loss of business information, or any other pecuniary loss) arising from the use of or inability to use the Book or the Software, even if HMI has been advised of the possibility of such damages.

(c) Because some jurisdictions do not allow the exclusion or limitation of liability for consequential or incidental damages, the above limitation or exclusion may not apply to you.

7. **U.S. Government Restricted Rights.** Use, duplication, or disclosure of the Software for or on behalf of the United States of America, its agencies and/or instrumentalities (the "U.S. Government") is subject to restrictions as stated in paragraph (c)(1)(ii) of the Rights in Technical Data and Computer Software clause of DFARS 252.227-7013, and in subparagraphs (a) through (d) of the Commercial Computer–Restricted Rights clause at FAR 52.227-19, and in similiar clauses in the NASA FAR supplement, when applicable.

8. **General.** This Agreement constitutes the entire understanding of the parties and revokes and supersedes all prior agreements, oral or written, between them and may not be modified or amended except in a writing signed by both parties hereto that specifically refers to this Agreement. This Agreement shall take precedence over any other documents that may be in conflict herewith. If any one or more provisions contained in this Agreement are held by any court or tribunal to be invalid, illegal, or otherwise unenforceable, each and every other provision shall remain in full force and effect.

GNU GENERAL PUBLIC LICENSE

Version 2, June 1991
Copyright © 1989, 1991 Free Software Foundation, Inc.
59 Temple Place - Suite 330, Boston, MA 02111-1307, USA
Everyone is permitted to copy and distribute verbatim copies of this license
document, but changing it is not allowed.

Preamble

The licenses for most software are designed to take away your freedom to share
and change it. By contrast, the GNU General Public License is intended to guaran-
tee your freedom to share and change free software--to make sure the software
is free for all its users. This General Public License applies to most of the Free
Software Foundation's software and to any other program whose authors commit
to using it. (Some other Free Software Foundation software is covered by the GNU
Library General Public License instead.) You can apply it to your programs, too.

When we speak of free software, we are referring to freedom, not price. Our
General Public Licenses are designed to make sure that you have the freedom to
distribute copies of free software (and charge for this service if you wish), that
you receive source code or can get it if you want it, that you can change the
software or use pieces of it in new free programs; and that you know you can
do these things.

To protect your rights, we need to make restrictions that forbid anyone to deny
you these rights or to ask you to surrender the rights. These restrictions translate
to certain responsibilities for you if you distribute copies of the software, or if you
modify it.

For example, if you distribute copies of such a program, whether gratis or for a
fee, you must give the recipients all the rights that you have. You must make sure
that they, too, receive or can get the source code. And you must show them these
terms so they know their rights.

We protect your rights with two steps: (1) copyright the software, and (2) offer
you this license which gives you legal permission to copy, distribute and/or modify the software.

Also, for each author's protection and ours, we want to make certain that everyone understands that there is no warranty for this free software. If the software is
modified by someone else and passed on, we want its recipients to know that what

they have is not the original, so that any problems introduced by others will not reflect on the original authors' reputations.

Finally, any free program is threatened constantly by software patents. We wish to avoid the danger that redistributors of a free program will individually obtain patent licenses, in effect making the program proprietary. To prevent this, we have made it clear that any patent must be licensed for everyone's free use or not licensed at all.

The precise terms and conditions for copying, distribution and modification follow.

TERMS AND CONDITIONS FOR COPYING, DISTRIBUTION AND MODIFICATION

0. This License applies to any program or other work which contains a notice placed by the copyright holder saying it may be distributed under the terms of this General Public License. The "Program", below, refers to any such program or work, and a "work based on the Program" means either the Program or any derivative work under copyright law: that is to say, a work containing the Program or a portion of it, either verbatim or with modifications and/or translated into another language. (Hereinafter, translation is included without limitation in the term "modification".) Each licensee is addressed as "you".

Activities other than copying, distribution and modification are not covered by this License; they are outside its scope. The act of running the Program is not restricted, and the output from the Program is covered only if its contents constitute a work based on the Program (independent of having been made by running the Program). Whether that is true depends on what the Program does.

1. You may copy and distribute verbatim copies of the Program's source code as you receive it, in any medium, provided that you conspicuously and appropriately publish on each copy an appropriate copyright notice and disclaimer of warranty; keep intact all the notices that refer to this License and to the absence of any warranty; and give any other recipients of the Program a copy of this License along with the Program.

You may charge a fee for the physical act of transferring a copy, and you may at your option offer warranty protection in exchange for a fee.

2. You may modify your copy or copies of the Program or any portion of it, thus forming a work based on the Program, and copy and distribute such modifications or work under the terms of Section 1 above, provided that you also meet all of these conditions:

   a) You must cause the modified files to carry prominent notices stating that you changed the files and the date of any change.

   b) You must cause any work that you distribute or publish, that in whole or in part contains or is derived from the Program or any part thereof, to be licensed as a whole at no charge to all third parties under the terms of this License.

   c) If the modified program normally reads commands interactively when run, you must cause it, when started running for such interactive use in the most ordinary way, to print or display an announcement including an appropriate copyright notice and a notice that there is no warranty (or else, saying that you provide a warranty) and that users may redistribute the program under these conditions, and telling the user how to view a copy of this License. (Exception: if the Program itself is interactive but does not normally print such an announcement, your work based on the Program is not required to print an announcement.)

These requirements apply to the modified work as a whole. If identifiable sections of that work are not derived from the Program, and can be reasonably considered independent and separate works in themselves, then this License, and its terms, do not apply to those sections when you distribute them as separate works. But when you distribute the same sections as part of a whole which is a work based on the Program, the distribution of the whole must be on the terms of this License, whose permissions for other licensees extend to the entire whole, and thus to each and every part regardless of who wrote it.

Thus, it is not the intent of this section to claim rights or contest your rights to work written entirely by you; rather, the intent is to exercise the right to control the distribution of derivative or collective works based on the Program.

In addition, mere aggregation of another work not based on the Program with the Program (or with a work based on the Program) on a volume of a storage or distribution medium does not bring the other work under the scope of this License.

3. You may copy and distribute the Program (or a work based on it, under Section 2) in object code or executable form under the terms of Sections 1 and 2 above provided that you also do one of the following:

    a) Accompany it with the complete corresponding machine-readable source code, which must be distributed under the terms of Sections 1 and 2 above on a medium customarily used for software interchange; or,

    b) Accompany it with a written offer, valid for at least three years, to give any third party, for a charge no more than your cost of physically performing source distribution, a complete machine-readable copy of the corresponding source code, to be distributed under the terms of Sections 1 and 2 above on a medium customarily used for software interchange; or,

    c) Accompany it with the information you received as to the offer to distribute corresponding source code. (This alternative is allowed only for noncommercial distribution and only if you received the program in object code or executable form with such an offer, in accord with Subsection b above.)

    The source code for a work means the preferred form of the work for making modifications to it. For an executable work, complete source code means all the source code for all modules it contains, plus any associated interface definition files, plus the scripts used to control compilation and installation of the executable. However, as a special exception, the source code distributed need not include anything that is normally distributed (in either source or binary form) with the major components (compiler, kernel, and so on) of the operating system on which the executable runs, unless that component itself accompanies the executable.

    If distribution of executable or object code is made by offering access to copy from a designated place, then offering equivalent access to copy the source code from the same place counts as distribution of the source code, even though third parties are not compelled to copy the source along with the object code.

4. You may not copy, modify, sublicense, or distribute the Program except as expressly provided under this License. Any attempt otherwise to copy, modify, sublicense or distribute the Program is void, and will automatically terminate your rights under this License. However, parties who have received copies, or rights, from you under this License will not have their licenses terminated so long as such parties remain in full compliance.

5. You are not required to accept this License, since you have not signed it. However, nothing else grants you permission to modify or distribute the Program or its derivative works. These actions are prohibited by law if you do not accept this License. Therefore, by modifying or distributing the Program (or any work based on the Program), you indicate your acceptance of this License to do so, and all its terms and conditions for copying, distributing or modifying the Program or works based on it.

6. Each time you redistribute the Program (or any work based on the Program), the recipient automatically receives a license from the original licensor to copy, distribute or modify the Program subject to these terms and conditions. You may not impose any further restrictions on the recipients' exercise of the rights granted herein. You are not responsible for enforcing compliance by third parties to this License.

7. If, as a consequence of a court judgment or allegation of patent infringement or for any other reason (not limited to patent issues), conditions are imposed on you (whether by court order, agreement or otherwise) that contradict the conditions of this License, they do not excuse you from the conditions of this License. If you cannot distribute so as to satisfy simultaneously your obligations under this License and any other pertinent obligations, then as a consequence you may not distribute the Program at all. For example, if a patent license would not permit royalty-free redistribution of the Program by all those who receive copies directly or indirectly through you, then the only way you could satisfy both it and this License would be to refrain entirely from distribution of the Program.

   If any portion of this section is held invalid or unenforceable under any particular circumstance, the balance of the section is intended to apply and the section as a whole is intended to apply in other circumstances.

   It is not the purpose of this section to induce you to infringe any patents or other property right claims or to contest validity of any such claims; this section has the sole purpose of protecting the integrity of the free software distribution system, which is implemented by public license practices. Many people have made generous contributions to the wide range of software distributed through that system in reliance on consistent application of that system; it is up to the author/donor to decide if he or she is willing to distribute software through any other system and a licensee cannot impose that choice.

This section is intended to make thoroughly clear what is believed to be a consequence of the rest of this License.

8. If the distribution and/or use of the Program is restricted in certain countries either by patents or by copyrighted interfaces, the original copyright holder who places the Program under this License may add an explicit geographical distribution limitation excluding those countries, so that distribution is permitted only in or among countries not thus excluded. In such case, this License incorporates the limitation as if written in the body of this License.

9. The Free Software Foundation may publish revised and/or new versions of the General Public License from time to time. Such new versions will be similar in spirit to the present version, but may differ in detail to address new problems or concerns.

Each version is given a distinguishing version number. If the Program specifies a version number of this License which applies to it and "any later version", you have the option of following the terms and conditions either of that version or of any later version published by the Free Software Foundation. If the Program does not specify a version number of this License, you may choose any version ever published by the Free Software Foundation.

10. If you wish to incorporate parts of the Program into other free programs whose distribution conditions are different, write to the author to ask for permission. For software which is copyrighted by the Free Software Foundation, write to the Free Software Foundation; we sometimes make exceptions for this. Our decision will be guided by the two goals of preserving the free status of all derivatives of our free software and of promoting the sharing and reuse of software generally.

NO WARRANTY

11. BECAUSE THE PROGRAM IS LICENSED FREE OF CHARGE, THERE IS NO WARRANTY FOR THE PROGRAM, TO THE EXTENT PERMITTED BY APPLICABLE LAW. EXCEPT WHEN OTHERWISE STATED IN WRITING THE COPYRIGHT HOLDERS AND/OR OTHER PARTIES PROVIDE THE PROGRAM "AS IS" WITHOUT WARRANTY OF ANY KIND, EITHER EXPRESSED OR IMPLIED, INCLUDING, BUT NOT LIMITED TO, THE IMPLIED WARRANTIES OF MERCHANTABILITY AND FITNESS FOR A PARTICULAR PURPOSE. THE ENTIRE

RISK AS TO THE QUALITY AND PERFORMANCE OF THE PROGRAM IS WITH YOU. SHOULD THE PROGRAM PROVE DEFECTIVE, YOU ASSUME THE COST OF ALL NECESSARY SERVICING, REPAIR OR CORRECTION.

12. IN NO EVENT UNLESS REQUIRED BY APPLICABLE LAW OR AGREED TO IN WRITING WILL ANY COPYRIGHT HOLDER, OR ANY OTHER PARTY WHO MAY MODIFY AND/OR REDISTRIBUTE THE PROGRAM AS PERMITTED ABOVE, BE LIABLE TO YOU FOR DAMAGES, INCLUDING ANY GENERAL, SPECIAL, INCIDENTAL OR CONSEQUENTIAL DAMAGES ARISING OUT OF THE USE OR INABILITY TO USE THE PROGRAM (INCLUDING BUT NOT LIMITED TO LOSS OF DATA OR DATA BEING RENDERED INACCURATE OR LOSSES SUSTAINED BY YOU OR THIRD PARTIES OR A FAILURE OF THE PROGRAM TO OPERATE WITH ANY OTHER PROGRAMS), EVEN IF SUCH HOLDER OR OTHER PARTY HAS BEEN ADVISED OF THE POSSIBILITY OF SUCH DAMAGES.

*****END OF TERMS AND CONDITIONS*****

How to Apply These Terms to Your New Programs

If you develop a new program, and you want it to be of the greatest possible use to the public, the best way to achieve this is to make it free software which everyone can redistribute and change under these terms.

To do so, attach the following notices to the program. It is safest to attach them to the start of each source file to most effectively convey the exclusion of warranty; and each file should have at least the "copyright" line and a pointer to where the full notice is found.

```
one line to give the program's name and an idea of what it does.
Copyright (C) yyyy  name of author

This program is free software; you can redistribute it and/or
modify it under the terms of the GNU General Public License
as published by the Free Software Foundation; either version 2
of the License, or (at your option) any later version.

This program is distributed in the hope that it will be useful,
but WITHOUT ANY WARRANTY; without even the implied warranty of
MERCHANTABILITY or FITNESS FOR A PARTICULAR PURPOSE.  See the
GNU General Public License for more details.
```

```
You should have received a copy of the GNU General Public License
along with this program; if not, write to the Free Software
Foundation, Inc., 59 Temple Place - Suite 330, Boston, MA
02111-1307, USA.
```

Also add information on how to contact you by electronic and paper mail.

If the program is interactive, make it output a short notice like this when it starts in an interactive mode:

```
Gnomovision version 69, Copyright (C) yyyy name of author
Gnomovision comes with ABSOLUTELY NO WARRANTY; for details
type 'show w'.  This is free software, and you are welcome
to redistribute it under certain conditions; type 'show c'
for details.
```

The hypothetical commands 'show w' and 'show c' should show the appropriate parts of the General Public License. Of course, the commands you use may be called something other than 'show w' and 'show c'; they could even be mouse-clicks or menu items--whatever suits your program.

You should also get your employer (if you work as a programmer) or your school, if any, to sign a "copyright disclaimer" for the program, if necessary. Here is a sample; alter the names:

```
Yoyodyne, Inc., hereby disclaims all copyright
interest in the program `Gnomovision'
(which makes passes at compilers) written
by James Hacker.

signature of Ty Coon, 1 April 1989
Ty Coon, President of Vice
```

This General Public License does not permit incorporating your program into proprietary programs. If your program is a subroutine library, you may consider it more useful to permit linking proprietary applications with the library. If this is what you want to do, use the GNU Library General Public License instead of this License.